ESTRANGED BY LIES

ESTRANGED BY LIES

HOW NARCISSISTIC PARTNERS USE POWER & CONTROL TO DESTROY YOUR FAMILY

TRACY A. MALONE

ESTRANGED BY LIES

How Narcissistic Partners Use Power & Control To Destroy Your Family

ISBN number: Paperback - 978-1-7365078-5-8 Copyright ©2025

Library of Congress – Control Number: 2025910521 All rights reserved.

NO REPRODUCTION WITHOUT PRIOR WRITTEN CONSENT

All rights reserved. Printed in the United States of America. No part of this publication may be used or reproduced by any means, graphic, electronic, or mechanical, including photocopying, recording copy, taping or by information storage retrieval systems, without the prior written permission of the author, except in the case of brief quotations embodied in critical articles and reviews, with proper attribution.

Request permission at info@narcissistabusesupport.com

Copy editing: Karla Crawford

Connect
Website: narcissistabusesupport.com
Website: tracyamalone.com

A WORD ABOUT THIS BOOK

LIABILITY

The author, Tracy A. Malone, is not a medical doctor, psychologist, licensed therapist, or licensed attorney.

This book is not intended to, nor is it to be interpreted as diagnosing any condition, nor is it to be interpreted as providing medical, psychological, legal, financial, or other professional advice. This book should not be used to diagnose anyone with a narcissistic personality disorder. If you believe that you or a loved one is suffering from narcissistic abuse, please seek help from a trained professional familiar with narcissistic abuse.

This book is intended solely to provide non-professional information and assistance to persons seeking information regarding common situations experienced by individuals involved in a narcissistic son or daughter in-law, and to provide strategies based on anecdotal experiences shared by thousands of surTHRIVERs.

The surTHRIVER stories in this book were donated for use in this book to help educate others. The names and identifying details of characters associated with events described in this book have all been changed. Any similarities to your own story would make sense because thousands of stories submitted described the common behaviors of narcissists going through estrangement. Every effort has been made to rotate the sexual identity of the victims to further conceal their identities, understanding that the behavior patterns of narcissists are essentially the same, regardless of gender or sexual orientation.

REFERENCE TO INDIVIDUAL PERSONS

Nothing in this book, or any of the accounts shared herein, is intended to describe the factual circumstances of any specific person's experiences. The names of all individuals contributing information for use in this book have been changed. Any resemblance to any person, whether living or not, is purely coincidental.

DEDICATION

To every parent who has felt the deep, unrelenting pain of estrangement this book is for you.

Your heartache is seen, your resilience is honored, and your love for your child is never in vain. To the countless souls I have had the privilege of coaching, to those who have found comfort in my words and videos, and to you brave enough to open this book in search of understanding and hope, I thank you. Your strength in facing the unimaginable is a testament to the power of love. May this book offer you the guidance, validation, and solace you deserve.

TABLE OF CONTENTS

Introduction	9
SECTION 1: Estrangement & Narcissistic Abuse - The Hard Facts	**11**
Chapter 1: Understanding Estrangement and Narcissistic Abuse	13
Introduction – Poem by Tracy	13
What Is Estrangement?	16
Common Reasons and Claims - Why Estrangement?	17
The Narcissistic In-Law Journey: Love Bombing and the Truth Beneath	18
Recognizing/Reflecting On Red Flags	21
You Are Not Alone - Estrangement Statistics	24
Why Are So Many Parents Facing Estrangement?	27
Chapter 2: The Narcissist's Playbook	31
What Is Narcissistic Abuse	31
Traits Of Narcissists	41
The Role of Gaslighting	42
Have You Seen These Tactics?	43
How The Narcissist Controls Your Child	48
Chapter 3: Your Child's Vulnerability	55
Why Can't My Smart Child Recognize Manipulation?	61
Do Parents Have Accountability?	61
Does The In-Law's Family Understand What is Happening?	62
Does Your Child Recognize the Behaviors?	65
The Impact on Your Child: Why They Comply or Cut Ties	66
Your Child and Family Are Equal Victims of Narcissistic Abuse	67
Chapter 4: Ground Yourself	69
Remember the Truth: Holding on to Reality	69

SECTION 2: From Charm to Harm - When Allegations Erase Your Family   71

Chapter 5: How Did We Get Here?   73

   The Family: Before And After   73
   No Two Cases Are Alike: Understanding Your Unique Estrangement Predicament   75
   False Allegations - The Crazy Has Begun!   77
   The Divide or The Discard   80
   You Need Therapy!   83

Chapter 6: Erasing Your Family's Life   87

   The Targeted Parent – When One Is Estranged and One Is Not   87
   When Estrangement Meets Marriage: How Adult Children's Narcissistic Partners Divide Their Parents   91
   The Only Parent or Only Child Differences   93
   We Don't Agree: The Parental Conflicts   95
   The Ripple Effect of Estrangement As It Washes Over the Entire Family   99
   The Pain of Losing Your Grandchildren   102

SECTION 3: Navigating The Pain   105

Chapter 7: Navigating the Pain of Estrangement   107

   The First Few Months: When It Feels Like Your World Is Falling Apart   107
   Endless Rumination: Searching For Answers in a Lifetime of Memories   115
   Where Are You Living? Understanding Emotional Time Zones   116
   What Am I Making This Mean?   117
   Recognizing and Maneuvering Through Emotional Triggers   119
   Hypervigilance - Beating the Anxiety Loop   122
   Healing from Shame and Guilt   126
   Healing the Need for Their Love   128
   Releasing Self-Blame and Finding Peace   129
   Overcoming Rejection and Betrayal in Estrangement   131
   The Fear of Never Reuniting with Your Child or Grandchildren and What to Do About It   133
   Traversing Judgement from Others   135

SECTION 4: The Art Of Communication In Estrangement   137

Chapter 8: Understanding the Narcissist's Communication Style: The Eggshell Dance   139

   Am I Talking to My Child or the Narcissist?   141
   Narc-Speak: Decode Their Communication and How to Respond   143
   Strategies to Prevent Conflict from Escalating - DARVO, BIFF, EAR, JADE   144

Chapter 9: Reaching Out to Your Child: Broaching the Situation — 147

- Should I Keep Reaching Out? Weigh the Pros and Cons — 147
- Finding the Right Moment and Tone for Communication — 149
- Contacting Your Child: Common Letter Writing Mistakes to Avoid — 150
- Navigating Manipulative Tactics in Communication — 152

Chapter 10: They Called—Now What? Preparing for the Unexpected — 155

- Understanding Their Messages: Plan Your Response Effectively — 155
- Stop Being Blindsided: How to Plan Conversations and Responses — 161
- The Cruel Lies: Maintain Composure in the Face of Attacks — 162
- Planning Your Next Steps: Learn to Stay Grounded in Reality — 163

Chapter 11: Planning To Meet Your Child In Person — 167

- Preparing for the First Meeting and Choosing a Neutral Location — 167
- Why It's Important Not to Show Fear When Meeting Your Child — 169
- Setting Boundaries: Will They Come Alone? — 172
- Understanding The Adult Child's Needs in an In-Person Meeting — 173
- How the Narcissistic In Law Can Present — 175
- Understanding How Parents Present and How It May Be Interpreted — 180
- Bracing for Impact: Prepare for Potential Attacks — 199
- Planning Your Next Steps: Know When It's Safe to Ask — 200
- Planning the Conversation: Key Lessons Learned — 201
- Managing Emotional Anxiety Before the Talk — 202
- Rebuilding Trust: Small Steps Forward — 203
- Celebrating Small Wins: Progress Over Perfection — 204

Chapter 12: Going to Therapy with Your Estranged Child — 207

- Choosing the Right Therapist: Yours, Theirs, or Neutral? — 207
- Navigating Therapy – What to Expect — 209

Chapter 13: Hostage Letters and Demands — 221

- Apology Demands – Why Does It Feel Like Santa's Naughty List? — 221
- The Apology Barrier: Why They Won't Accept It — 223
- Crafting an Apology Letter - Sample Letters — 225
- Normal vs. Narcissistic Expectations: Understanding the Difference — 239
- Learn To Analyze Your Child Or In-Laws Texts Or Emails — 240
- Evaluating What Needs a Response — 242
- When Things Go Wrong: Unraveling the Breakdown — 244

Chapter 14: Explaining Estrangement to Those Who
Don't Understand   247

    Explaining Estrangement: Protecting Your Story and Your Heart   247
    The Three-Bucket Strategy for Estrangement Conversations   248

SECTION 5: What Now?   **253**

Chapter 15: What To Expect Going Forward   255

    Be Mindful of What to Expect   257
    Managing Your Expectations: Things to Consider   260
    Rebuilding Trust After Estrangement   262
    Setting Boundaries for Your Mental Health   266
    Practicing Self-Compassion   267
    Winning the Game You Never Wanted to Play   268
    How to Stop Playing the Game Without Giving Up   270
    Navigating the Silence: How Journaling Can Bring Peace   273
    Legacy Ideas to Keep You Busy   276

CHAPTER 16: Financial and Legal Considerations   279

    Protecting Your Child from Financial Abuse and Manipulation   279
    Planning Your Estate in Estranged Family Situations   280
    Grandparent's Rights: What You Need to Know   284

SECTION 6: Conclusion   **287**

Chapter 17: A Message of Hope   289

About the Author   293

Bibliography   295

INTRODUCTION

Family estrangement is an increasingly prevalent and distressing issue that more parents are confronting than ever before. The emotional toll of losing a relationship with a child - particularly when the separation occurs suddenly, without explanation, or under the influence of a controlling partner - can be a profound and difficult grief to put into words. While some estrangements unfold gradually, due to miscommunication or emotional distance, others occur abruptly, leaving parents shocked and searching for answers. Although not every adult child is married to a narcissist, many parents are beginning to identify concerning patterns in their child's partner that suggest manipulation, control, and emotional abuse.

This book is not intended to diagnose anyone, nor is it designed to label your child or their partner. It is not about assigning blame but rather about fostering *understanding*. If you suspect that your adult child is in a relationship with someone displaying narcissistic traits, this book will help you navigate the complexities of the situation. You will gain insight into how narcissistic influence can distort communication, fracture family bonds, and use power and control to isolate your child from you. More importantly, you will learn strategies for responding effectively, safeguarding your emotional well-being, communicating thoughtfully, and preparing for the potential of healing, even in the face of manipulation.

Throughout this book, you will find practical tools, scripts, real-life examples, and supportive guidance - not only for writing letters or preparing for conversations but also for staying grounded in your truth. While I cannot promise to resolve the estrangement, I can help you navigate it with dignity, clarity, and resilience. If you have been made to feel like the villain in a narrative you don't recognize, this book is here to remind you that you are not alone and that there *is* a path forward, even when the road ahead seems unclear.

SECTION 1
Estrangement & Narcissistic Abuse
The Hard Facts

"Parents often make mistakes, not out of malice, but because they don't realize they've been pulled into a game a game only the narcissistic son- or daughter-in-law knows they're playing."

CHAPTER 1
Understanding Estrangement and Narcissistic Abuse

Introduction – Poem by Tracy

The hardest part is **not knowing.**
Not knowing **why...**
Not understanding **why...**
Not having answers...
Not being given a chance to talk...

Worrying if they're struggling ... are they struggling?
Do they care? How could they not?
How could they **not remember** how much you loved them?

Worrying they are gone forever...

Missing the sound of their voice, the sight of their face, the knowledge that you were—or are—loved.

The false accusations are bewildering...
How could they say such things?
They know you better than anyone; why?

Not knowing if you will ever see them again...
Not knowing if you will ever see your grandchildren again...
Worrying that your grandchildren wonder where you are...

Worrying that you caused your child pain...

Not knowing if you can go on without them...
Wondering if they have regrets, if they ever think about you...
Worrying that if something happens to you, would they care?
Would they live with regret over the loss of a loving parent?
Wondering why...

Seeing that everything you tried to teach them about a loving family now exists without you...
The vacillation between the **deepest pain** you've ever felt, to anger and rage.

The rumination over every moment of their life...
The shame...
The pain that pierces your heart, unlike anything you've ever felt...

Reflecting on your choices, lessons, and teachings...
The **internal shame** as you question your role and accountability.

The judgment from friends and family, who believe "children don't walk away from a healthy parent..."

The silence from once-loving friends, who either couldn't fathom facing the same situation or simply don't understand, leaving you isolated in your deepest struggle and greatest loss...

The self-blame, wondering if the trauma you tried to protect them from ended up hurting them too...

Questioning if your own childhood wounds played a role in this...

And asking yourself if life is worth living...

Grieving a child who is alive but chooses to walk away...
The hopelessness...
The silence, the confusion...
The darkness...

Losing a child to death and grieving a child who has chosen to walk away are both profound and painful experiences, yet they carry vastly different kinds of sorrow. When a child passes away, a parent faces an irreplaceable loss, mourning a life that was needlessly cut short and the future that will never be. The pain is immense yet there is often an eventual sense of closure, a societal acknowledgment of their grief, and support from others who understand that loss.

On the other hand, when a child chooses estrangement, the grief is ongoing and filled with uncertainty. There are no answers, no finality, just unresolved questions and the agony of harsh rejection, peppered with a lingering hope that one day they may return. This kind of grief is often silent and isolating, as the world may not recognize or validate the heartbreak of being cut off from a living child. Perhaps it is even assumed that the parent is at fault, or how else would a child turn their back on those who raised them? Both losses leave an ache in a parent's heart, but estrangement adds layers of self-doubt, shame, and an ever-present longing for reconciliation.

If you are reading this, you may know the heartbreak all too well. You may be searching for answers, questioning every moment that led to this loss, and wondering if there is any hope of reconciliation.

This book was created to help you understand what has happened, why it happened, and most importantly, how to not make fatal mistakes that could extend your silence sentence. It is critical to understand and believe that it is *not your fault*.

What Is Estrangement?

My goal, when I first began thinking of this book, was to be a guide; to lead you through this educational journey, starting with the fundamental facts about estrangement and then delving in to take a deeper look at the role narcissism plays in it. As the chapters progress, we will focus on your emotional state, at which time I will help you develop emotional regulation skills to enable you to grow stronger. From there, we'll tackle the crucial aspects of communication: how to engage without triggering further conflict, how to navigate therapy if that opportunity arises, and how to approach seeing your child again. Most importantly, I'll provide guidance on methods to avoid perceived mistakes that could unintentionally make things worse, ultimately helping you move forward with confidence and clarity.

Estrangement is a deeply painful and complex experience. While narcissists tend to use similar patterns of manipulation and control, every family's situation is unique with its own dynamics, history, and emotional layers. When a child chooses estrangement, a parent's grief is ongoing and filled with uncertainty.

Estrangement caused by a narcissistic in-law is particularly devastating. Narcissists thrive on control and often view their spouse's parents as a threat to their dominance. Through tactics like gaslighting, triangulation, and playing the victim, they strategically sow seeds of doubt and conflict, convincing their partner that their family is toxic or unsupportive. Over time, this manipulation erodes the bond between the adult child and their parents, leading to reduced contact, strained relationships, and, in some cases, complete cutoff from the family.

For parents, this type of estrangement often follows a period of closeness and harmony. Everything felt perfect. The sudden shift to distance and hostility is confusing and hurtful. Parents are left grappling with feelings of rejection, guilt, and grief, wondering what they did wrong or how they could have prevented the rift. The emotional toll is compounded by the loss of access to grandchildren and the fear that their child is being manipulated or mistreated. What can you do?

Common Reasons and Claims - Why Estrangement?

Influence and Manipulation: Narcissistic partners work tirelessly to isolate their spouse from family and friends, creating a bubble of control. They may subtly or overtly encourage the adult child to cut ties, claiming the parents are toxic or manipulative. "Look what they did."

Rewriting Family History: Narcissists are experts at reframing the narrative. They may convince the adult child that past family dynamics were abusive or unhealthy, even if they were not. Over time, the adult child starts to see their parents through the narcissist's lens. "Wow, you were right. How did I not see this?"

Setting Unrealistic Expectations for Loyalty: Narcissistic partners often demand absolute loyalty, which can pit the adult child against their parents. Any support or connection to the parents may be seen as a betrayal, forcing the adult child to choose sides. "It's either them or me. Do you want to throw everything we have away?"

False Accusations and Smear Campaigns: The narcissist may spread false accusations about the parents, painting them as harmful or abusive. These accusations are often designed to justify the estrangement and solidify the narcissist's control over the adult child. "I'm saving you from their toxicity."

Control Through Conflict: Narcissists thrive on drama and conflict. By creating tension between the adult child and their parents, they keep the focus off their own abusive behaviors while maintaining control over the situation. ~ Look there, not here. ~

Jealousy Over the Parent-Child Bond: Narcissistic partners are often jealous of any close relationship that threatens their dominance. A strong bond between the adult child and their parents can trigger jealousy, leading the narcissist to sabotage the relationship. "It's your fault we can't be together because you love your parents more than you love us."

Exploitation of the Adult Child's Vulnerabilities: Narcissists often exploit their partner's emotional wounds or insecurities. If the adult child has unresolved issues with their parents, the narcissist will amplify and weaponize those feelings to drive a wedge between them. "They will continue to hurt you because they won't change how they treat/see you."

Financial or Emotional Dependency: If the parents provide financial or emotional support, the narcissist may see them as a threat to their control. Cutting off the parents eliminates competition for influence and ensures the adult child is entirely dependent on the narcissist. "You don't need them. I can give you everything you need."

Boundary Violations Fabricated by the Narcissist: Narcissists often accuse parents of overstepping boundaries, even if no violation has occurred. They may frame normal parental behavior, such as offering advice or expressing concern, as controlling or invasive. "Your parents continue to be in our business, and this is the only way to make it stop."

Preventing Access to Grandchildren: Narcissists often use children as pawns in their manipulations. Estranging the adult child from their parents can prevent grandparents from having a relationship with their grandchildren, further isolating the family. "We don't want our children to be negatively influenced by them."

The Narcissistic In-Law Journey: Love Bombing and the Truth Beneath

A tale as old as time: boy meets girl, they fall in love, get married, and live happily ever after. But in every fairy tale, there's a villain. In today's world of love, it is the people with narcissistic personality disorder (NPD) who have claimed the role of the love villain. They wield control and manipulation, pretending to love someone only to use them for their own gain - what narcissists call "supply." This supply can take many forms: someone to give them children, provide for them financially, or handle all the responsibilities of home and family life. The list of possible reasons is endless. Narcissists demand total control in relationships, and in today's younger generation of narcissists, they have added a new tactic to their playbook: isolating their partner from the people who love them most - their family.

For your family, the journey may have started with what seemed like a dream come true. You met your son or daughter's new partner and were instantly charmed. They appeared to have it all, potential, charm, intelligence, and impeccable manners. They seemed like the perfect match for your child, and you welcomed them with open arms. You took them on family vacations, celebrated holidays together, and maybe even helped with the wedding, a house, or a car. What you didn't realize was that you were being love bombed, a calculated tactic used by narcissists to win over not just their partner, but their partner's entire support system.

Idealization is the first stage in the narcissistic cycle, love bombing is a tactic used in this part of the game. It's a whirlwind of charm, flattery, and grand gestures designed to make everyone feel special and valued. For your family, this meant that the narcissist presented themselves as the ideal addition to your lives. They mirrored your values, laughed at your jokes, and seemed genuinely invested in building a relationship with you. But beneath the surface, this was all part of their strategy to secure control over your child and, by extension, your family. Creepy, right!?

Once the narcissist feels they've secured their position, whether through marriage, moving in together, or some other milestone, the mask begins to slip. The charming, attentive person you once knew starts to change. Suddenly, the lyrics from the old song "Cats in the Cradle" feel eerily familiar: "When you coming home, dad? I don't know when, but we'll get together then." The distance grows. Calls and texts go unanswered. First, your child might try to maintain contact, calling you only when they're alone. But over time, the narcissist tightens their grip, cutting off these lifelines and isolating your child further.

When you do manage to see your child, things feel... off. The narcissist's mood swings and anger become more apparent. They might pick fights over trivial matters, creating tension that forces an early exit. These encounters leave you feeling confused and hurt, wondering what went wrong. The truth is this is all part of the narcissist's plan. They thrive on chaos and control, and by driving a wedge between your child and your family, they ensure their dominance in the relationship.

Donna never imagined she would one day be erased from her only daughter's life. She had spent years as a devoted single mother, guiding Cindy through childhood, supporting her education, and sharing a home with her well into adulthood. Their bond was strong... at least, that's what Donna believed.

When Cindy met her soulmate, Donna was overjoyed. Her daughter had finally found love, and her fiancé seemed like a promising match: intelligent, ambitious, and charming. However, as time passed, subtle changes began to emerge. Cindy and her fiancé became harder to pin down for plans. Canceled visits became the norm, and though Donna missed her daughter, she reassured herself that this was just part of young love - the natural pull toward independence.

Still, something felt off. When they did visit, her future son-in-law often seemed tense, his irritation barely concealed. Cindy would brush it off, explaining that he was under a lot of stress. Donna wanted to believe her, so she ignored the unease creeping into their once effortless relationship.

Then, everything shattered.

Out of nowhere, Cindy called with accusations that blindsided Donna, claims that she had been unsupportive, that she had crossed boundaries she didn't even know existed, that she was toxic. Before Donna could process what was happening, her daughter cut off all contact. No explanations, no discussion, just silence. Calls, emails, and texts went unanswered.

Two years have passed. Donna has never met her grandchildren, never received a photo, never been given the chance to make things right—because, in Cindy's world, she no longer exists. Through whispers from a mutual friend, Donna learned that Cindy and her husband built a life together, a life in which Donna was not welcome.

This is the painful reality of narcissistic in-law estrangement, when a controlling spouse isolates their partner from family, rewriting history to serve their own narrative. While there are countless reasons why adult children become estranged from their parents, this book is dedicated to those who have been deliberately cut off due to the influence of a narcissistic partner.

Not all estrangements follow the same path as Donna's; many, over time, lead to reconciliation.

The Love Bombing of Your Entire Family

What makes this situation so insidious is that the love bombing wasn't just directed at your child, it was directed at your entire family. The narcissist knew that to fully control your child, they needed to win you over too. They showered you with attention, compliments, and gestures of goodwill, making you feel like they were truly part of the family. But this was all a facade, a carefully constructed illusion designed to disarm you and make it harder for you to see the truth when their behavior changed.

The love bombing stage is intoxicating. It feels good to be appreciated, to feel like you've gained a new family member who truly cares. For the narcissist, however, it's just a means to an end. Once they've secured their position, they no longer need to keep up the act. The charm fades, the attention dwindles, and the manipulation begins. What was once a warm, welcoming relationship turns cold and distant, leaving you wondering what you did wrong.

Recognizing/Reflecting On Red Flags

Estrangement rarely happens overnight. There are often early warning signs that, in hindsight, seem glaring. Some red flags include:

Subtle Shifts in Behavior: One of the earliest warning signs of a narcissistic son- or daughter-in-law's influence is a noticeable change in your child's behavior. They may become increasingly distant, defensive, or unresponsive, leaving you feeling like you're walking on eggshells during interactions. You might notice that they only feel comfortable talking to you when their partner isn't around, as if they're being monitored or judged. In the beginning, the narcissist may stop attending family gatherings altogether, leaving your child to visit alone, and even then, these visits often come with a strict time limit or a sense of urgency to leave. This subtle shift in behavior is often the first clue that something is off, signaling the beginning of isolation and control.

Tension at Family Gatherings: Family gatherings, once a source of joy and connection, may become fraught with tension when a narcissistic son- or daughter-in-law is involved. The narcissist often thrives on drama and will deliberately create conflict or discomfort to assert control and shift the focus onto themselves. They might make passive-aggressive comments, criticize family traditions, or pick fights over trivial matters, leaving everyone on edge. Their mood swings or sudden outbursts can turn what should be a happy occasion into a stressful ordeal. Over time, their behavior may escalate to the point where your adult child feels compelled to leave early or avoid family events altogether to prevent further conflict. This deliberate disruption not only isolates your child from their family but also reinforces the narcissist's dominance in the relationship, leaving everyone else walking on eggshells and dreading the next gathering.

Increased Criticism: A narcissistic son- or daughter-in-law may suddenly begin accusing you of overstepping boundaries or being overly involved in your adult child's life, even if your actions were once welcomed and appreciated. This criticism often comes out of nowhere and feels disproportionate to the situation, leaving you confused and defensive. For example, offering to help with childcare, giving advice, or even expressing concern about your child's well-being might be framed as "intrusive" or "controlling." The narcissist uses these accusations to paint you as the problem, driving a wedge between you and your child. Over time, this narrative can erode your child's trust in you, raising questions about your intentions and eventually creating a distance in your relationship. The increased criticism is not about your actions; it's a tactic to assert control, isolate your child, and position the narcissist as the sole source of support and guidance in their life.

Tolerating and Repeating Disrespectful Behavior: Your in-law initiates the devaluation stage by showing blatant disrespect toward your family. They reinforce the false narratives they've fed to your child, and the heartbreaking reality is when your child adopts their mindset, mirroring their behavior, speaking to you with disrespect, and even resorting to yelling and swearing.

Your Services Are No Longer Needed: One of the most telling signs of a narcissistic son- or daughter-in-law's influence is the sudden and unexplained withdrawal of tasks or responsibilities you were once trusted with. Whether it's babysitting your grandchildren, helping around the house, or offering support during busy times, you may find yourself abruptly sidelined. Tasks that were previously embraced and even requested start being met with resistance followed by excuses like, "We've got it covered," or "We don't want to burden you." This shift often feels jarring, especially if you've always had a close, collaborative relationship with your child. The narcissist may frame this change as a desire for independence or boundaries, but in reality, it's a calculated move to limit your involvement and weaken your bond with your child and grandchildren. By cutting off these opportunities for connection, the narcissist further isolates your child and solidifies their own control over the family dynamic, leaving you feeling unappreciated and excluded.

You Are No Longer Welcome in Their Home: A particularly painful red flag in this dynamic is when you are suddenly no longer welcome in your child's home. This exclusion often comes with vague or outright false accusations of an offense you supposedly committed, perhaps a misunderstood comment, a misrepresented action, or even a completely fabricated incident. The narcissistic son- or daughter-in-law may exaggerate or twist the situation to paint you as the villain, claiming you were "disrespectful," "intrusive," or "overbearing." These accusations are rarely based on reality but are instead a deliberate tactic to justify cutting you out. Over time, your child, under the influence of the narcissist, may begin to believe these narratives, further straining your relationship. Being barred from their home not only limits your ability to spend time with your child and grandchildren but also reinforces the narcissist's control by isolating your child from your support and influence. This exclusion is a heartbreaking and clear sign that the narcissist is working to sever familial ties and dominate the relationship.

Relationships and Passions Are Stripped Away: One of the most insidious red flags in a relationship with a narcissistic son- or daughter-in-law is the gradual erosion of your child's connections with their friends and the activities they once loved. The narcissist may subtly or overtly discourage your child from spending time with their friends, often by criticizing those relationships or creating unnecessary drama to make socializing feel like a burden. Over time, your child's friendships may fade as they become increasingly isolated. Similarly, the passions and hobbies that once brought them joy, whether it's a creative pursuit, a sport, or a community activity, may be dismissed as "unimportant" or "a waste of time." The narcissist's goal is to monopolize your child's time and energy, ensuring they have no outside sources of fulfillment or support. By stripping away these relationships and passions, the narcissist weakens your child's sense of identity and independence, making them more reliant on the narcissist for validation and companionship. This loss of self is a heartbreaking consequence of the narcissist's control, leaving your child a shadow of the vibrant person they once were.

You Are Not Alone - Estrangement Statistics

Think back to when you held your child for the first time and vowed to love and protect them for life. You nurtured them, celebrated their milestones, and dreamt of the future you will share. Then, without warning, the bond you've built begins to crumble; not because of a falling out or a mistake, but due to the subtle, deliberate influence of someone you blindly welcomed into your family.

For many parents, estrangement doesn't come from a single argument or misunderstanding. It creeps in slowly, often orchestrated by a son or daughter-in-law whose narcissistic traits erode family connections. You may feel blindsided, heartbroken, and even ashamed. How did it come to this?

You are not alone. Estrangement caused by a narcissistic in-law is an increasingly common and devastating dynamic.

Estrangement Stats

According to Psychology Today, one in four people experience estrangement from a family member, and another study indicates that one in ten have cut ties with a parent or child. Sadly, estrangement is becoming increasingly common and causes profound emotional pain for both parents and the wider family. It can dramatically alter family dynamics, leading to situations where grandchildren are cut off from their grandparents, siblings lose their bond, and extended family members like aunts, uncles, and cousins are suddenly estranged.

Statistics on parental estrangement vary by region and the criteria used in studies. A commonly cited figure suggests that 10-12% of parents in the U.S. are estranged from at least one adult child, while some studies show that as many as one in four families may experience estrangement at some point.

These figures fluctuate across different surveys, often depending on whether the estrangement is seen as temporary or permanent, as well as the underlying causes. As family dynamics continue to shift in modern society, estrangement has become a growing and critical area of research.

Why Does Estrangement Happen?

Estrangement is a painful and complex experience, and there are several common factors that can lead to adult children distancing themselves from their parents. These include:

Control and Isolation by a Narcissistic Partner: A narcissistic partner often seeks to dominate your child's life by isolating them from their family and support system, creating a wedge in the relationship.

Lies and False Allegations: Narcissists are skilled at twisting narratives, often spreading untrue accusations to sever bonds and maintain control.

Personality or Value Clashes: Differences in beliefs, lifestyle, or ways of communicating can escalate into major conflicts over time.

Perceived Abuse or Neglect: Adult children may cite unresolved pain or trauma from their upbringing as a reason for stepping away.

Disagreements Over Parenting or Lifestyle Choices: Disputes about how life should be lived or how grandchildren should be raised can create significant tension.

Understanding these underlying reasons is the first step toward navigating the complexities of estrangement and finding a way to move forward.

Length of Time of Estrangement

Estrangements are not necessarily permanent. The variation in the length of estrangement ranges from less than 6 months to more than 10 years. This is a case-by-case basis and there is no way to judge what an estranged family member should expect.

Percentage of Estranged Children That Return

The percentage of estranged children who reconcile with their parents varies. Some studies suggest that about 10-30% of estranged children eventually reconcile with their parents, but reconciliation is often a gradual and complex process. Many factors influence whether reconciliation occurs, including the cause of estrangement, communication efforts, and external support (such as therapy).

Are More Men or Women Estranged from Their Families?

Studies indicate that daughters are more likely than sons to initiate estrangement from parents. A survey conducted by sociologist Karl Pillemer found that about 70% of estranged adult children are daughters. This may be due to emotional dynamics and relational factors, as women are often more involved in family relationships and may have stronger reactions to perceived emotional issues. If we look at the statistics showing that approximately 62% of people diagnosed with Narcissistic Personality Disorder (NPD) are men, it makes sense that the majority of victims are women. This imbalance helps explain why so many women find themselves entangled in relationships marked by narcissistic abuse.

Common Age Children Walk Away

Estrangement often occurs when children are in their "late 20s to mid-30s," a period during which individuals are forming their own identities, establishing relationships outside the family, and reevaluating past family dynamics.

These trends may vary depending on family backgrounds, cultures, and specific circumstances, but this age range is commonly observed in studies related to estrangement.

Why Are So Many Parents Facing Estrangement?

More and more parents are waking up to the painful reality of estrangement, especially when a narcissistic in-law is involved. I often hear the question, *Why is this happening so much now?* Having spent years in the narcissistic abuse recovery world, I've watched awareness grow. When I first started my YouTube channel in 2018, there were far fewer conversations about narcissism, let alone the impact of a controlling son- or daughter-in-law. Now, in my support groups, we see this pattern repeating over and over, and it's clear that the landscape of parenting has changed.

Parenting has evolved dramatically over the last few decades, shaped by cultural shifts, psychological research, and new societal expectations. These generational changes play a key role in why estrangement seems to be happening more frequently. While understanding these shifts won't take away the pain, it can offer clarity, and with clarity comes the ability to respond in ways that support your own healing and, hopefully, create a path toward reconnection.

The 1950s, 1960s and early 1970s: The Era of Independence

From the 1950s through the early 1970s, parenting was often hands-off. Many parents prioritized their own lives, whether it was socializing, work, or personal interests, while children were expected to entertain themselves and develop independence early. It was not uncommon for young children to roam the neighborhood unsupervised, take on responsibilities far beyond their years, and receive little emotional nurturing. "Children should be seen and not heard" was still a lingering mindset in many homes. This was my parents' mantra, and they were proud of it.

Parents of this era were not neglectful in a malicious way; they were simply raising children in the way they had been raised. Emotional needs were often overlooked because survival and discipline were seen as more important. Children learned resilience, but many also grew up feeling unheard or unseen.

The mid-1970s, 1980s and 1990s: The Overcorrection

As these children grew up and had families of their own, many took a completely different approach. Having felt emotionally neglected, they vowed to be more involved with their children. Parenting books, therapy, and psychology became more mainstream, emphasizing emotional intelligence, self-esteem, and the importance of bonding.

This generation of parents, now raising children in the mid-70s, 80s and 90s, pushed their kids to succeed, micromanaged their schoolwork, and made sacrifices to ensure their children felt loved and supported. However, in doing so, many also coddled their children, shielded them from failure, and overcompensated for their own childhood wounds.

The 2000s to Today: The Age of Emotional Boundaries

Fast-forward to today, and we see an entirely new trend: the rise of emotional awareness, therapy culture, and boundary-setting. Adult children are encouraged to cut off relationships that feel "toxic" or do not serve their well-being. While these methods of protection are a good in theory, too much of any one thing usually isn't. Social media and self-help movements reinforce the idea that estrangement is a healthy step in protecting one's mental health, sometimes without deep exploration of the full family history.

This generation has more language for trauma and dysfunction than ever before, which in many ways is a positive shift. However, in some cases, it may also mean they are more likely to see their parents' imperfections as irreparable wounds rather than normal human flaws. A parent who was once deeply involved may now be perceived as controlling or overbearing, leading some adult children to distance themselves.

Are Generational Parenting Styles Contributing to Estrangement?

It's possible that the pendulum has swung too far in each direction. The neglect and emotional absence of the 50s, 60s and 70s led to over-involvement in the 70s,

80s and 90s, which may have left today's adult children yearning for more autonomy and separation.

Estranged parents often find themselves heartbroken, wondering what went wrong when they did so much for their children. The truth is, parenting has never been a perfect science, each generation reacts to the one before it, often overcorrecting in the process. What is sometimes forgotten is that a parent did not receive training on how to do everything perfectly. They make mistakes along the way and learn as they go. The children may feel like they receive the fallout for that – but they will be in the same situation when they become parents.

This doesn't mean estrangement is always justified, but it does suggest that a larger societal shift is at play. Many estranged parents are not abusive or toxic; they are simply products of their time, raising children in ways they believed were best.

For parents facing estrangement, understanding these generational patterns may help lessen self-blame. Healing may come not from questioning every past decision, but from recognizing that each generation struggles to balance love, independence, and boundaries in its own way. When a narcissistic in-law is involved, however, the way a child was brought up is a non-issue; faults will be found and everything you did will be considered wrong, no matter the circumstance or how you raised them.

CHAPTER 2
The Narcissist's Playbook

What Is Narcissistic Abuse

At its core, narcissism is defined by a need for control, validation, and dominance. A narcissistic son or daughter-in-law often views family relationships as a threat to their authority and will work to dismantle them, leaving parents confused and adult children caught in the middle.

Narcissistic individuals are masters of manipulation. They create division, paint themselves as victims, and turn your child against you, all while convincing everyone else they are blameless. If you've felt powerless in the face of this behavior, it's not your fault.

The awareness of narcissistic abuse has magnified in the last decade. I have witnessed how the younger generation has learned to take the silent treatment to the next level resulting in total estrangement and no contact.

Narc-education and the DSM-5 guidelines.

In the game of narcissistic son or daughter in-laws, it is important to understand the enemies who will place the landmines and idiosyncrasies in your path.

Understanding the dynamics of narcissistic abuse is the first step toward reclaiming your peace and taking back your life.

Narcissistic Personality Disorder (NPD) falls under the category of Cluster B Personality Disorders within the DSM-5.

To be clear, NPD is a personality disorder that typically displays on a spectrum. A narcissism spectrum means people can present with just a few traits (low) such as healthy self-love or self-centeredness to the opposite extreme with full blown personality disorder (high) and a larger number of the more dangerous traits and malevolent behaviors. The narcissist that constantly belittles you is as dangerous as the one who covertly ebbs away your sense of self. Those with NPD can appear mild, sweet, and kind until the something or someone threatens the image they have been portraying, at which point they could instantly morph to straight up devious. If you're wondering how you could have possibly missed that side of their personality, it's because they intentionally hide it. Narcissists often keep their true nature masked until they've fully secured their target, only revealing their darker traits once they believe you're emotionally invested and less likely to walk away.

It is technically and medically incorrect to call someone by the name of their personality disorder. There is not a separate type of human called a narcissist. Just like you would never say, "My mother is a bi-polar," the same holds true for "I am married to a narcissist," since it is technically their personality disorder. You would be correct if you said, "My husband is bi-polar," or "My wife has Narcissistic Personality Disorder." With this said, for the ease in understanding when I refer to narcissists in this book, I will sometimes refer to them as a narcissist or a person with NPD.

Narcissists can be male or female and they traditionally display telltale behaviors by late childhood. It is estimated that 6.2% of the United States population has

Narcissistic Personality Disorder (NPD). That equates to approximately 20 million people – 62% men and 38% women (Stinson et al. 2008). If we assume that each person with NPD negatively impacts three people, 60 million victims would be accounted for in the USA alone. Many experts believe that the number be extremely low and feel a more realistic multiplier would be at least ten (or 200 million victims). These numbers are staggering; there are over 325 million people in the US and the victim count grows daily.

According to the DSM-5, a person can be professionally diagnosed with narcissistic personality disorder by having at least five of the following characteristics:

- A grandiose sense of self-importance (e.g. exaggerates achievements and talents or expects to be recognized as superior without commensurate achievements).
- Preoccupied with fantasies of unlimited success, power, brilliance, beauty, or ideal love.
- Beliefs that they are "special" and unique and can only be understood by, or should associate with, other special or high-status people (or institutions).
- Requires excessive admiration
- Has a sense of entitlement (i.e., unreasonable expectations of especially favorable treatment or automatic compliance with their expectations)
- Displays interpersonally exploitative tendencies (i.e., take advantage of others to achieve their own ends)
- Lacks empathy and is unwilling to recognize or identify with the feelings and needs of others
- Often envious of others or believe that others are envious of them
- Shows arrogance, haughty behaviors, or attitudes

While these characteristics outline the DSM's criteria, the way narcissistic personality disorder presents are not always reflective of this list.

Covert (or Fragile) Narcissist

If you put a frog in a pot of cold water and steadily turn up the heat, the frog will adjust to the raising temperature and will boil to death.

Narcissistic covert abuse is often compared to this analogy because it happens slowly. Once caught, the heat (abuse) gets turned up. Most victims of covert narcissists report that they felt something was off, but it didn't feel like abuse because it was subtle and hard to put their finger on the changes.

The typical pattern of a covert narcissist is to come on fast and intense, claim their soulmate, and propose quickly. It's the idealize phase of the relationship where the victim is placed high on a pedestal and not allowed the chance to really get to know the person or see their true self. The intensity of being the center of someone's world sounds like a fairy tale; but then there is a noticeable change in availability and the victim is no longer the priority…the first of many confusing moments that showcase the reality they will experience going forward.

These tactics are common from a covert narcissist. They are unoriginal, often cowardly, and exceptionally low on the emotional intelligence scale. Most victims don't notice these methods or understand their meaning. They don't see the person as they really are until they leave. The strategies are stealthy and designed to confuse.

Covert narcissists are exceedingly difficult to recognize and even harder to expose because they have built a fake persona with everyone they know. Most that are unaware of the covert traits see a charming, helpful, caring, compassionate, and often enlightened individual. However, this type tends to stick with the same tricks and methods, don't learn from them, and are extremely persistent.

I've compiled a list of covert narcissist traits that you may recognize. I encourage you to examine this from two perspectives: the ways these behaviors have influenced your child and also how they have impacted your family as a whole. Your in-law may use a combination of some or all of these tactics to create division and control the narrative.

- rushes relationships with very intense love bombing (idealizing phase) that "prove" how much they cherish your child
- charming yet socially awkward and less skilled than the grandiose or malignant narcissist
- introvert – withdrawn and self-centered
- lack of empathy for you or others – fake empathy can be exhibited as a technique to get something they want or to find new supply. It is an act to make people think they have true empathy.
- Passive-aggressive communication and behaviors, usually done behind closed doors
- subtle insults
- shaming
- blaming
- gaslighting
- passive-aggressive anger
- procrastination
- ghosting
- silent treatment
- stubbornness
- a sarcastic or argumentative attitude
- deliberately not doing the things they say they will do
- victimized – they play the victim, the world is out to get them, in estrangement you are out to get them, they use their victimhood to trap victims, and they share stories of trauma and neglect.
- sullen, angry, and never content with a quiet rage simmering just below the surface
- overly critical and always believe they are better and smarter than everyone else, even their boss
- needy and vulnerable
- anxious
- resentful and jealous
- hostile and argumentative; must always be right

- not typically good in social situations – if they do go to events, they will ruin them with passive-aggressive behavior.
- no genuine friends – only admirers and people they can use for supply
- constantly seek validation – always bragging to convince others how great they are. In extreme cases this manifests as a God-like mask to be the savior to those lucky enough to be in their presence.
- arrogant and dismiss other's opinions because they believe they are better
- entitled and believe that they deserve the best of everything and seek those who will give it to them, even though they are not worthy of it.
- hypersensitive to feedback or criticism – they react with rage: "How could you!" This is also known as a narcissistic injury.
- need to control everyone around you – the need for control controls them.
- smug with an air of superiority: they don't need you
- expert justifier of their behaviors and usually present it by turning the mirror on you. If you catch them cheating, it was because you weren't being a good partner to give them what they wanted.
- intense need to win and prove they did nothing wrong, so they point fingers at you to deflect the accusations
- no remorse – able to apologize, but the apology is not genuine. They never learn from their actions. The apology is an act to give hope. They will turn around and pull the rug of hope out from under you again at another time.
- emotional actors to control the victim. Crying on demand creates drama, sells them as a sensitive person, moves the attention to them and garners sympathy.
- pathological liars – if their lips are moving, they're lying.
- Even when the truth serves them better, they lie. They can't help themselves and you will wonder how they keep all the fake facts straight.

How many do you recognize?

Weapons of passive-aggressive Covert Narcissists:

- the silent treatment – to punish and abuse their victims. When the covert narcissist goes dark (ghosting) and refuses to engage, the victim feels rejected and wonders what they did to provoke this behavior, making them feel like they did something wrong. Ultimately, the victim will get angry causing resentment from the narcissist because they believe they are entitled to treat people this way.
- ignoring you – pretending not to hear you or understand your request, completely aware that this is aggravating behavior.
- reactive response – pushing the victim to react with anger and then placing blame regarding their anger issues
- playing the victim – a control tool to garner emotions and evoke sympathy by always having a sad story about past mistreatment or making others believe they are team players by consistently accepting the short end of the stick.
- the joke is on you – off-handed jokes are designed to make the victim feel bad. Humor to tease and belittle someone is followed by a "just kidding" in an insincere attempt to ease the pain, but the objective is achieved.
- name calling and constant verbal abuse – typically done in private but sometimes the line is crossed, and it's done in front of family or friends.
- pretending to forget the things they promised to do – intentionally not doing something after they said they would and expressing anger or exasperation if it is mentioned.

How many have you witnessed?

Grandiose Narcissist

The grandiose narcissist is the poster child of what is characteristically described in the DSM-5 as charming, charismatic, confident, attractive, and entitled. This is how most imagine narcissists to present themselves as the "constant mirror gazing" or "let's take a selfie" type.

They tend to hold jobs that put them in a place of power and marry easy-to-control people who will also boost their image and careers. In order to be in a relationship with them, they require someone who appears worthy of being on their arm. Status is necessary but even that cannot outshine them.

Usually soon after marriage, the devalue stage will begin to knock their partner down a peg or two from the status that originally attracted them. It is important that the victim have insecurities so that they need the narcissist.

Grandiose Narcissist traits:
- superiority
- entitlement
- flamboyance
- pompous
- brash
- forcefulness
- never plays the victim
- charming extravert
- controlling
- rages quickly if they don't get their way
- hypersensitive to feedback
- unable to accept that they are not perfect, so they deny criticism and put anyone down that does not get fully on board idealizing them.

How many have you seen?

Malignant Narcissist

Malignant narcissists are on the higher end of the narcissistic spectrum because they usually exhibit an evil side, possibly with sadistic traits. They share the lack of empathy and the poor sense of self-worth with their lesser narcissistic comrades but because of this darkness, they tend to be the ones who derive joy from taking down their enemies.

Where a narcissistic injury often launches other types of narcissists into black-and-white thinking, a malignant narcissist only sees people as friend or foe. Anyone they determine as lesser than them automatically falls into the enemy camp and they are not shy about voicing their opinions. Their amplified lack of empathy will be evident in everything they do.

Malignant Narcissistic traits you may have seen:

- limited capacity to show empathy
- pathological liars
- power and social influence – motivated by the greed of power, they hang with successful people, have great jobs, lead companies, and throw their weight around against their victims.
- grandiosity
- demand validation
- exploitative
- evil tendencies – straddle the line that other types of narcissists only touch
- stalkers
- dangerous – more so than other types as they are more calculated in planning attacks
- more likely to have criminal charges brought against their victim
- takes pleasure in humiliating and causing pain
- master of all skills – unlike the other types of narcissists, they learn from their efforts. They test a strategy, evaluate its success, and then look for additional ways to serve up endless abuse.

If you recognize these malignant narcissist traits, it's likely that your family will continue to face even greater levels of manipulation and cruelty.

The Narcissistic Mask

Narcissistic traits can overlap, or your narcissist may only have a few, because everything NPD-related is on a spectrum, which is as wide as it is long. While behaviors do converge, your in-law might be a hybrid with combination characteristics. Not everyone yells, not everyone gaslights, not everyone is charming, but they all wear masks. Don't bog yourself down trying to label your narcissist in-law because chances are good that you have only seen the tip of the malevolent iceberg. It really doesn't matter what we call them; what matters is the tricks they pull, the behaviors they exhibit and how they make you feel.

While I have outlined the definitions of the different types of narcissists earlier in this chapter, I want to remind you that the same behaviors are often not shared from one covert narcissist to another. Narcissists have created many masks throughout their lives that they present to the world. Imagine a mask as a character, role, or a false persona that they play. Masks of normalcy are routinely invoked to create the illusion to the world that they are normal and not disordered. Designed to entice the people they want to attract for various supply, it's ultimately all about the status, services, money, accolades, dedication, sex, and servitude. The masks are interchangeable so you may identify or cross-identify with several depending on the target of their influence. Narcissists don't need friends or partners; they need an audience so the mask must be selected very carefully.

The narcissistic mask is used as a tool to build a carefully tailored persona in order to friend people who they will later use for supply (your child). When you see a contradiction to what they do in public and what they say in private, you observe the public mask being removed behind closed doors. The masks may seem familiar to you but look a bit deeper and observe other relationships they have and the way the "show" might have always been interchangeable depending on the crowd. Once an actor, always an actor and this performance theater will carry over in every social circle in their lives.

A quote from one of my favorite movies, Sabrina, is apropos – *"Illusions are dangerous people. They have no flaws."* The mask chosen for your child is customized to their needs; the narcissist made your child's dream illusion. The role was defined by your child's own imagination and carefully orchestrated to trap them. I envision the mask being removed at the door and placed on a hook like a hat. Once you see through the fantasy and catch a glimpse of the real person, you can't unsee it. It's scary and the sense of betrayal may be overwhelming.

Narcissists do not want to be exposed. After their mask falls and they realize you have seen the truth; a narcissistic injury usually occurs.

How do these masks relate to your narcissistic son or daughter-in-law?

Traits Of Narcissists

A narcissistic son- or daughter-in-law wields a range of psychological weapons to control their spouse and manipulate their in-laws, with manipulation and lack of empathy being their primary tools. Manipulation often takes the form of emotional blackmail, guilt-tripping, or playing the victim to gain sympathy and control. For instance, they might twist situations to make it seem like their spouse's parents are the source of conflict or unhappiness, even when they themselves are the instigators. They may also use triangulation, pitting family members against each other by spreading lies or exaggerating grievances, creating division and mistrust. This manipulative behavior keeps everyone off-balance and ensures that the narcissist remains the central figure in their spouse's life, free from outside interference.

Another key weapon in their arsenal is their profound lack of empathy. Narcissists are unable to genuinely understand or care about the feelings of others, which allows them to exploit and hurt without remorse. They may dismiss or invalidate the emotions of their spouse and in-laws, making them feel unimportant or irrational. For example, if a parent expresses hurt over being excluded from family events, the narcissist might coldly respond, "You're being too sensitive," or "It's not a big deal." This emotional invalidation not only silences the parents but also reinforces the narcissist's control by making their spouse question their own feelings and loyalty. Over time, this lack of empathy creates an emotional chasm, leaving the family feeling isolated and powerless.

In addition to manipulation and lack of empathy, narcissistic in-laws often employ tactics such as isolation from their support system. Isolation is perhaps the most damaging tactic, as the narcissist systematically cuts off their spouse (your child) from their family and support network, ensuring they have no one to turn to but the narcissist. Together, these weapons of control create a toxic dynamic that leaves the family fractured, the spouse dependent, and the narcissist firmly in charge. For parents, recognizing these tactics is the first step toward understanding the situation and finding ways to protect themselves and their relationship with their adult child.

The Role of Gaslighting

A narcissistic son- or daughter-in-law often uses gaslighting as a powerful tactic to confuse and control both their spouse and their in-laws. Gaslighting involves manipulating someone into doubting their own perceptions, memories, and sanity. For example, they might deny saying or doing something hurtful, even when there's clear evidence to the contrary, or twist events to make it seem like the parent is overreacting or imagining things. They may also rewrite history, claiming that past positive interactions never happened or that the parents were always critical or unsupportive. This constant distortion of reality leaves the targeted family members feeling disoriented, guilty, and unsure of themselves, making it easier for the narcissist to maintain control over the narrative and the relationship.

In the context of estrangement, gaslighting becomes a tool to isolate the adult child from their parents. The narcissist might convince their spouse that their parents are "toxic," "manipulative," or "overbearing," even when there is no evidence to support these claims. They may fabricate stories about things the parents supposedly said or did, painting themselves as the victim and the parents as the villains. Over time, this erodes the adult child's trust in their parents and strengthens their dependence on the narcissist. The gaslighting creates a fog of confusion, making it nearly impossible for the adult child to see the truth or maintain a healthy relationship with their family. For the parents, this manipulation feels like a cruel and unjust rewriting of reality, leaving them powerless and heartbroken as they watch their child drift further away.

Have You Seen These Tactics?

One of the most challenging aspects of estrangement is the exasperating behaviors that come with it. Whether intentional or not, these behaviors can feel like a deliberate effort to wound, alienate, or dismiss the parent's role in their child's life. From dismissing advice to ignoring family traditions, these actions cut deep, leaving parents feeling unseen and invalidated.

I'll explore the common frustrations faced by estranged parents. By shedding light on these experiences, I hope to validate the pain you may feel and provide a deeper understanding of the complex dynamics at play. If you've ever found yourself wondering why your child dismisses your input or why family traditions are disregarded, you're not alone. These experiences are shared by many estranged parents navigating this difficult and emotional journey.

Exercise: Understanding What You've Experienced and How It Made You Feel

Take some time to reflect on the things your child and their narcissistic partner have done to you and your family. Begin by identifying and categorizing their frustrating behaviors, using the examples below. Placing their behavior into specific patterns can bring clarity and validation, especially when you begin to see that these aren't isolated actions, but familiar tactics straight out of the narcissist's playbook.

Once you've categorized their behaviors, take a moment to connect those actions to your emotional responses. Understanding how their treatment is making you feel will help you process the emotional roller coaster of estrangement.

Here are common feelings parents report—use this list as a starting point, and feel free to add your own:

- Excluded
- Powerless

- Unheard
- Scolded
- Judged
- Blamed
- Disrespected
- Silenced or afraid to speak up
- Lonely
- Ignored
- Like the "bad guy"
- Forgotten
- Unsafe
- Unloved
- Betrayed
- Frustrated
- Disconnected
- Trapped
- Emotionally depleted
- Manipulated
- Controlled
- Like nothing you do is ever good enough

This exercise isn't about staying stuck in the pain—it's about naming it, owning it, and beginning to understand how deep the impact has been. Awareness is the first step toward healing.

Brushing Off Advice

Comments like, "We don't do it like that, Mom!" can be dismissive and hurtful, leaving parents feeling like their input is unwelcome or irrelevant. Parents often feel judged, blamed, disrespected, forgotten, or they feel like the bad guy because their integrity is being attacked.

Dismissing Your Pain

The emotional toll of estrangement is often ignored. Adult children may fail to acknowledge how deeply their actions hurt the parent, invalidating their experiences and struggles. Parents often feel judged, blamed, unloved, unheard.

Perceived Judgment

Estranged children often claim their parents are judging their lifestyle choices, even when that may not be the parent's intention. This perception creates a barrier to communication and understanding. Parents often feel judged, blamed, disrespected, unsafe, trapped, controlled.

Overlooking Important Occasions

Family traditions and milestones are often disregarded in estrangement. Birthdays, anniversaries, and weddings may pass without acknowledgment, and even in times of illness, an estranged child may fail to check in. Funerals, in particular, can become a source of family tension. If your child attends, their presence may stir emotions, creating conflict during an already difficult time. On the other hand, they may ignore the loss entirely, leaving the family to grieve not only for their loved one but also the absence of their estranged child. In other cases, the narcissistic in-law may manipulate the situation, turning a funeral into an opportunity to draw attention to themselves, shifting focus away from the person being honored. Parents often feel excluded, powerless, disrespected, ignored, forgotten, unloved, ignored.

Judging Parenting Skills

Estranged children often attack their parents' past decisions, claiming they were abusive or inadequate. They critique and judge their upbringing, often without considering the full context of their parents' actions. Parents often feel unheard, scolded, judged, blamed, feel like the bad guy, forgotten, unsafe, unloved, disconnected.

Judging Grandparenting Skills

Estranged children, often influenced by their narcissistic partner, may criticize how their parents interact with their grandchildren. They nitpick harmless behaviors, impose unrealistic expectations, or claim their parents are unfit to be involved—using grandparenting as another excuse to justify the estrangement. Parents often feel unheard, judged, blamed, disrespected, feel like the bad guy, unsafe.

Refusing to Spend Time Together

Parents may hear excuses like, "We don't have time for you," as their child prioritizes everything and everyone else overspending time together. Well-meaning friends might say, "It's just new love, give them time to adjust," but this situation is different. Those who haven't experienced narcissistic abuse struggle to understand the deep manipulation at play. This isn't just about a busy schedule, but rather control, isolation, and a gradual erasure of the parent-child bond. Parents often feel excluded, blamed, disrespected, ignored, forgotten, unloved, frustrated, disconnected.

Clinging to Past Mistakes

Estranged children often refuse to forgive, repeatedly bringing up past missteps no matter how much time has passed or how many apologies have been made. Narcissists fuel this by keeping a running tally of perceived offenses, using it as a tool to reinforce resentment and control. This constant rehashing of the past becomes a form of emotional brainwashing, ensuring your child remains focused on grievances rather than healing. Parents often feel scolded, blamed, disrespected, feel like the bad guy, unsafe, unloved, frustrated, disconnected, manipulated, controlled.

Unfair Comparisons to Other Grandparents

Estranged children may unfairly compare their parents to the other grandparents or friends' parents, holding them to unrealistic standards. They use these comparisons to criticize, diminish, or justify their distance, making it seem like their parents are never good enough. Parents often feel unheard, scolded, judged, blamed, disrespected, feel like the bad guy, forgotten, unsafe, unloved, felt like it was unfair, frustrated, disconnected, manipulated, controlled.

Failing to Show Gratitude

Instead of appreciating their parents for past or present efforts, estranged children often withhold gratitude, framing everything their parents did as wrong or inadequate. Parents often feel judged, blamed, disrespected, unloved, frustrated, used.

Ignoring Family Traditions

Narcissistic partners or influences may exacerbate this by intentionally disrupting family traditions, leaving the estranged parents and extended family members feeling isolated and hurt. Parents often feel disrespected, forgotten, unloved, felt like it was unfair, frustrated, disconnected.

Mocking Habits or Quirks

Rather than seeing their parents' quirks as harmless or endearing, estranged children may criticize or ridicule them, further demonizing their parents' character. Parents often feel scolded, judged, blamed, disrespected, lack of affection, feel like the bad guy, forgotten, unsafe, unloved, frustrated, disconnected, controlled.

Neglecting Parental Needs

Estranged children often ignore their parents' emotional or physical needs, seemingly as a deliberate act of indifference or punishment, leaving parents feeling abandoned and dehumanized. Parents often feel excluded, powerless, unheard, blamed, disrespected, could speak up, lonely, ignored, forgotten, unsafe, unloved, frustrated, disconnected, manipulated, controlled.

Estrangement carries a profound sense of grief, made even heavier by these painful behaviors. It's completely natural to feel discouraged, confused, and heartbroken. The first step toward healing is recognizing these challenges for what they are: evidence of the deep complexities at play, not a reflection of your worth as a parent. You are not alone in this, and with the right tools and support, you can navigate this difficult journey with strength and clarity.

Social Games They Play

Social media has become a powerful tool for narcissists—a curated stage where they showcase their perfectly polished, yet often fake, lives. It's no surprise that they also use these platforms to manipulate estranged parents. They may impose strict boundaries, insisting that you post nothing about your grandchildren, while they flood their own feeds with daily updates. They might unfollow or block you entirely, sometimes even severing online ties between you, your child, and your child's siblings. And in a final twist of control, they'll follow *your* friends and extended family, ensuring that everyone but you get to see glimpses of the life you've been shut out of. It's calculated, cruel, and designed to deepen the emotional divide.

How The Narcissist Controls Your Child

Understanding Coercive Control in Estrangement

Losing a relationship with your child is an agonizing experience, and when a narcissistic in-law is involved, that separation is often not their conscious choice. It's about control, manipulation, and self-preservation. Your child may still love you deeply, but they are caught in a psychological battleground where pleasing the narcissist is the only way to avoid conflict.

I know this can feel overwhelming, so below, I have outlined the tactics narcissists use to maintain their grip and keep your child from reconnecting with you. Understanding these patterns can help you navigate this painful situation with greater knowledge and compassion.

Cognitive Dissonance: The Psychological Tug-of-War

Your child holds two conflicting beliefs:

- They love and cherish you.
- They must believe the narcissist's narrative that you are toxic.

This internal conflict, known as *cognitive dissonance,* creates deep emotional distress. Instead of confronting the uncomfortable truth that the narcissist is manipulating them, they adopt the narcissist's version of reality to ease their discomfort. Over time, this rewiring of their beliefs leads them to push you away, not out of hatred, but as a survival strategy.

The narcissist fuels this process by:

- Rewriting family history to make you the villain.
- Framing themselves as the victim and the hero who is "saving" your child from you.
- Instilling fear that if your child reconnects with you, there will be consequences.

The Fear That Keeps Them Silent

Your child isn't just estranged; they're being **coerced into staying silent.** The narcissist ensures this by:

- Isolating them: *"Your parents are toxic. They never respected your boundaries."*
- Gaslighting them: *"Your childhood wasn't happy. You just don't remember how bad it was."*
- Using guilt: *"After everything I've done for you, how could you betray me?"*
- Threatening them: *"If you go back to them, I don't know if I can stay with you."*

Your child isn't freely choosing estrangement. **They are surviving.**

How Narcissists Achieve Control: Coercive Tactics in Estrangement

Narcissists use a variety of psychological tactics to isolate their victims and dominate their relationships. These tactics are not random; they are calculated tools used to maintain power that they have honed to perfection.

Gaslighting

They distort reality to make their partner question their past experiences and family relationships. While we have already reviewed gaslighting, this is how it sounds to your child:

- "Your family never listens to our boundaries or respects us. They always try to control you."
- "I know they helped us financially, but do you see how they use money to manipulate us? We're adults, we don't need their control."

Guilt & Obligation

They create a sense of duty and shame, making your child feel responsible for their emotional well-being. This sounds like:

- "I am your family now. How could you betray me by choosing them over me?"
- "After everything I've done for you, you're just going to let them disrespect me like this?"

Victim or Hero Complex

They either paint themselves as the tragic victim or the savior, ensuring the victim remains emotionally dependent. This sounds like:

- "Your family never truly loved you. Can't you see how toxic they are? I'm the only one who truly understands and supports you."
- "They don't think I am good enough for you."
- "They've never accepted me. They're so cruel to me, and I need you to stand up for me."

Triangulation

They pit family members against each other, deepening the estrangement. This sounds like:

- "Your parents always favored your sister's kids over you. Haven't you noticed how unfair they are?"
- "I overheard your mom say something awful about you. You'd be shocked at what they really think of you."

Manipulation

They use charm, deception, and emotional blackmail to keep control. This sounds like:

- *"I'm the only one who's ever truly supported you. Your family has only ever held you back."*
- *"I just want what's best for you. They don't. If they did, they wouldn't treat me this way."*

Fear Tactics

They use intimidation to make sure their victim never challenges their control. This sounds like:

- *"If you let them back into your life, they'll ruin everything. Do you really want to risk that?"*
- *"If they keep interfering, I might have to take legal action to protect our family from their toxicity."*

Reinforcement of Dependency

Narcissists create chaos and instability to keep their partner emotionally reliant on them. Even if your child is financially independent or the primary breadwinner, the narcissist ensures they feel emotionally incapable of standing on their own. I have seen it too many times—the narcissist dismantles their confidence, rewrites their reality, and fosters self-doubt, ultimately convincing them that reconnecting with you is too overwhelming or even dangerous. When everything in their world feels uncertain, clinging to the narcissist feels like the only stable option, even when it's the source of their pain. This sounds like:

- *"Look at what a mess your family has made of things. You don't need them—you only need me."*
- *"No one else will ever love you the way I do. Without me, where would you even go?"*

These tactics are designed to trap your child, making reconciliation with you feel unsafe or impossible. Recognizing them is the first step in breaking their hold.

How Do You Recognize the Signs of Coercive Control in Your Estranged Child

If your child has cut contact, it is not because they suddenly stopped loving you. Their behavior reflects coercion, not choice. To recognize the impact of narcissistic control, understand that their rejection isn't a choice; it's an unknown survival strategy to them. Your child is proving their loyalty to the narcissist because reconnecting with you comes with consequences they cannot afford.

They're Repeating, Not Believing

Every estranged parent eventually realizes, "My child is starting to sound just like the narcissist." When you hear accusations and phrases that sound just like their spouse's words, it's because they've been conditioned to repeat the narcissist's narrative, not because they truly believe it.

They Comply to Avoid Consequences

Your child follows the narcissist's rules, even when it's against their own well-being. This isn't about preference, it's about self-preservation. They have learned that obedience prevents punishment.

They Avoid Talking About Their Experience

When you ask how they're doing, they shut down or change the subject. It's not that they don't want to share, it's that speaking openly risks punishment from the narcissist.

They Internalize the Narcissist's Devaluation

Years of being manipulated have worn them down. You may hear them say things like:

- *"I'm always the problem."*
- *"I always mess up."*
- *"Maybe I don't deserve better."*

This isn't low self-esteem; it's conditioning or as I like to say, reprogramming. They have been trained to believe that they are the problem.

Your child isn't pushing you away by choice; they are trapped in a cycle of coercion, manipulation, and fear, even if it is subconscious. The narcissist keeps them tethered through a relentless push-and-pull dynamic, pulling them back in with love and validation whenever they waver, only to reinforce control once again. Their estrangement isn't a reflection of their love for you; it's a testament to how deeply they have been conditioned to comply.

CHAPTER 3
Your Child's Vulnerability

Estrangement is an unimaginable heartbreak, and when a narcissistic partner is involved, it's rarely about personal choice - it's about control, manipulation, and survival. As a parent, it's devastating to watch your child become unrecognizable, wondering how they end up trapped in a relationship that isolates them from the people who love them most.

Your adult child's vulnerability to marrying or being with a narcissist can often be traced back to their personality traits, life experiences, and emotional needs. If your child is an introvert, a people pleaser, or someone who is deeply kind, loving, and forgiving, they may be more susceptible to falling under the spell of a narcissist. These traits, while beautiful and admirable, can make them an ideal target for someone who seeks to exploit their generosity and desire for harmony. A narcissist is drawn to individuals who are empathetic and selfless, as they are more likely to tolerate abusive behavior and prioritize the narcissist's needs over their own.

If your child is spiritual or highly values forgiveness, they may be more inclined to give the narcissist endless chances, believing in their capacity to change or seeing the good in them despite glaring red flags. Additionally, if your child is successful, has a promising career, or comes from a wealthy family, they may attract a narcissist who sees them as a source of financial gain or social status. The narcissist's charm and love bombing can feel like a dream come true to someone who is desperate for love or validation, making it difficult for your child to see the manipulation beneath the surface.

Common Vulnerabilities That Narcissists Exploit

Limited Relationship Experience

If your child did not have many serious relationships before meeting their narcissist, they may lack the emotional experience to recognize manipulation, gaslighting, and control. Without past heartbreaks or betrayals, they may idealize their partner and overlook red flags. Without a clear understanding of what abuse looks like beyond physical harm, they may dismiss emotional or psychological manipulation as normal relationship challenges rather than the dangerous red flags they truly are.

How it feels to your child:

- They've never felt love like this before.
- They don't see the red flags because they have no comparison.
- The narcissist becomes their entire world, making them emotionally dependent.

Overprotective or Sheltered Upbringing

If your child was raised in a highly protective environment, they may have been shielded from hardship, making it more difficult for them to recognize when they are being mistreated. They may lack the ability to set strong boundaries, which a narcissist quickly exploits.

- They never learned how to say no to authority figures or partners.
- They may be more trusting and naiver, believing the best in people.
- They weren't exposed to manipulation tactics, making them more susceptible.

Deeply Spiritual, Forgiving, or Conflict-Avoidant

Some children are naturally empathetic, forgiving, and inclined to see the good in others. If your child was raised with strong spiritual or religious values, they may believe in unconditional love and second chances, even in the face of abuse.

- They rationalize the narcissist's bad behavior as something they can 'fix' with love.
- They believe setting boundaries is unkind or 'not what a good person does.'
- They think enduring hardship makes them strong or loyal.

Abuse & Control

Even if your child grew up with a narcissistic parent, their perception of abuse may be shaped by what they witnessed in childhood. If the narcissist in their life now presents differently from what they previously experienced, they may not see the warning signs. For example, if they grew up with an overt narcissist, one who was explosive, argumentative, or physically aggressive, they might assume that as long as their partner isn't screaming or throwing objects, they are in a healthy relationship.

I've seen this happen time and again, and I personally understand how easy it is to miss the signs. In my own life, my parents fought like cats and dogs. My mother threw plates. That was my normal, what I (later) understood to be abuse. Fast forward to adulthood when a covert narcissist entered my life, quietly manipulative, emotionally controlling, and cruel in subtle ways. I naturally compared it to what I knew of abuse and assumed I was safe. I fell for it, hook, line, and sinker. It wasn't until much later that I realized abuse doesn't always come in the form of yelling or physical violence, it can be hidden in charm, guilt, silent punishment, and emotional withholding.

The cycle of intermittent reinforcement in childhood had me believing that the sudden flips between rage, flying plates, and tearful apologies were signs of love. I convinced myself their anger was my fault. The fear that I had done something wrong was enough to trigger my shame and justify the abuse I was enduring. Your child may be experiencing this same blind spot, unknowingly rationalizing or minimizing the behaviors of their partner because it doesn't match their idea of what abuse looks like.

Understanding this can help you approach their situation with compassion and patience, knowing that their lack of awareness isn't willful ignorance, but rather a gap in experience and understanding that has left them vulnerable to manipulation.

- They think abuse only looks like physical violence, not psychological tactics.
- They don't understand why the narcissist's behavior is harmful.
- They dismiss concerns as 'drama' or 'family misunderstandings.'

People-Pleasing & Codependency

Children who grow up as people pleasers are prime targets for narcissists. If your child seeks external validation or struggles with confrontation, they may prioritize keeping the narcissist happy over maintaining family relationships.

- They avoid conflict by giving in to the narcissist's demands.
- They feel responsible for the narcissist's happiness and wellbeing.
- They don't want to 'rock the boat' by defending their parents.

Coming from a Divided or Dysfunctional Family

If your child grew up in a household with divorced parents, family tension, or estranged relatives, the narcissist may exploit this by deepening the divide.

- They believe cutting off family is normal or necessary.
- They already feel pulled between family members, making it easier for the narcissist to step in as their 'protector.'
- They see estrangement as an acceptable conflict resolution strategy

Exposure to Narcissistic Behavior in Childhood

If your child was raised by or around a narcissist, they may find the narcissist's behavior familiar, even comforting. They may not realize they are being manipulated because it feels "normal."

- They mistake control for love because they grew up with it.

- They unconsciously repeat patterns from childhood.
- They don't see how unhealthy the relationship really is.

Vulnerability Through Disability or the Need for Extra Care

If your child lives with a disability—physical, emotional, or neurological—or simply needs extra care and support, they may be especially vulnerable to narcissistic partners. The narcissist may initially appear nurturing, understanding, and accepting. This can feel like a rare and precious connection to someone who has often felt overlooked or misunderstood. The narcissist seizes this opportunity to gain control under the guise of love and support.

Sadly, I often see this happen when a child receives disability benefits, has a trust fund, or relies on family financial support. A low-level narcissist will cling to your child—not out of love, but as a source of income and security. What looks like a caregiving relationship can quickly turn into a parasitic one.

- They feel lucky someone finally 'sees' them and accepts their challenges.
- They confuse dependence for intimacy, mistaking control for care.
- They fear no one else will love or accept them, so they cling to the relationship.
- They feel too overwhelmed by life to question or challenge the narcissist's behavior.
- The narcissist quietly takes control of finances or living arrangements under the pretense of helping.

Strong Independence & Success

Many narcissists target highly capable, self-sufficient individuals because they want:

- A partner who makes them look good.
- Financial stability (without having to earn it themselves).
- Someone who handles responsibilities for them.

How it looks:

- The narcissist takes credit for their achievements.

- They drain them emotionally and financially.
- They keep them so busy and exhausted that they don't have time to question the relationship.

Exploitation of Emotional Wounds & Insecurities

If your child has unresolved emotional wounds or insecurities, the narcissist will use them to gain further control. They may position themselves as the only one who truly understands your child, deepening their dependency.

How it sounds to your child:

- *"No one else really gets you like I do."*
- *"Your family never appreciated you, I'm the only one who does."*
- *"You're too sensitive; they don't care about you the way I do."*

How Narcissists Exploit Your Child's Unmet Needs

Another vulnerability that can play a powerful role in estrangement is unmet needs. Every person carries wounds from childhood needs that were never fully met, even in the best of families. Narcissists are experts at spotting these vulnerabilities and exploiting them. If your child grew up as an only child, they might have longed for a big, close-knit family, and the narcissistic in-law swoops in offering that dream. If they grew up in a large family where they sometimes felt overlooked or unvalidated, the narcissist offers endless attention, admiration, and the illusion of deep understanding. The narcissist becomes the fulfillment of whatever ache your child carries, weaving themselves into a false sense of healing only to later use that attachment as leverage to alienate them from you. Understanding this dynamic can help parents see that the estrangement isn't solely about past grievances, it's about how the narcissist weaponized their child's deepest unmet emotional needs.

Understanding your child's vulnerabilities doesn't mean blaming yourself or them.

Your child's vulnerabilities were not weaknesses until someone weaponized them. It's devastating to watch them be used, manipulated, or isolated, but awareness is the first step to healing. By recognizing how they were pulled into this dynamic, you can better understand their vulnerabilities for why they were targeted. They didn't choose a narcissist; they chose the mask the narcissist carefully crafted and sold them as love.

Why Can't My Smart Child Recognize Manipulation?

Estrangement from an adult child is a heartbreaking experience, especially when you believe their narcissistic spouse or partner is the driving force behind the divide. One of the most common questions parents ask in this situation is, "My child is so smart, why can't they see what's happening?" The answer lies in the intricate and calculated tactics used by narcissists to manipulate and control their partners.

Intelligence doesn't protect against manipulation.

It's important to recognize that intelligence isn't a shield against emotional manipulation. Narcissists are masterful at creating an alternate reality, subtly isolating their partners from their support systems while presenting themselves as the victim or hero. They often use techniques which can entangle even the most perceptive individuals.

Your child's intelligence may even work against them in this scenario. They might rationalize or excuse the narcissist's behavior, believing they can "fix" the situation or that they're seeing a side of their partner others can't understand. This misplaced loyalty can deepen their entanglement and prevent them from seeing the harm being done.

Do Parents Have Accountability?

Parents can find themselves absorbing the blame for their estrangement. Narcissists are skilled at weaving a narrative that positions them as the victim and you as the villain, and they often sprinkle in a small kernel of truth to make their accusations seem more credible. While no parent is perfect, and mistakes happen in every family, the difference here is that the narcissist takes those imperfections, real or fabricated, and weaponizes them to drive a wedge between you and your child.

Many parents, desperate to maintain or restore their relationship with their child and grandchildren, are willing to take responsibility for things they may not have even done or accept blame for actions that were never intended to harm. The pain of estrangement can make them question themselves: *Did I really fail as a parent? Could I have done something differently?* These questions are normal, but they become dangerous when the narcissist uses them to manipulate you into self-blame and compliance with their demands.

True accountability requires self-reflection, but it does not mean accepting false blame or groveling in the hope of regaining a relationship. It's important to separate genuine moments of parental imperfection from the exaggerated or distorted accusations the narcissist feeds your child. You may have made mistakes, as all parents do, but that does not justify complete estrangement or the cruelty of being cut off from your child's life. The key is to acknowledge what is fair without allowing the narcissist to rewrite history or hold you hostage to an unattainable standard of perfection.

So, do parents hold accountability in these situations? Only for their real actions, not the twisted version the narcissist has painted. The challenge is learning to distinguish between healthy accountability and the manipulative guilt that keeps you trapped in a cycle of blame, hoping for reconciliation on terms that will never be fair.

Does The In-Law's Family Understand What is Happening?

One of the most frustrating aspects of this is wondering whether their own family sees the truth. Do they recognize the manipulation, control, and abuse their child is inflicting on your son or daughter? Do they acknowledge the destruction left in their wake? Or are they complicit, either through enabling, denial, or outright participation in the behavior?

In some cases, the narcissist's parents are fully aware of who their child is but believe that marriage or parenthood will "fix" them. They may have lived through years of their child's chaos and mistreatment, hoping that a strong partner would come along and stabilize them. They might even express relief that their child has "found someone," without fully grasping, or choosing to acknowledge, that their child is continuing the same destructive patterns in their new relationship.

Other times, the in-laws are enablers, having spent their lives making excuses for their child's toxic behavior. These parents may have covered for them as they manipulated others, overlooked their deceit, or ignored the emotional damage they caused within the family. They might justify their child's actions by saying things like, "That's just how they are," or even blame others, including you, for "provoking" the estrangement. When a narcissist is enabled rather than held accountable, they learn that their behavior is acceptable and continue using the same tactics into adulthood.

Then, there are families where estrangement is a repeated pattern, passed down through generations. If your in-law has cut off multiple people before or has a history of burning bridges, their parents may have been victims of the same tactics themselves. Some narcissists turn against their own families first, training themselves in the art of isolation and control before applying it to their romantic partners. If their parents have already been discarded, they may silently watch the cycle repeatedly, either resigned to it or unwilling to confront the truth.

In the most extreme cases, the narcissist's parent is the source of the dysfunction. If they were raised by a narcissistic parent, they may have learned everything from them, how to gaslight, manipulate, and emotionally dominate others. A narcissistic parent may actually encourage their child's behavior, viewing relationships as a game of control rather than connection. These are the families that breed estrangement and division, where emotional abuse is normalized, and loyalty is demanded rather than earned.

When the Narcissist's Parents Turn Against You

The relationship with a child's new in-laws often begins on a hopeful note, filled with warm intentions, shared support, and the shared excitement of two families coming together. During the engagement, these in-laws may seem kind, helpful, and eager to create a blended extended family. They might host showers, help with the wedding, and include you in celebratory gatherings. You might believe a genuine bond is forming - one rooted in mutual care for your children and their new marriage.

What catches many parents off guard is how drastically things shift after the wedding. The warm, welcoming relationship suddenly turns cold, distant, or even hostile, and you're left wondering what happened.

What's happening behind the scenes is something I've seen time and time again in estrangement cases: the narcissistic son- or daughter-in-law begins a calculated smear campaign almost immediately after the wedding. They start planting seeds of doubt in their own parents' minds, playing the victim and spinning stories that cast you and your family in a negative light. It can be as subtle as claiming you gave them a judgmental look walking down the aisle, or as extreme as accusing you of refusing to include them in family photos or ignoring them at the reception. These false narratives are carefully crafted to turn their parents against you, gaining sympathy and support by portraying you as cruel, disrespectful, or dismissive - when none of that is true.

This strategy serves multiple purposes. First, it isolates your child by aligning both sides of their new family against you. Second, it gives the narcissist control over the narrative, shaping how others view you without your knowledge or ability to respond. And lastly, it sets the stage for estrangement. With their parents now "on their side" and a growing list of supposed slights and offenses, they can justify cutting you off completely – casting themselves the innocent victim of a toxic parent. By the time you realize what's happening, the damage is often done, and the narcissist's family has become a silent - or active - accomplice in your estrangement.

Understanding the role the in-laws' family plays in your child's estrangement can be helpful, but it doesn't always change the outcome. Whether they are aware of their child's narcissism or in complete denial, your focus should remain on protecting your own emotional well-being and setting healthy boundaries. Recognizing that your in-law's family dynamic is likely complex, dysfunctional, or complicit can help you make sense of their behavior, even if it doesn't bring you closer to the resolution you seek.

Exercise: Reflecting on the In-Laws' Family

Take a few minutes to write down everything you know about your in-laws' family. This exercise can help you gain clarity about whether their parents are trustworthy or if it's wiser to proceed with caution. Be mindful: sharing concerns with the narcissist's parents could easily make their way back to your son- or daughter-in-law and potentially be used against you.

That said, not all in-laws' parents are toxic. Some estranged parents have found unexpected allies in the narcissist's family, especially when those relatives don't display narcissistic traits themselves. These individuals have at times shared photos of grandchildren or offered insights into patterns they've seen in their own child's relationships. While it's important to protect yourself, it's equally important to stay open to the possibility of support in unexpected places.

Does Your Child Recognize the Behaviors?

One of the most painful questions estranged parents wrestle with is: Does my child see what is happening? Do they recognize the manipulation, control, and emotional abuse inflicted by their narcissistic spouse? It's natural to hope that deep down, your child knows something is wrong, that they can see the toxic dynamics unfolding. However, it's important to revisit our discussion on coercive control, a powerful psychological force that shapes the way your child thinks, reacts, and even justifies their partner's behavior. Narcissists do not manipulate with outright force; they reshape reality, slowly training their victims to question their own thoughts, memories, and instincts. Your child may have once expressed doubts or frustrations about their partner, but under the narcissist's influence, those moments are quickly erased, rewritten, or dismissed.

In the early stages of the relationship, your child may have voiced or shared concerns or even confided in you about things they didn't like. They may have asked, "Do you think this is normal?" or "I don't like when they do that." But narcissists are masters of intermittent reinforcement, showering their victims with love, charm, and affection just when they start to pull away. This cycle creates emotional confusion, keeping your child tethered to a toxic relationship. Every time they begin to question or push back, the narcissist skillfully reels them back in, making them forget the cruelty, convincing them that they overreacted, or making them believe they are the problem. Over time, the doubts fade, replaced by the narcissist's version of reality.

Most victims of narcissistic abuse eventually stop fighting back, not because they don't see the manipulation but because they have been conditioned to accept it. They begin to think, *"This is just how they are..."* or *"If I just don't argue, things will be easier."* Slowly, they lose the ability to distinguish between what is healthy and what is toxic. Your child may not be blind to the dysfunction; they may simply be too exhausted, too confused, or too afraid to challenge it. The best thing you can do as a parent is to remain a steady, loving presence outside of their manipulated world, providing a safe space for them to turn to if and when they finally recognize the truth.

The Impact on Your Child: Why They Comply or Cut Ties

When a narcissistic partner enters the picture, your child may feel trapped in a no-win situation. They might:

- Comply to Keep the Peace: Agreeing with their spouse to avoid conflict.
- Internalize Manipulation: Believing the lies told about you and themselves.
- Fear Retaliation: Avoiding contact with you because of the backlash it could provoke from their spouse.

The psychological toll this dynamic takes on your child and how their choices are often driven by fear, not malice. Understanding this perspective can help you process the estrangement with compassion, even if their actions feel deeply hurtful.

Your Child and Family Are Equal Victims of Narcissistic Abuse

When I work with parents in this situation, they often struggle to accept that their child has become a victim of narcissistic abuse. It's heartbreaking for them to feel powerless, unable to help or protect their child from the manipulation and control of a narcissistic partner. This is especially painful when they reflect on the loving, close relationship they once shared with their child before the narcissist entered the picture. My hope is that by sharing these insights, you're able to see more clearly how the behaviors of narcissists align with what you've observed in your in-law. Recognizing these patterns is the first step toward understanding the dynamics at play and finding ways to navigate this difficult situation.

What's important to understand is that your child isn't the only victim of this narcissistic abuse, your entire family is affected. Siblings, nieces, nephews, cousins, aunts, uncles, and grandparents all feel the ripple effects of the narcissist's control. The narcissist has taken your once-loving, kind child and transformed them into someone who may feel unrecognizable to you. This estrangement is not a reflection of your love or your relationship with your child; it's the result of the narcissist's calculated efforts to isolate and dominate.

I often hear parents say, "I hesitate to label my daughter-in-law as a narcissist, it feels like such a trendy buzzword." You don't need an official diagnosis to recognize narcissistic behavior: if it walks like a duck and talks like a swan, it's likely a narcissist. In the same way, if your in-law consistently displays the hallmarks of narcissism, manipulation, lack of empathy, control, and a pattern of exploiting others, then the advice for dealing with a narcissist will likely apply. Trust your observations and instincts. When their actions align with the traits and patterns of narcissism, it's reasonable to treat the situation as such, even without a clinical label. The goal isn't to diagnose but to understand and respond effectively to protect yourself and your family. If the behaviors fit, the strategies for navigating narcissistic relationships will too.

There is, however, reason to hold onto hope. Many adult children eventually see through the narcissist's manipulation and find their way back to their families. The fog of control can lift, often when the narcissist's behavior becomes too extreme to ignore or when the victim begins to reclaim their sense of self. While the journey to reconciliation may take time, it's important to never give up hope. Hold onto faith. Faith is believing in something even when you can't see how it will work out. Your love, patience, and unwavering support can be a lifeline for your child, even if they can't fully acknowledge it yet. Keep the door open, and trust that healing and reconnection are possible, even in the face of such profound challenges.

CHAPTER 4
Ground Yourself

Remember the Truth: Holding on to Reality

Your greatest tool in navigating the chaos created by a narcissistic in-law is your mind. While the narcissist works tirelessly to rewrite your family's story, casting you as the villain and distorting the truth, your strongest defense is to hold firmly to reality—the reality of who you are and the love you've shared with your child. You know the parent you were, the sacrifices you made, the support you have offered, and the unconditional love you gave. The narcissist's goal is to erase that truth, making you question your own reality just as they have conditioned your child to doubt theirs.

Many parents don't realize that the narcissist's lies are a form of gaslighting. Their rewriting of your family's history isn't just manipulation, it's deliberate psychological warfare designed to confuse, distort, and weaken your child. Their tactics are meant to make you second-guess yourself, to wonder: *Did I really do those things? Was I really a bad parent?* If you allow their false narrative to take hold, even for a moment, then their manipulation is working. The narcissist wants you to internalize their poison, to believe their version of events so that, in your pain and self-doubt, you shrink away from your child and give up on rebuilding your relationship.

Resist this. Hold onto your truth. The love, history, and connection you built with your child are real. No amount of distortion can erase the years of care and commitment you shared. These truths are your anchor, keeping you grounded when the narcissist's lies threaten to pull you into despair. By staying focused on the reality of your actions and intentions, you protect yourself from their gaslighting and remain steady in your love, so that when your child is ready to see through the manipulation, they have a strong, unwavering parent waiting for them.

It's also important to revisit your memories not with pain, but with joy. Reflect on the moments that define your relationship with your child, the laughter, milestones, and quiet moments of connection. These memories are proof of the love you share, and they belong to you, no matter how the narcissist tries to distort them. Allowing yourself to embrace the sweetness of those memories, rather than the pain of estrangement, can help you maintain emotional resilience. When you hold onto joyful remembrance, you remind yourself that the love you built is real and enduring, even if it feels distant right now.

Finally, don't let the narcissist's lies overshadow your truth. They may try to convince your child, and even you, that you were never a good parent, that your actions were selfish, or that you caused harm. But you know the truth. You know the love you've poured into your family, the efforts you've made, and the genuine care you've always shown. Hold onto that truth, even when the world tries to rewrite it. By staying rooted in reality, you not only protect your own mental and emotional well-being, but you also create a foundation of truth, a safe place for your child to return to when they are finally ready to break free from the narcissist's grip.

Your truth is your strength—never let it go.

SECTION 2
From Charm to Harm
When Allegations Erase Your Family

"A narcissistic son- or daughter-in-law doesn't just enter your child's life they slowly eclipse it, dimming the light of friendships, silencing the warmth of family, and stealing the spark of every passion once cherished."

CHAPTER 5
How Did We Get Here?

The Family: Before And After

Families that experience estrangement due to a narcissistic partner often share a deep bond prior to the separation from their child. These families tend to be close-knit, supportive, and emotionally connected, with strong traditions, shared values, and a history of being there for one another. Parents and children in these families probably enjoyed open communication, heartfelt conversations, and a foundation of trust that made them feel secure. Siblings may have been best friends, and extended family members likely played significant roles in each other's lives.

Due to this closeness, your child has become the prime target for a narcissistic partner who seeks control. Why? Think back to chapter 1 where we outlined what a narcissist looks for in their supply. It Is all these positive attributes that they desire for themselves and find in your child and, ultimately, your family. At the same time, narcissists recognize that these strong family ties threaten their ability to isolate and manipulate their partner. They want what you have and represent but they don't want you to as part of the package. In fact, they need you completely out of the picture. They know that a person with a loving, involved family is more likely to have emotional support, outside perspectives, and the courage to leave if the relationship becomes unhealthy. To prevent this, narcissists often employ subtle but deliberate tactics to create division. They sow doubt by making the adult child question their family's intentions, twisting words and past events to paint the family as intrusive, judgmental, or even harmful. Over time, the partner being manipulated may start to believe that their family is unsupportive or toxic, leading them to withdraw in an attempt to keep peace in their relationship.

For the estranged family, this separation is devastating. They don't just lose their child or sibling, they lose a lifelong relationship built on love, trust, and shared experiences. The absence is particularly unnerving because it is not rooted in conflict that naturally arises between family members but in the distortion of reality caused by an outsider (the narcissistic partner). Parents who once had daily conversations with their child may be left in silence, unsure of what went wrong. Siblings who were once inseparable may feel like strangers. The pain is compounded by the knowledge that their loved one is likely suffering under the influence of their partner, yet any attempt to reach out may be met with resistance, anger, or even complete rejection.

Unlike estrangement due to direct abuse from a parent where the child seeks protection and distance, this unwarranted estrangement leaves families feeling helpless. They were once a source of comfort and safety, and now they are perceived as a threat. The grief is profound, not only for the loss of connection but for the fear that their loved one is enduring emotional, and possibly physical, harm without the support system that once held them up.

No Two Cases Are Alike: Understanding Your Unique Estrangement Predicament

Estrangement varies widely from family to family. Some parents find themselves completely cut off, while others experience a strained, distant relationship with minimal contact. The level of estrangement often depends on how much influence the narcissistic in-law exerts and how enmeshed the child has become in their spouse's family dynamic.

Common Estrangement Scenarios:

Conditional Contact: Communication and visits are allowed, but only under strict and unspoken rules, usually dictated by the in-law. The boundaries are unclear, shift frequently, and leave parents feeling confused or punished for unknowingly crossing invisible lines. The ever-changing nature of the "rules" makes it difficult to know what is acceptable, creating a constant sense of walking on eggshells.

Superficial Contact: The relationship exists in name only, maintained more out of obligation than genuine care. There's little to no emotional depth, and your well-being is rarely, if ever, a concern. They may never ask how you are or acknowledge if you're sick and although you might still receive a token "Happy Birthday, Dad" text, it will always be only enough to maintain minimal contact without true connection.

Total Cutoff: All forms of contact are severed. Your child blocks phone calls, emails, and social media, and you are completely shut out of their life, including access to the grandchildren. In some cases, parents who attempt to break through this boundary have faced legal consequences, including police involvement or threats of arrest.

Relationship Stages and Their Impact:

Dating & Engagement: Estrangement can begin subtly at this early stage. A controlling or narcissistic partner may start testing your child's loyalty by planting seeds of doubt about you. If they succeed in dividing your family early on, it often signals their intent to dominate and isolate later. This is when the groundwork for control is quietly laid.

Married Without Children: Once married, the influence may intensify. The spouse might begin to enforce rigid boundaries that seem disproportionate or out of step with your history. These limits are often based on distorted narratives or emotional manipulation, making it nearly impossible to understand what changed or why.

Married With Children: This stage often brings the deepest pain. Grandchildren can be used as leverage, with access restricted or revoked altogether. Grandparents are frequently accused of being overbearing, inappropriate, or even abusive, claims that reflect more about the narcissist's need for control than any real threat. This vilification isolates the parent further and strengthens the in-law's hold over the family.

Each estrangement is shaped by personal history, family dynamics, and external influences. Some estrangements happen suddenly, while others unfold gradually over the years. Occasionally parents receive a direct explanation, while many are left in silence trying to piece together what went wrong. In other cases, only one parent is cut off, while the other remains in contact, creating division. Sometimes, siblings stay connected, but most narcissistic partners who push estrangement ensure the complete dismantling of an entire family unit, leaving grandparents, aunts, uncles, and lifelong family friends confused and heartbroken.

A key factor in narcissistic estrangement is the accusations made against the family. Parents might be labeled as controlling, manipulative, or emotionally abusive, claims that are often exaggerated or completely false. Other allegations may be vague, such as being "negative" or "toxic," without any clear explanations. Narcissistic partners excel at rewriting history, persuading the estranged child to view past interactions through a distorted lens that serves their agenda.

Demands also vary. Some estranged children impose strict rules: no discussing the past or offering opinions, no mentioning of certain people, or even requiring all communication to go through their partner. Others demand financial support, compliance with specific behaviors, or apologies for things to which the parent is oblivious. These conditions may shift over time, leaving parents feeling like they are walking on thin ice, never sure what will be acceptable or how to rebuild the relationship.

Many parents make numerous attempts to reconnect, writing heartfelt letters, respecting boundaries, offering to participate in counseling, or seeking mediation, only to be met with silence, resistance, or further accusations. If a narcissistic partner is involved, efforts to reconcile may be twisted as proof of wrongdoing.

Recognizing that no two estrangement cases are alike should help parents avoid comparing their situation to others. While patterns exist, each instance is deeply personal, influenced by history, personalities, and outside pressures. Understanding these nuances can help parents make sense of their experience and focus on preserving their emotional well-being, even in the face of uncertainty.

False Allegations - The Crazy Has Begun!

It all starts with what's known as the **love bombing stage (idealize)**, when your narcissistic in-law carefully crafts a false persona to win over your child, and your entire family. They hide their true nature, presenting themselves as kind, loving, and deeply invested in your child's happiness. Most recall welcoming this person with open arms, taking them on family vacations, celebrating holidays together, and embracing them as part of the family.

During this stage, generosity flows altruistically. Parents help with wedding expenses, assist with purchasing a car, contribute to a down payment on a home, or provide other financial assistance. After all, this is your child's partner, someone they have chosen to build a life with. There is no reason to suspect that all the kindness and support you gladly offer will one day be twisted against you.

The Devalue Stage – The Shifting Narrative Begins

Slowly, the **devalue stage** creeps in. The warmth fades, replaced by subtle criticisms and passive-aggressive remarks. Little jabs disguised as humor. Comments about your parenting style, your traditions, or even your personality. At first, they seemed small, even ignorable. But over time, the message becomes clear: *you're the problem*.

Here are some things your child might hear in the devalue stage:

- *"Your family is so overbearing. I don't know how you survived growing up with them."*
- *"Your mom means well, but she has no boundaries. I can't believe the way she just invites herself into our business."*
- *"Your dad is always trying to control everything. No wonder you have anxiety."*
- *"I don't feel comfortable at your family gatherings, they're just... too much."*
- *"Your parents seem nice, but they're actually manipulative if you think about it."*
- *"I just want to protect you from all the negativity your family brings into our life."*

Your child, initially resistant, may start to internalize these ideas. They begin to question their upbringing, seeing problems where none existed before. What was once a happy childhood, filled with love and encouragement, is now redefined as dysfunctional. The narcissist plants seeds of doubt, warping their perception of the past.

The False Allegations – When Reality is Rewritten

Next comes the **false allegations** - a full-blown recreation of your family history. These are not just misunderstandings but outright lies, distorted memories that reshape your child's past into something dark and abusive.

You may hear things from your child like:

- *"I am reevaluating everything about my childhood."*
- *"I've been talking to my therapist, and I realize now that I grew up in a toxic environment."*
- *"You always controlled me. I was never allowed to have my own opinions."*
- *"You were emotionally abusive, and I never saw it until now."*

- *"You prioritized my sibling(s) over me, and I've finally realized how much damage that did."*
- *"You manipulated me my entire life. I can't believe I didn't see it before."*
- *"I have trauma from the way I was raised, and I need to protect myself from you."*

These accusations come out of nowhere, blindsiding parents who had no indication that their child felt this way. Deep down, they don't, but the reality is that the narcissistic in-law has spent months or even years rewriting the narrative, twisting normal childhood events into something sinister. The love and sacrifices you made for your child are now seen as control. The discipline and guidance you provided are now labeled as abuse.

False accusations go far beyond the pain of estrangement; they strike at the very core of who you are as a parent. When your parenting is called into question, your integrity dismissed, and your judgment considered harmful, it creates a sense of profound loss, confusion, and undoubtedly some anger. The child you lovingly raised, the one who once laughed with you, leaned on you, and shared their milestones, now sees you through a distorted lens, cast as the villain in their revised story. No amount of reasoning seems to reach them, because this new version of the past feels real to them. This is what it's like to be erased inside a one-person cult, where the truth has been replaced by a narrative crafted by manipulation and control.

The Purpose Behind the Lies

Narcissistic in-laws craft false allegations with a clear intent: to sever the bond between you and your child, gaining full emotional control in the process. By rewriting history and naming you as the problem, they isolate your child from their foundational support system. The more your child buys into these distortions, the more emotionally dependent they become on their partner. Any hesitation or red flags they may have seen in the narcissist are overshadowed, because now, the focus shifts. You are framed as the threat, not the one manipulating them. This shift solidifies the narcissist's power and leaves you, the loving parent, on the outside looking in.

Understanding this process won't take away the pain, but it can help you see that this isn't your fault. You are not the person they claim you are. This is a carefully orchestrated manipulation designed to disconnect your bond and ensure your child remains fully under their partner's influence.

The Divide or The Discard

The Divide or The Discard – When Parents Are No Longer "Needed"

One of the most devastating aspects of narcissistic estrangement is the moment a parent realizes they are no longer "needed" in their child's life. This is not a natural drifting apart but a deliberate and calculated process, where one or both parents are either divided against each other or completely discarded. The goal of the narcissistic partner is to ensure absolute control, and that means eliminating any parental influence that doesn't serve their agenda. In some cases, the parent is left to quietly feel replaced or irrelevant; in others, the message is loud and clear, spoken through words, behavior, or total silence.

The Methods of Discarding a Parent

The "You're Toxic" Narrative: The narcissistic in-law convinces your child that their relationship with you is unhealthy, labeling you as toxic, controlling, or emotionally abusive.

Childhood memories are twisted—guidance becomes "manipulation," discipline turns into "abuse," and parental concern is reframed as "suffocation."

Your child may say things like:

- *"I need to protect my peace, and that means stepping away from you."*
- *"I've realized you were never really supportive of me."*
- *"Talking to you brings up too much trauma. I need space."*

The Selective Discard – Dividing Parents

Rather than cutting off both parents, a narcissistic in-law will often target just one, usually the parent who shares the closest bond with the adult child. This is not accidental; it's a calculated move. The stronger the connection, the greater the threat it poses to the narcissist's control. By singling out one parent for exclusion and keeping the other at a controlled distance, the narcissist creates hesitancy, guilt, and emotional pain.

The parent left out is left wondering, "*What did I do wrong?*" when in truth, it's their deep love and connection that made them the target. Meanwhile, the "tolerated" parent is often forced to walk a fine line, afraid that speaking up could cost them even their limited access. This tactic also drives a wedge between the parents, causing conflict and mistrust. For the narcissist, this added division is not just a side effect, it's a bonus.

The discarded parent often hears statements like:

- *"Mom/Dad understands me, but you never did."*
- *"I can still have a relationship with one of you, but I can't be around both."*
- *"I don't feel safe talking to you anymore."*

The Grandparent Erasure

If grandchildren are involved, the discard is even more painful. Your in-law may paint you as a danger to the children, ensuring that you are completely cut off. You may be accused of overstepping boundaries, being emotionally harmful, or even something as extreme as being unfit to be around them.

Common phrases include:

- *"We need to limit contact because it's not healthy for the kids."*
- *"We're setting boundaries, and that means you won't be seeing the grandchildren for a while."*
- *"Your presence is too stressful, and that's not good for the children."*

Silent Disappearance – The Ghosting Discard

Without warning, your child simply vanishes from your life. Calls go unanswered, texts are left unread, and the silence becomes deafening. There's no explanation, just an abrupt and unacknowledged absence. Some parents have driven to their child's home, knocked on doors, or even shown up at workplaces, only to be met with cold rejection or threats of restraining orders or arrests.

In these cases of complete cutoff, it's not uncommon for siblings and extended family to be cut off too, creating a ripple effect of uncertainty and heartbreak. Parents are left trying to emotionally hold the pieces of the family together, while everyone spins in disbelief, wondering what just happened.

You're left replaying every interaction, every word, searching for answers to a question that may never be answered: *What did I do wrong?*

The Pain of Being Discarded

Being discarded by your own child is a wound few can truly understand. You've poured your heart into raising them, loving, nurturing, and sacrificing, only to be cast aside as if none of it ever mattered. The sense of betrayal runs deep. Many parents describe feeling used, followed by waves of anger, and then guilt for feeling that anger, because at the end of the day, all you want is your child back, whole and safe.

To make matters worse, the discard is often justified with false narratives designed to wound and distance:

- *"You were always controlling."*
- *"I can't have a relationship with someone who hurt me so much."*
- *"I've realized I need to heal from my childhood, and that means cutting ties with you."*

The most heartbreaking part? The person saying these things barely resembles the child you knew. You no longer recognize them: their words feel foreign, rehearsed, almost as if someone else is speaking through them. In many cases, especially when emails or messages don't sound like your child at all, parents can see the fingerprints of the narcissistic partner behind the scenes. It's not just the loss of connection; it's the devastating realization that your child has been emotionally hijacked and rewired.

Why This Happens

This process isn't about anything you did wrong. It's only ever about control. The narcissistic in-law needs full dominance over your child's thoughts, emotions, and relationships. Parents are discarded not because they fail but because they pose a threat to that control.

Some children eventually register the manipulation and return. Others remain trapped in the narcissist's web for years, or even a lifetime. The journey is unpredictable but understanding that this is not your fault is the first step toward healing.

No matter how discarded you feel, your love for your child is real, and nothing can erase that truth.

You Need Therapy!

You need therapy, Mom! One of the most painful and infuriating lies a narcissistic in-law, or estranged child, can use against a parent is the accusation that they are mentally unstable or in need of therapy to "fix" their supposed issues. This is not only pure projection, where the narcissist accuses you of the very things they are guilty of, but it's also a trap designed to keep you in a cycle of compliance and false hope.

The Psychology Behind the Demand

Narcissists need control, and what better way to control a parent than to pathologize them? By framing you as mentally unwell, they create a justification for estrangement and shift the blame away from their own manipulations. They turn your pain into "proof" of your instability:

- If you cry or beg for answers → *"See? You're emotionally unstable."*
- If you defend yourself → *"You're in denial and need help."*
- If you get angry → *"This is why we cut you off—you're toxic."*

This tactic is devastating because it invalidates your reality and forces you to fight against an invisible accusation. The more you try to prove you're not "crazy," the more they claim you are.

When a narcissistic in-law or estranged child demands that a parent attend therapy, it's typically not a genuine gesture of reconciliation, it's another form of control. In some cases, they even request proof of attendance, such as canceled checks or therapist confirmations, as if parents must *prove* their willingness to "change." The implication is clear: *you* are the problem. Even when a parent agrees to therapy in good faith, it can be twisted as evidence that the assertions against them were valid all along. Instead of fostering healing, the demand becomes a weapon, used not to reconnect, but to reinforce blame and continue the cycle of shame.

The False Hope of Compliance

When your estranged child or their narcissistic partner demands that you seek therapy as a condition of reconciliation, it feels like a lifeline. You want to see your child... You want to mend the relationship... so, you comply, believing that if you show you're willing to change, things will improve.

But here's the devastating truth: it's a moving goalpost.

- If you go to therapy → *"That's a good start, but we're still not ready."*
- If you show personal growth → *"You need more time to work on yourself."*
- If you ask what specifically needs to change → *"See? You're still not taking accountability."*
- If they feel you haven't changed enough → *"Your therapist isn't helping, you need someone better who can actually deal with your deep issues. Try again and do the real work."*

No matter what you do, it will never be enough because therapy is not actually the goal, the goal is to keep you under their thumb while they hold reuniting just out of reach.

Weaponizing Therapy Against You

Another cruel twist in this cycle is that they don't demand therapy for the real reason you need it: to heal from the trauma of estrangement - created by them. Instead, they claim it's because you are the problem. They want you to admit to things you never did, take responsibility for things that never happened, and "prove" that you are no longer abusive.

This isn't a path toward healing or reconciliation, it's a demand for your compliance.

If you express pain over being cut off, they call it narcissistic injury.
If you grieve the loss of your child, they call it emotional manipulation.
If you defend yourself against false accusations, they call it denial and gaslighting.

The truth? No matter how much you grow or change or how many i's you dot or t's you cross, it will never be enough for them to welcome you back. Why? Because you can't fix what was never broken.

Why You Really Need Therapy

You don't need therapy to prove you are worthy of love or a relationship with your child. You need therapy to process the betrayal, navigate the sadness, and protect your emotional well-being. Therapy should be for you, not a hoop you jump through to gain their approval.

True healing begins when you recognize that you do not have to prove your sanity to people who thrive on keeping you powerless. You are not crazy. You are not broken. You are a parent grieving a loss that never should have happened, and that pain is real, no matter how much they try to dismiss it.

CHAPTER 6
Erasing Your Family's Life

The Targeted Parent – When One Is Estranged and One Is Not

When an estranged child maintains a relationship with one parent but not the other, it can create a variety of emotional and practical side effects for everyone involved. This dynamic not only impacts the estranged parent but also affects family relationships, personal well-being, and even the child-parent relationship that is still maintained. Here are some of the primary side effects that can arise in this difficult situation:

Emotional Pain and Isolation for the Estranged Parent

Feelings of Rejection and Sadness: The estranged parent may experience deep feelings of rejection, sadness, and grief, as they are cut off from their child and grandchildren. It's common to question what they may have done to cause the estrangement, especially when the other parent is still welcomed, leading to self-doubt and anguish.

Increased Anxiety and Depression: Prolonged estrangement can contribute to mental health struggles, including anxiety and depression. Without contact with their child, the estranged parent may feel isolated and disconnected from a significant part of their life.

Loss of Role and Purpose: The estranged parent may feel as if they've lost their identity as a parent (or grandparent if they are also cut off from their grandchildren). This can lead to a sense of purposelessness or diminished self-worth.

Strain on the Marriage or Co-Parenting Relationship

Division in the Household: If one parent maintains a relationship with the child while the other is estranged, it can create tension and resentment between the two parents. The estranged parent may feel envious or even betrayed by their spouse, leading to arguments and misunderstandings.

Communication Challenges: This imbalance in family relationships can create challenges in communication, as one parent may feel hesitant to discuss their interactions with the child out of respect for their estranged partner's feelings. On the other hand, the estranged parent might feel left out or disconnected from family matters.

Divided Loyalty: The parent who maintains the relationship with the child may feel caught in the middle, experiencing divided loyalty between their spouse and their child. They may feel pressure to keep peace between both parties, which can be emotionally exhausting. In many cases, the parent who is still allowed to see the child and their family is encouraged to keep that connection alive, partly to preserve some thread of family support. While this can be a practical and sometimes necessary strategy, it often leaves the targeted parent feeling even more isolated, abandoned, excluded, and painfully aware of what they've lost. The targeted parent may unintentionally put the other parent in an uncomfortable position by asking for details about visits—wanting to remain in the loop but coming across as interrogating. This can create tension and make the parent who remains in contact feel as though they're being asked to share secrets or choose sides or raise fears that they could also easily be cast aside. It becomes another sticky layer of an emotional spiderweb, caught in the middle of a heartbreaking situation.

Manipulation by the Narcissistic In-Law

Control and Influence: A narcissistic in-law may use this dynamic to control the relationship, often setting conditions or dictating terms for the child's relationship with each parent. This can lead to one parent feeling manipulated, while the other may feel obligated to comply with the in-law's demands to keep contact.

Triangulation: Narcissistic individuals often use triangulation to create conflict or manipulate family members. In this situation, the in-law may feed misinformation to the child about the estranged parent, furthering the divide and reinforcing what they believe to be their decision to cut off one parent.

Emotional Blackmail: The narcissistic in-law may also pressure the child to take sides or threaten to withdraw their affection if attempts to reconcile with the estranged parent are made. This type of manipulation can make it even harder for the family to heal.

Feelings of Guilt and Confusion for the Child

Conflicted Emotions: The child may experience remorse and indecision about maintaining a relationship with one parent while excluding the other. They may feel loyalty to the estranged parent but feel pressured to comply with the wishes of their spouse or partner.

Difficulty in Boundary Setting: The child may struggle with setting boundaries with the narcissistic in-law, fearing that any attempt to reconnect with the estranged parent could lead to conflict in their own relationship. This often results in strained communication or limited interaction with the estranged parent.

Identity Confusion: If the child was close to the estranged parent prior to the separation, they may experience identity confusion as they distance themselves.

They could feel uncertainty as they are being forced to choose between two integral people in their life.

Disrupted Family Dynamics

Extended Family Alienation: This estrangement can extend beyond the immediate family, affecting relationships with siblings, cousins, and grandparents. Extended family members may feel caught in the middle, pressured to take sides, or unsure about how to support each family member.

Unresolved Family Conflict: Estrangement often brings unresolved family issues to the surface, which can lead to lingering resentment or misunderstandings within the family unit. Without open communication, these issues can remain unaddressed, impacting family gatherings and future interactions.

Impact on Children and Grandchildren: If grandchildren are involved, they may not fully understand why they can see one grandparent but not the other. This can lead to feelings of confusion, culpability or being caught in the middle and may affect their immediate mental health as well as their own family relationships as they grow older.

Personal Health and Well-being

Chronic Stress: The emotional toll of estrangement, especially when one parent remains involved, can lead to chronic stress and poor behavioral health for everyone involved. Over time, this burden can manifest physically, contributing to issues such as high blood pressure, headaches, digestive problems, insomnia, and more.

Social Isolation: Estranged parents may withdraw socially, feeling ashamed or hesitant to discuss the situation with friends or extended family. This social isolation can exacerbate feelings of loneliness and make it difficult for them to seek support.

Legal and Financial Complications

Challenges with Estate Planning or Inheritance: If a parent is estranged, they may face difficult decisions around estate planning, such as whether to include or exclude the estranged child. These decisions can lead to additional family conflict and further complicate the situation.

When Estrangement Meets Marriage: How Adult Children's Narcissistic Partners Divide Their Parents

Estrangement from an adult child is heartbreaking for a parent and it becomes even more complex when the estrangement is influenced by a narcissistic spouse. In these situations, the child adopts the narcissist's cruel worldview, isolating or targeting one parent more heavily than the other. The imbalance in treatment frequently creates tension between the parents themselves, as they gravitate toward different perspectives on how to handle the situation.

Understanding these dynamics can shed light on why disagreements occur and how this conflict can further strain a marriage.

The Targeted Parent vs. the Lesser-Targeted Parent

When a narcissistic spouse enters the picture, they aim to control and isolate the adult child by undermining their relationship with one, or both, parent. Typically, the parent who is closest to the child often becomes the primary target of the narcissist's smear campaigns, manipulations, or outright rejection.

This parent may face:

- Harsh criticism for imagined or exaggerated faults.
- Accusations fueled by the narcissistic spouse's lies.
- Complete exclusion from their child's life.

The lesser-targeted parent may still experience dismissive behavior, but perhaps more subtly, such as reduced contact or being treated as a peripheral figure. This energy can create a rift between the parents, as they experience estrangement in different ways.

Differing Approaches to Handling Estrangement

Parents often respond to estrangement based on their emotional coping mechanisms and the degree of their exclusion. The following are some common ways these distinctions play out:

The Parent Who Chooses to Let Go

This parent may decide that they have exhausted every possible solution and comes to the painful conclusion that letting go is the healthiest option for their own well-being. They might advocate focusing on the life they can control, avoiding further conflict with their child or the narcissistic spouse.

The belief that continuing to reach out only empowers the narcissist or reinforces the cycle of manipulation may influence their decision to maintain distance.

The Parent Who Cannot Let Go

This parent struggles to accept estrangement and is willing to endure ongoing mistreatment to maintain even minimal contact with their child or grandchildren. They may repeatedly apologize for things they didn't do, in hopes of regaining access to their child's life.

Some allow themselves to be continually persecuted or humiliated by the narcissistic spouse, believing it's a necessary sacrifice to preserve the relationship.

Areas of Disagreement

These differing approaches often lead to conflict between the estranged parents, who may argue about how to best navigate the situation effectively. Some common areas of disagreement include:

Frequency of Contact - One parent may advocate for limited or no contact to protect their mental health, while the other pushes for regular outreach, even at the cost of their dignity.

Responding to Mistreatment – The parent who chooses to let go may refuse to accept abusive behavior, while the other parent may justify enduring it to maintain any form of relationship with the child.

Grandparenting Access - One parent may believe they need to step back entirely, while the other is determined to maintain a relationship with their grandchildren, regardless of the toll it takes.

Apologies and Accountability - Endless apologies for false accusations may feel intolerable to one parent, while the other views it as a necessary step toward reconciliation.

Conflict with the Narcissistic Spouse – While one parent may prefer to confront the narcissistic spouse's behavior directly, the other might believe that appeasement is the best way to prevent further estrangement.

Setting Boundaries - Disagreements often arise over whether to set firm boundaries or to accommodate the couple's demands in hopes of rebuilding the relationship.

The Only Parent or Only Child Differences

For most parents, their child is the center of their world, but when you have only one, that bond can feel even deeper. You poured every ounce of love, energy, and hope into raising them. You spoiled them when you could, lifted them when they stumbled, and cheered them on through every major event. They aren't just your child, they are your universe, your greatest investment, your legacy, your joy, your connection to the future...your everything.

But when your only child marries a narcissist, that bond can shatter in a blink of an eye in ways you never imagined. Suddenly, the child you adored becomes distant, cold, and controlled. The narcissistic partner pulls them into a web of manipulation, alienating them from you and reworking the narrative of your relationship.

This estrangement feels like the ultimate betrayal. You're left with a profound sense of sorrow, grieving not only the loss of your child but also the life and future you envisioned. And unlike parents with multiple children, there's no sibling to share your pain or bridge the gap. The silence is deafening, the loneliness overwhelming.

The Additional Pain Parents Feel from Estrangement from an Only Child

A Lifetime of Love Dismissed: You devoted your life to raising and loving your child, and being tossed aside feels like all your sacrifices and efforts meant nothing. The narcissist's influence changes everything, painting you as the villain in a story where you were once the hero.

Loss of Identity: For many parents, especially those with an only child, your identity is intertwined with your role as a parent. Estrangement robs you of that role, leaving you to question your purpose and place in the world.

No Buffer from the Pain: When you have only one child, estrangement cuts even deeper as there is no emotional cushion, no sibling relationships to soften the blow. Parents of multiple children may find some comfort and connection through their other kids, but with an only child, the loss feels total. The heartache is isolating, and when two parents share the pain, they are often left clinging to each other, trying to make sense of a quiet that echoes through every corner of their lives. Alternatively, the parents are unable to cope with the torment of rejection and are torn apart from each other as well. The emptiness can feel absolute.

Fear for the Future: When estranged from your only child, fears about the future can become overwhelming. You may worry about facing your later years alone, with no one to carry on your legacy or be by your side when you need comfort and love of family the most. Practical concerns like updating your medical power of attorney or revising your estate plan only deepen the emotional ache. The mere fact that you're having to contemplate these changes can make the estrangement feel more permanent, especially for single parents, where it feels like all hope is lost. These fears go beyond loneliness; they intensify the heartbreak and make it even harder to hold onto any hope for reconciliation or peace.

If You're Navigating This Alone

The pain of estrangement is hard enough, but going through it without the support of another parent or partner can feel unbearable. Whether you're a single parent, divorced, or widowed, isolation can amplify the anguish.

Carrying the Weight Alone: Without another parent to share the burden, you may feel solely responsible for the estrangement. You will replay every decision you ever made, wondering what you could have done differently to prevent it.

No Partner for Validation: Having another parent to validate your memories and experiences can provide a sense of sanity. Without that, you may feel as though you're living in a surreal nightmare, questioning what's real and what's been twisted by the narcissist's influence. Gaslighting will do its work on you.

Lack of Emotional Support: Estrangement can feel like an impossible weight to bear alone. You may lack a partner to lean on, confide in, or simply hold you as you cry.

Seek support, join one of my groups, or find a safe outlet to process your emotions. Navigating this kind of pain alone can feel formidable, and no one should have to face these deep waters without a lifeline.

We Don't Agree: The Parental Conflicts

Estrangement doesn't just strain the bond between parent and child, it often creates tension between the parents themselves. When both parents are navigating the loss of connection with their adult child, it's common for them to have very different coping styles, perspectives, and ideas on what to do next. These differences can lead to misunderstandings, resentment, and even deeper hurt. Unfortunately, these feelings can lead to more conflict and isolation during an already difficult time.

In many families, one parent is clearly "targeted" by the estranged child, blamed for the problems or completely cut off, while the other is still somewhat tolerated or occasionally contacted. This dynamic can be mystifying and painful. The targeted parent may feel discarded, misunderstood, and desperate to reunite, while the other may take a more distanced or protective stance, seeing the child's behavior as abusive or manipulative.

It's not uncommon for one parent to say, *"I'll do anything to see them again,"* while the other says, *"I'm not going to grovel or let them treat us this way."* One parent may suggest writing yet another letter, sending a gift, or apologizing again... anything to open a door. The other might refuse, feeling it only rewards bad behavior and compromises their integrity.

These differences can create a painful rift in a marriage. Each may feel isolated in their unhappiness, questioning whether they're handling things the "right" way, and sometimes even feeling judged by their partner for not loving their child enough to keep trying.

It's important to remember that these responses aren't about who loves the child more. They are simply different methods of managing deep pain and powerlessness by two separate individuals who both desperately want the same outcome. One parent may need hope to survive. The other may need boundaries. And both can be true at the same time.

If this is your situation, try to create space for each other's suffering. You may not agree on every step, but staying united in your care, love, and desire for peace, however it may come, can make all the difference in your survival. Two heads and hearts rather than one would certainly be helpful in this instance. Don't let the narcissist have any power over this relationship too.

To help you feel less alone, I've gathered some of the most common themes of disagreement between estranged parents. If you find yourself caught in this maze, know that you're not the only one navigating this difficult terrain but recognize it for what it is and fight with that knowledge. Go down swinging, metaphorically speaking.

Whether or Not to Reach Out: One parent may feel the need to send regular messages, birthday cards, or updates to "keep the connection alive," while the other believes silence might invite healing. To one, reaching out shows love. To the other, it feels like self-betrayal.

Who's to Blame: One parent may point to a manipulative in-law, the cult-like influence, or a mental health issue; the other may believe their adult child is making their own conscious decisions. This difference can make you feel like you're not even in the same story.

How Much to Accept: Some parents are willing to meet any condition, no matter how humiliating, just to remain in contact. Others draw the line at being treated unfairly, even if it means losing access completely. This can cause one parent to accuse the other of "giving up" or "not caring."

How to Talk About It with Others: One parent may want to be private, while the other needs to talk it out, share with others, and seek validation. Disagreements can emerge over what to say to extended family, friends, or even therapists and support groups.

Accepting Conditional Contact: Some children offer limited or heavily monitored contact. One parent might welcome anything, while the other refuses to be "put on probation." These unequal arrangements often lead to more tension between the parents, especially if only one is granted occasional communication.

Seeking Support: Not all parents are ready for therapy or support groups. One may dive into research and healing work, while the other avoids it altogether. It can feel like one is "doing all the work" or like the other is "making it worse by overanalyzing."

What to Say to Siblings: Parents often disagree on how much to share with the other children. One might believe the siblings have a right to know what's going on, while the other worries it could cause more pain or division. The age of the siblings as well as their current relationship status with the child in question could be the deciding factor in these cases.

Hope vs. Acceptance: Perhaps the most painful difference: one parent may still be holding on to hope for reconciliation, while the other has emotionally shut the door. The process is a deeply personal one, and mismatched timelines often create silent suffering between partners.

Many of these differences stem from the emotions each parent is carrying. One might be overwhelmed by shame, guilt, or fear, driving them to do anything to restore contact. The other could feel anger, betrayal, or a deeper understanding of the manipulation at play, allowing them to step back more easily. These emotional responses can pull parents in opposite directions, even though both are mourning the same loss.

Impact on the Estranged Parents' Marriage

The differences in a preferred approach can place enormous strain on the estranged parents' marriage. Without mutual understanding or support, they may experience:

Resentment: The parent who chooses to let go may feel unsupported or undermined by the other's willingness to tolerate mistreatment. Conversely, the parent who refuses to give up may feel abandoned or judged by their spouse's decision to disengage.

Communication Breakdowns: Disagreements about how to handle the situation can lead to heated arguments and an inability to reach a shared approach. It's important to remember that you both want the same outcome – different approaches that come together in the end.

Emotional Burnout: Both parents may feel emotionally drained, compounding the stress and leading to withdrawal from each other.

Divided Loyalties: One parent may perceive the other as being more aligned with the adult child or the narcissistic spouse, further fracturing their partnership.

Isolation: If one parent retreats to avoid conflict, it can leave the other feeling isolated and unsupported. Lack of support can take additional tolls on the person affected such as loneliness and low self-esteem. Without a supportive network, some struggle to cope, leading to increased anxiety, depression, and other mental health disorders.

It's important to recognize that one of the narcissist's key tactics is division, turning people against one another to maintain control. Don't let them take anything more from your family than they already have. Staying connected and unified with your partner, even if you see things differently, can help you feel grounded and mentally reinforced. This doesn't mean you have to convince each other of your views, but rather, make space to talk about your experiences without blame. Open, respectful conversations can reduce tension and help you face the situation as a team.

The Ripple Effect of Estrangement As It Washes Over the Entire Family

Estrangement is a complex issue that doesn't just affect the immediate individuals involved; it sends shockwaves through the entire family. When an adult child cuts ties with a parent, the emotional toll ripples outward, affecting siblings, grandparents, aunts, uncles, nieces, nephews, cousins, and even future generations. Estrangement is more than a private dispute; it is a familial fracture that can result in lifelong wounds for generations.

The Sibling Divide

When one child becomes estranged from their parents, siblings are often caught in the middle. The estranged sibling may feel justified in their decision, while the others may remain loyal to the parents, causing divisions within the family. These opposing loyalties can create resentment, misunderstandings, and even result in siblings cutting ties with each other. A sibling who maintains a relationship with the estranged parent may be seen as taking sides, while the estranged sibling might feel unsupported or betrayed. What starts as one broken relationship can multiply, leading to sibling rivalry with lasting effects.

These divisions can be particularly harmful when siblings have previously had close relationships. When communication breaks down, and unresolved grievances pile up, the divide becomes even harder to bridge.

"I feel like I lost my best friend. I don't know who he is anymore."
– surTHRIVER sibling

It's important to be mindful of how much you lean on your other children during an estrangement. No matter where they stand, supportive of you, neutral, or unsure, they are carrying their own pain, and it can look very different from yours. While it's okay to talk about the situation if they're open to it, try not to make them your "emotional pillow." Oversharing or venting too aggressively can place a heavy emotional burden on them and, in some cases, create health complications of their own. I have a client who, while angrily oversharing with her adult daughter, caused her a medical emergency from the stress. This misjudgment can cause long-term damage to your healthy children as well as sibling relationships. Aim to protect their space to form their own views, process their own feelings, and maintain their own relationships.

Your Child's Grandparents' Grief

Grandparents are often among the most affected by estrangement. They treasure the time spent with their grandchildren, forming deep bonds. However, when an adult child severs ties with their parents, it often means that the grandparents are cut off as well. This abrupt loss can cause immense grief, as grandparents may feel powerless, isolated, and abandoned; they truly are fallout in a very unfortunate situation. They lose not only the relationship with their adult grandchild but also the opportunity to be involved in their great grandchildren's lives.

For the great grandchildren, this loss is significant too. Growing up without access to grandparents may deprive them of a rich source of love, wisdom, and family history. Grandparents often play a nurturing role in a child's life, and their absence can lead to questions about why the family isn't whole, fostering turmoil or even resentment as children grow older.

The Silent Battles Among Cousins

Estrangement within a family can also create distance among cousins, who may become collateral damage in the family's division. Without regular family gatherings or communication, cousins can become strangers, missing out on shared experiences, traditions, and bonding opportunities. This loss can be subtle but profound, as the cousin relationship is often one of the first social bonds outside of the immediate family.

The separation of cousins further deepens the rift, isolating children who may have otherwise built strong relationships within their extended family. Family functions such as holidays, weddings, and funerals become emotional minefields that everyone must carefully navigate. Questions arise like: Will the estranged child attend their cousin's wedding? If so, where will they sit, and how will they avoid interacting with family members they no longer speak to? What once were joyous, or solemn, family gatherings will now be filled with anxiety, pressure, and uncertainty.

Over time, the lack of connection can lead to awkwardness and discomfort, making future reconciliation even more challenging.

Family Tensions and Fights

Estrangement doesn't just affect the immediate relationships; it has the potential to cause friction throughout the entire extended family. Relatives may feel pressured to "choose sides" in a conflict they were never directly part of, leading to heightened tensions at family events. The once harmonious environment can become a battleground, with every interaction being colored by underlying resentment or unresolved issues.

In some cases, family members may try to act as intermediaries, attempting to repair the broken relationship. However, these efforts can backfire, as pushing for reconciliation without addressing the root causes of the estrangement may only make the situation worse. Well-meaning family members may find themselves entangled in arguments, causing further distance and frustration.

The Emotional Toll on Everyone

The emotional toll of estrangement on an entire family is substantial. The absence of a loved one leaves a void that is difficult to fill, and family members may experience a wide range of emotions, from anger and sadness to remorse and bewilderment. Family traditions and holidays will never feel the same for anyone. Estrangement can lead to a breakdown in communication and a loss of shared history, leaving family members feeling disconnected from one another. Over time, these emotional scars can have lasting effects on the mental and emotional health of everyone involved.

Estrangement doesn't just sever one relationship; it creates a domino effect that can divide entire families. Siblings, grandparents, and even aunts, uncles, and cousins all feel the repercussions of a fractured family. The emotional toll of estrangement is massive, as it disrupts family connections, causing hurt and detachment that can last for generations. Healing requires patience, understanding, and an openness to rebuilding relationships, but the journey to repair these deep wounds can be long and complicated.

The Pain of Losing Your Grandchildren

Being cut off from your grandchildren is a devastating aspect of estrangement. For many grandparents, these children were not just a part of their lives, they were their joy, their purpose, and often a daily presence. Some were full-time caregivers or regular babysitters, helping to raise the children while their adult child worked. Bonds developed through holidays, school pickups, bedtime stories, meals cooked with love, and everyday moments that created a deep, irreplaceable attachment. When that relationship is suddenly severed, especially with little explanation or based on a false or exaggerated accusation, the emptiness can feel akin to torture.

It's particularly heartbreaking when the cutoff is tied to an alleged mistake, something minor, misunderstood, or even fabricated. A diaper change that wasn't done the right way. A scraped knee while playing. A misinterpreted comment. These events are twisted into justifications for cutting off contact, especially when there is a narcissistic in-law involved who thrives on control. It's a classic tactic: find a flaw, magnify it, and use it as a reason to isolate. The result? Loving, well-intentioned grandparents are left feeling ashamed, perplexed, and utterly heartbroken, all while fearing their grandchildren will forget them, or worse, be taught that they are unsafe.

Another deep concern for grandparents is the well-being of their grandchild who is being raised in a home with a narcissistic parent. The thought of a child growing up in an environment where manipulation, control, emotional neglect, or even abuse is normalized is agonizing. Grandparents worry about the values being modeled, the lack of empathy being taught, and the emotional toll it may take on the child. The helplessness of knowing a child you love may be suffering, yet being unable to protect or guide them creates a constant undercurrent of fear and sorrow.

Navigating this loss requires incredible strength and intentional emotional care. It's natural to want to defend yourself, to set the record straight, to scream into the void that none of it is true. But often, pushing back too hard only leads to further punishment. The path forward begins with acknowledging your grief and giving yourself permission to mourn what has been lost. If appropriate and safe, you can write letters to or create videos for your grandchildren that you may one day share, so they know how deeply they were loved and missed. Most importantly, try not to lose yourself in the injustice. The love you gave was real. The bond you shared mattered. And even if you're being kept away today, your love leaves an imprint that cannot be erased.

SECTION 3
Navigating The Pain

"For strong, loving families where parents and children once shared deep bonds estrangement often becomes the first true trauma. The pain cuts deeper because it follows so much love."

CHAPTER 7
Navigating the Pain of Estrangement

The First Few Months: When It Feels Like Your World Is Falling Apart

When you first hear the words from your adult child that they want nothing to do with you, it feels like the ground has been pulled out from under you. The first six months of estrangement are nothing short of a parent's worst nightmare. Losing a child to estrangement is a unique kind of pain - one that isn't often acknowledged or understood.

Searching for Answers

One of the most difficult aspects of estrangement is the lack of clarity. Many parents don't understand what happened. You replay every moment, every interaction, desperately searching for the moment things began to unravel. Sometimes, the only clue is the arrival of a narcissistic son- or daughter-in-law who slowly isolates your child from you.

In cases of estrangement influenced by a narcissistic partner, the first months are especially cruel. The sadness is unrelenting. You ruminate over everything leading up to that moment, followed by the sudden and unexpected discard. You apologize repeatedly, even when you don't know what you're apologizing for; you condemn yourself – for what, you're not sure – but how would your child say something like this if it wasn't true? You're coldly informed that your apologies aren't sincere, you once looked at the in-law "the wrong way," and the list goes on and on. Are you really that bad of a person?

This spirals into self-blame: *"Why did I say that?"* or *"What could I have done differently?"* You wonder why your child won't accept your apology, why nothing you do is enough to repair the relationship. There must be a solution, but the panic begins to set in. The hopelessness feels like a heavy weight pressing on your chest every second of the day. You start to fear for your sanity.

The Physical and Emotional Toll

The misery of estrangement isn't just emotional, it's gutterly physical. Eating becomes a chore, sleep elusive, and basic functioning a struggle. The uncertainty of *"Is this permanent?"* and *"Will I ever see my child again?"* is all-consuming.

You reach out, pleading: *"Please talk to me. I need to understand."* Instead of answers, however, you're met by a silence thick enough to choke on. The rejection feels unbearable; it's not just pain, it's a tidal wave crashing through your chest, splintering something vital inside you. You cry constantly, unable to stop the waves of anguish.

For some, the torment becomes so enormous that they feel like they can't go on. Most are not suicidal, although there is limited data on the suicide rates of parents who are estranged from their children, but the desire to escape the unrelenting heartbreak makes them pray for release: *"Take me, God. Free me from this pain."*

The Isolation and Judgment of Others

No one expects this to be the story you tell. First, friends express shock. They remember how close you and your child were and can't understand how this happened. *"What did you do?"* But as time passes, friends slowly pull away. Your pain is too much for them, they don't know what to say, and their own fears of estrangement tickle their brains. *"What if this were to happen to me?"* drives them into silence, leaving you feeling even more isolated.

Family dynamics also suffer. Instead of uniting to support each other, families become divided. Spouses argue over how to handle the estrangement. Siblings may feel angry or betrayed by the child who left, resent the focus on the estranged sibling, or feel guilty for not being able to help, while the parent most affected by the estrangement carries the heaviest emotional burden, unintentionally affecting everyone in the family.

Anxiety, sadness, and shame ripple through the entire family.

The Physical and Mental Fallout

Estrangement wreaks havoc on your physical and mental health. The constant stress raises cortisol levels, triggering your fight-or-flight response. You become a zombie, unable to sleep or eat properly. The elevated cortisol causes your body to hold onto extra weight when the stress slows your metabolism, or you lose massive amounts of weight and look ill. Your body weakens, your mind feels numb, and the only thing you can do is cry.

You question everything about your role as a parent and your ability to cope with this new reality. Life feels bleak and senseless, and you wonder how—or if—you'll ever find peace again.

The first months of estrangement are dark, but it's important to remember you're not alone. Millions of parents share your pain, even if society doesn't always understand or acknowledge it. While this chapter is unbearably difficult, there are steps you can take to begin healing—by seeking support, focusing on self-care, and finding ways to get through this devastating experience with hope for the future.

You are not defined by your estrangement. You are still a parent, still deserving of love and connection, and still capable of moving forward... one step at a time.

Understanding Your Emotional Pain Level

Estrangement is one of the most emotionally intense experiences a parent can endure. The hurt is real, immeasurable, and unpredictable. One moment you may feel a sense of acceptance, and the next you're overwhelmed by sadness, anger, or helplessness. Your emotional state may spike with a memory, a holiday, or even the continued silence from your child.

When I work with clients, I use a simple but powerful tool to help them understand and regulate their pain: the emotional pain scale. You've probably seen something similar in a doctor's office: *"On a scale from 1 to 10, how bad is your pain?"* I ask my clients to apply that same concept to emotional pain. For example, how high does your anger or sadness feel today?

Now, go deeper: what *kind* of anger are you feeling? Is it irritation? Frustration? Bitterness? Or are you hovering near rage? By naming the emotion, you gain clarity. Next, assign it a number to help you measure how close you are to the emotional edge.

This is an important exercise because reaching out to your child when you're sitting at an emotional level of 9 (on a scale of 10) would be risky. I don't advise it. If you receive silence, rejection, or an angry reply, your emotional state could quickly skyrocket to a 12 or 13. There may be no scale for suffering, but there is a limit to how much a heart can bear - and every soul has its breaking point. Guard yours like your life depends on it, because sometimes, it does.

So... before you send a message, make that call, or try to take a bold step, check in with yourself first. *"What am I feeling?" "Where am I on the emotional scale?"* If you're already teetering near the edge, wait. Breathe. Care for yourself.

Learning how to manage emotional vulnerability is a large part of your healing because protecting your peace is just as important as protecting your heart.

The Emotional Stages of Estrangement: Navigating the Grief Cycle

Estrangement from a child is a profound emotional wound that a parent could never anticipate. The sudden and unexplained detachment can leave parents grappling with feelings they never expected to feel. Much like grief in its rawest forms, parental estrangement unfolds in painful stages.

The emotions estranged parents feel fall into two dire categories: disenfranchised grief and ambiguous loss. *Disenfranchised grief* is the gut-wrenching sorrow that goes unrecognized or invalidated by society: there are no casseroles, no funerals, and no one checking in, because the world doesn't quite know how to support a scenario that doesn't involve death. *Ambiguous loss*, on the other hand, is the deep ache that comes from losing someone who is still alive. Your child is out there somewhere, alive but absent - gone not by fate, but by choice. That kind of loss - grieving a relationship that still breathes - feels like an endless, gaping wound, raw and pulsing, with salt ground into it every time your thoughts wander to them. They're alive, just not in your life—and that's the agony. It's mourning in slow motion. Together, these make estrangement feel isolating, maddening, and impossible to heal from. Understanding these terms can offer a layer of validation to help parents realize something vital: you're not grieving *wrong*; you're grieving something incredibly complicated. Be gentle with yourself and seek the support you deserve. This is potentially the most difficult thing you will encounter as a parent, and you don't have to (and shouldn't) face it alone.

While everyone's experience is unique, understanding these stages can help parents navigate the intense emotions and find a path toward healing.

Shock and Denial - The initial stage of estrangement is often marked by disbelief. It is a struggle to accept that a child has chosen to sever the relationship with their parents. This stage can feel surreal, because how could a bond that once seemed unbreakable be so drastically altered? Most parents will replay conversations or events in their minds, searching for answers or moments where things went wrong. Denial often emerges as a defense mechanism, allowing parents to hold on to the hope that this is a temporary situation or that their child will "snap out of it."

During this phase, parents may reach out repeatedly to their child, sending messages, cards, or gifts in the hope of mending the relationship. Perhaps to jolt their child into an a-ha moment. Be aware that these efforts can sometimes backfire, particularly if the child is seeking space. It's important to recognize that shock and denial are natural responses.

Anger and Frustration - As the reality of estrangement sets in, parents often find themselves grappling with anger. This anger may be directed toward the estranged child, particularly if the reasons for the estrangement seem unclear or unjust. Parents may feel frustrated that their child has seemingly turned their back on the family, disregarding years of love, care, and support.

In cases where a narcissistic spouse or outside influence is involved, parents might direct their anger toward the person they believe is responsible for manipulating their child. There can also be frustration with oneself. Parents might question if they failed in some way, or if their actions inadvertently caused the rift.

During this stage, it's important for parents to process their anger in healthy ways, utilizing therapy, journaling, or speaking with others who've gone through similar experiences, remembering that all are alike although still very different. Holding onto anger for too long can lead to bitterness and damage future attempts at reconciliation.

Bargaining and Guilt - Bargaining is a stage where parents attempt to regain control of the situation, typically by reflecting on what they could have done differently. They may make promises to themselves or their child, saying, *"If I can just do this, maybe they'll come back."* This stage is marked by a deep desire to undo the estrangement, and parents may be willing to make personal sacrifices, change behaviors, or accept blame to repair the relationship.

Guilt often accompanies bargaining. Parents might endlessly replay the past, questioning their parenting decisions and wondering if they could have prevented the estrangement by being more lenient, more supportive, more attentive... more *something*. This stage is painful because it places the burden squarely on the parent's shoulders, whether or not they are truly at fault.

It's crucial to recognize that while reflection and self-improvement are valuable, parents must also set healthy boundaries and avoid taking sole responsibility for the estrangement or it will be used to extend your sentence of silence.

Depression and Grief - Estrangement is often described as a "living loss," a form of grief that is ongoing, with no clear resolution. When parents reach the stage of depression and grief, they begin to confront the emotional weight and gravity of their situation. They may feel hopeless, believing that their child will never return or that the relationship is damaged beyond repair. This stage can be marked by deep sadness, isolation, and even physical symptoms like sleeplessness, anxiety, or changes in appetite.

Grieving the loss of a relationship with your child is essential for healing. It's important to recognize that this is not just about losing contact with your child, but also mourning the hopes, dreams, and expectations you had for the future. Additional losses may include relationships with grandchildren, or other family connections that have been strained by the estrangement.

Acceptance and Growth - The final stage of estrangement grief is acceptance. This doesn't mean parents are "okay" with the situation or have stopped caring about their child. Instead, acceptance involves acknowledging the reality of estrangement without constantly trying to change it. In this stage, parents understand that they can't force their child to reconnect and that the future is uncertain.

With acceptance often comes a focus on personal growth. Parents may use this time to heal emotionally, focus on self-care, or find new meaning and purpose outside of the parent-child relationship. They may also begin to build or strengthen relationships with other family members or friends.

In some cases, acceptance can create a space for reconciliation. When parents let go of the desperate need to control the outcome, their child may feel more comfortable re-establishing contact, if they can get their narcissistic spouse to go along with it. However, even if reconciliation never happens, acceptance allows parents to move forward with their lives and find peace.

It's important to note that the stages of estrangement aren't always linear. Parents may find themselves moving back and forth between stages, depending on external events, emotional triggers, or new developments in their relationship with their child. For example, receiving a holiday card from the estranged child might reignite hope and trigger a return to bargaining, while a prolonged period of silence may lead to renewed feelings of grief.

Every parent's journey through estrangement is unique, but understanding the stages can provide a framework for processing the complex emotions involved. While the path to healing isn't straightforward, understanding the stages of shock, anger, bargaining, depression, and acceptance can help parents navigate their journey with knowledge, self-compassion, and resilience.

Mending a wounded soul takes time, and every emotion - no matter how messy or overwhelming - is a sign that you're still moving forward. You're allowed to feel it all. Though you may not be able to change the outcome, focusing on your own healing and finding support can lead to growth, strength, and, ultimately, peace.

Endless Rumination: Searching For Answers in a Lifetime of Memories

One of the most emotionally exhausting aspects of estrangement is the relentless rumination, the mental loop that plays over and over, searching for answers that may never come. Parents find themselves trapped in memories, replaying conversations, decisions, holidays, and moments, big and small, looking for the exact second when things shifted. This may or may not be before you understand how your child has been hijacked by a narcissist or that all of these new directives are coming from an outsider and not your child. A lifetime of love, sacrifice, and connection suddenly feels tainted, and the mind becomes consumed with "What did I miss?" "What could I have done differently?" and "How did we end up here?"

This mental rewinding often turns into a full-time job for the heart and soul, sapping energy, joy, and sleep. The danger of this loop is not just emotional; it can begin to impact physical health, relationships, and one's sense of identity and sanity. Rumination keeps you stuck in pain, distorts your ability to see the situation clearly, and prevents forward motion. It tricks the brain into thinking it's being productive when in truth, it's re-traumatizing you one memory at a time.

And yet, rumination can offer a clue to what's most meaningful. The fact that you return to these thoughts reflects your deep love and desire for connection and understanding. Instead of revisiting the past in a cycle of blame or shame, what if there was a way to transform rumination into reflection? Reflection brings awareness, while rumination keeps you spinning. The key is to start noticing your thoughts, gently interrupt the spiral, and redirect your mind to what you can control: your healing, your boundaries, your future.

How do you stop? It starts with awareness. Writing down the repetitive thoughts can help move them from the mind to the page. This is where journaling can help.

Create a new routine.
Ground yourself in the present moment.
Speak the words aloud.

"This thought isn't helping me heal" can begin to break the cycle. Therapy, coaching, and support groups can also create new pathways that help you feel less alone in your suffering. The past can't be changed, but how you live with it can.

Healing isn't forgetting, it's choosing to no longer be consumed by the rewind button.

Where Are You Living? Understanding Emotional Time Zones

When I work with estranged parents, one of the most useful tools I keep nearby is a simple, laminated sheet that maps out where we are emotionally "living": the past, the future, or the present. It's fascinating how much insight we gain by identifying which emotional time zone we're stuck in, and how that awareness can help us begin to shift our experience.

When we're emotionally living in the past, we often feel emotions like *grief, guilt, sadness, regret, shame, anger,* and *hopelessness*. These feelings are rooted in loss. We replay moments, wondering where it all went wrong, clinging to "why me?" and struggling to forgive ourselves or others. *"If you are depressed, you are living in the past."* ~Lao Tzu

When we're living in the future, our minds are consumed by *anxiety, fear, overthinking, pressure,* and *what-if scenarios*. We worry about the grandchildren forgetting us, about whether we'll ever hear from our child again, about dying alone. The unknown becomes a breeding ground for dread, and our nervous systems stay in a state of tension, waiting for something, *anything*, to shift. *"If you are anxious, you are living in the future."* ~Lao Tzu

But when we begin to root ourselves in the present, even just for a few moments, something powerful happens. We reconnect to *inner peace, calm, contentment, love, joy,* and a sense of being *grounded*. The present moment may not hold all the answers or resolutions, but it offers a soft place to land - one where we can breathe, feel, and simply be. *"If you are at peace, you are living in the present."* ~Lao Tzu

By gently noticing our emotional state, we can begin to ask ourselves: *Am I living in the past, the future, or the present right now?* This awareness alone can begin to reframe your thinking and offer a path back to peace. It doesn't mean ignoring your pain or pretending things are okay, it means honoring where you are while also creating space to heal. This is the emotional work of reclaiming your life, one breath at a time.

What Am I Making This Mean?

When I was deep in my own healing journey from narcissistic abuse, one of the tools I returned to time and again came from *A Course in Miracles*. In the Course, a miracle isn't some grand event, it's defined as a simple, small shift in perception. A subtle yet powerful change in how you choose to see something. That idea offered me countless, *ah-ha* moments. Instead of gripping tightly to one painful version of a story, I could allow myself to hold it differently, to see new angles, uncover gentler truths, and ultimately release the meaning I had assigned to it. And no, this doesn't mean ignoring reality or living in denial about what's happened; it means reclaiming your power to choose how you carry it.

One of the most meaningful takeaways from the Course for me, so much so that I had it engraved on a plaque that now sits behind my desk, was the question: "What am I making this mean?" I use it often in my practice with estranged parents. When we're hurting, it's natural to create meaning to make sense of the distress we're feeling. ...but sometimes the meaning we assign isn't only fabricated, it's deeply damaging.

When I ask parents what they're making the estrangement mean, the answers often reflect deep shame and grief: *"I must have been a terrible parent,"* or *"I've lost my child forever."* For others, it becomes an agonizing expression of anger: *"My child is cruel,"* or *"They've abandoned me for good."* These meanings are powerful. They shape how we feel, how we show up, and whether we can access hope. But they're also stories. Stories created in pain and fear. And they are immensely untrue.

With this in mind, I invite you to pause and ask yourself: "*What am I making this mean?*"

Write it down.

Then ask, "*Is this true? Is there actual proof of this meaning, or is it a fear dressed as fact?*"

Once you've explored the answers, try gently reframing the story. You're not rewriting what happened, you're choosing how to carry it. Shift the load like you would a heavy box. Maybe instead of *"I've lost my child forever,"* say, *"We're disconnected right now, and I don't know what the future holds — but I'm open to healing."* This small modification won't erase how you're feeling, but it may create space for grace. And in that space, healing can begin.

The following are a few self-compassionate and less arduous ways to rephrase the experience of estrangement. Each allows room for hope, healing, and emotional resilience while still honoring the truth of what's happening. These may feel incongruent with the depth of your pain, but the way you speak about and hold your experience directly impacts your emotional survival. Let these suggestions inspire your own compassionate rephrasing, ones that allow space for hope and healing without denying your truth.

"We are in a season of disconnection." - This frames the situation as temporary, like a season, not forever. It creates space for change, growth, and eventual reconnection.

"Our relationship is paused while we each work through our own paths."- This emphasizes individual growth and healing without finality. It implies that something is being worked through, not ended.

"We're not in contact right now, but the door isn't closed in my heart." - This offers warmth and openness while acknowledging the current distance. It reminds you (and possibly others) that your love remains strong.

"We are walking different emotional journeys at the moment." - This softens the sting by recognizing that both you and your child are navigating personal challenges, not that love, or connection has been permanently severed.

"We are apart right now, and I'm holding space for understanding and hope." - This centers your strength and intention. It shifts the story from helplessness to empowerment, and from despair to patience and love.

> Watch your thoughts, they become your words;
> Watch your words, they become your actions;
> Watch your actions, they become your habits;
> Watch your habits, they become your character;
> Watch your character, it becomes your destiny.
> ~ Lao Tzu

Recognizing and Maneuvering Through Emotional Triggers

A challenging part of estrangement is managing emotional triggers. Triggers often sneak up unexpectedly, especially around meaningful dates, such as holidays, birthdays, or the anniversary of the last time you saw your child. These are what I call *calendar triggers*. They're emotional landmines tied to love and loss. You might think you're prepared, bracing for impact, but the grief can still knock the wind out of you. One kind comment from a friend like, "Are you doing okay today?" and suddenly you're spiraling back into sadness, anger, or deep longing. That's how unpredictable and powerful triggers can be.

As I've shared previously, grief is not a linear process. You may wake up in acceptance, managing your day with strength and peace, only to find yourself sliding into depression or rage by afternoon. Triggers don't follow logic; they connect to emotional memories and pain points rooted in your history with your child or their narcissistic partner.

When I teach about emotional triggers, I encourage clients to break down the experience. Start by identifying what happened. *What exactly triggered you?*

Then ask, *What did the narcissist (or your child) do or say?* And more importantly, *What emotion did that stir in you?*

Use a 1–10 scale to rate the intensity of that emotion. Ask yourself, *When do I remember feeling this before? Why did this hit me so hard?*

Often, the answer is something like,

Because they lied.
Because they ignored me.
Because they turned my child against me.

However, beneath that explanation is a deeper emotional wound, one that may have been poked many times throughout your life. The behavior is upsetting, yes, but the emotional response it provokes is what lingers and causes the actual affliction.

Here's a list of common emotional reactions that lie underneath many triggers:

- I felt excluded
- I felt powerless
- I felt unheard
- I felt scolded
- I felt judged
- I felt blamed
- I felt disrespected
- I felt a lack of affection
- I felt I couldn't speak up
- I felt lonely
- I felt like the bad guy
- I felt forgotten
- I felt unsafe
- I felt unloved
- I felt it was unfair
- I felt frustrated

- I felt disconnected
- I felt trapped
- I felt ignored
- I felt manipulated
- I felt controlled
- I felt I couldn't be honest

Reviewing this list, most will often recognize that it wasn't just one emotion, but rather several layered-on top of each other. It's a compounded, multifaceted effect created from past unresolved trauma. The real impact of a trigger isn't always what someone did, but *how it made you feel*. That's where the emotional work begins, not in denying what happened, but in understanding and healing your response to it.

Let's look at a few real-life examples:

- When your child tells you that you did something wrong, you may feel judged, blamed, and disrespected.
- When your child shows no appreciation for your efforts, you might feel unheard, scolded, unworthy, and powerless.
- When a narcissist dictates the terms of your relationship, you may feel trapped, controlled, or like the villain in their narrative.
- When lies are being spread about you, you may feel erased, disrespected, and utterly powerless.
- When a child refuses to take any accountability for their actions, it can leave you feeling invisible, frustrated, invalidated—and as though your truth no longer matters.

There are endless things your in-law and child (and anyone, really) can do to hijack your emotional stability but understanding your triggers is a key part of reclaiming your emotional strength. This bears repeating: a trigger isn't just about *what* someone did, it's about *how it made you feel*. This is where your power lies. By recognizing that the emotional reaction is rooted in your experience, not in their behavior alone, you can begin to respond differently. It's not about dismissing how you were wronged, it's about learning effective ways to protect your well-being, so another person's actions no longer hold power over you. Over time, this awareness helps you regain control over your story, and your healing.

Hypervigilance - Beating the Anxiety Loop

Hypervigilance often feels like a storm inside your mind, doubt blended with a heightened state of alertness, intense emotion, and increased awareness of potential threats or dangers. Anyone in this state may struggle to eat, experience disrupted sleep, or feel mentally foggy and forgetful, even about things they'd normally remember with ease. It's as if the body and brain are stuck in survival mode, constantly scanning for emotional risks while trying to make sense of the chaos. This exhausting mental state is common in estrangement and will take a major toll on your well-being.

Many parents describe living in a state of constant alertness, waiting for the next shoe to drop, re-reading texts, analyzing silence, or bracing for holidays, birthdays, or milestones that once brought joy. This hypervigilance is the result of emotional unpredictability. When love feels conditional and communication is strained or cut off entirely, your nervous system stays on edge, bracing for impact. Over time, this can leave you burnt out, overwhelmed, and questioning yourself. Recognizing this pattern is the first step toward understanding your emotional triggers and taking your power back.

What Is Hypervigilance?

Hypervigilance is an exaggerated state of alertness, often a symptom of conditions like PTSD and anxiety disorders, triggered by trauma or prolonged emotional distress. For estranged parents, this can manifest as:

- Overanalyzing every interaction (or lack of interaction) with your child.
- Feeling on edge, anticipating the worst-case scenario.
- Avoiding certain places or conversations for fear of judgment or confrontation.

- Constantly seeking information about your child through social media or mutual acquaintances.
- Experiencing physical symptoms like fatigue, headaches, muscle tension, or digestive issues.

This hyperawareness develops as a survival mechanism. When you've been emotionally wounded, your brain goes into protection mode. However, when there is no immediate threat, this heightened state of awareness can become debilitating, making it hard to find peace.

Hypervigilance can be triggered by several factors, including:

- Fear of further rejection. Every interaction feels like an opportunity to either repair or worsen the relationship.
- Unresolved guilt or shame. Many estranged parents replay past mistakes, wondering what they could have done differently.
- Emotional abuse or manipulation. If a child or outside influence is using blame or control tactics, the parent may be left feeling powerless and anxious.
- Legal or financial threats. In cases where estrangement involves court battles or financial obligations, parents may remain on edge, anticipating the next crisis.

The Cost of Living in Hypervigilance

It's important to be conscious of the fact that being in a constant state of wariness will take a toll on your mental and physical health. Chronic stress can lead to:

- Insomnia or restless sleep
- Anger outbursts
- Loss of appetite
- Anxiety and depression
- High blood pressure and heart problems
- Social withdrawal and isolation
- Behavior changes
- Difficulty making decisions due to emotional exhaustion
- Catastrophize situations

Living in this state can also hinder the possibility of reconciliation because fear-based reactions can make communication more strained or defensive. It is not a temperament that goes unnoticed.

Breaking Free from Hypervigilance

The good news is that you can retrain your brain to find peace, even in the uncertainty of estrangement. Here's how:

Shift Your Focus to What You Can Control

You can't force your child to reconnect, but you can control your thoughts, actions, and self-care. Redirect your energy into healing yourself, rather than analyzing every move.

Set Boundaries with Information

If checking their social media or seeking updates from mutual acquaintances makes you anxious, set strict boundaries for yourself. Reduce or eliminate exposure to triggers that keep you stuck in the hypervigilant loop.

Developing a Grounding Practice

Techniques like deep breathing, meditation, counting, journaling, or gentle movement (such as yoga or walking) can help bring your nervous system back to a calmer state. Studies also provide empirical evidence suggesting the anxiolytic properties of 528 Hz music, a specific type of Solfeggio frequency, has healing and stress-reducing properties.

Challenge Catastrophic Thinking

Hypervigilance often leads to worst-case scenario thinking. When you catch yourself spiraling, ask:

- Is this fear based on fact or assumption?
- What evidence do I have that this will actually happen?
- If the worst happens, what is my plan to cope?

Reclaim Your Identity

Estrangement can feel like it defines your entire existence, but you are more than just an estranged parent. Reconnect with hobbies, friendships, and personal goals that bring you joy.

Finding Peace in the Present

Estrangement may feel like an open wound, but you don't have to live in a constant state of anxiety. By recognizing hypervigilance and actively working to calm your nervous system, you can begin to heal, whether reconciliation happens or not.

You deserve peace. You deserve healing. Most of all, you deserve to feel like yourself again. If you find that hypervigilance is lingering and interfering with your daily life, consider speaking with your doctor. In some cases, support through medication or professional guidance can make a meaningful difference in helping you find stability and begin reclaiming your emotional state.

How the Narcissist Creates Fear to Control Your Family

One of the most common tools in the narcissist's tool belt to manipulate and control in-laws is fear, specifically, the fear of permanent estrangement. They create an environment where parents believe that if they do not comply with the narcissist's unspoken rules, demands, or expectations, they will never see their child or grandchildren again. I often refer to these demands as hostage letters, which are emotional ultimatums designed to break your will and keep you under control.

This fear-based manipulation can make parents feel like they are constantly on edge, afraid to say or do the wrong thing in front of their adult child and their narcissistic in-law. However, the key to overcoming this manipulation is understanding the power dynamic at play and ensuring that your agitation does not become a visible weakness. Like an animal, once a narcissist smells it, they recognize that they have control, and they will continue using it to their advantage.

How Narcissists Use Fear to Control In-Laws

Threats of No Contact: The narcissistic son- or daughter-in-law may openly or subtly threaten estrangement. They might say things like, "*If you don't respect our boundaries, we won't be able to have a relationship.*" This often leaves parents in a state of panic, making them more likely to comply with unreasonable demands.

Creating Uncertainty: Narcissists thrive on ambiguity. They may not explicitly state that contact will be cut off but will imply it through their actions, such as giving silent treatment, canceling plans at the last minute, or making vague statements like, "*I'm not sure if we can make it next time.*"

Controlling Access to Grandchildren: Narcissistic in-laws know that nothing can break a grandparent's heart faster than being kept away from their grandchildren. This tactic will be used as leverage to force compliance, making grandparents feel powerless.

Guilt and Emotional Manipulation: They will frame themselves as the victim and make parents feel like they are the problem. "*Your son/daughter is always so stressed after seeing you. Why do you put them through that?*" This causes parents to second-guess their actions.

Public Shaming and Triangulation: Some narcissists use smear campaigns, involving extended family or friends to make the in-laws feel like they are the unreasonable ones, further isolating them from their adult child.

Healing from Shame and Guilt

Estranged parents often carry guilt, and also shame. Many people struggle to differentiate between the two. A helpful way to remember it is this:

- **Guilt** says, "*I did something bad.*"
- **Shame** says, "*I am bad.*"

Guilt can be resolved. When we've made a mistake, forgotten a birthday, said something hurtful, we can apologize and seek forgiveness. In healthy relationships, this opens the door to healing. However, with a narcissist, there is no forgiveness and no forgetting. The offense, real or imagined, becomes ammunition in a never-ending war.

Shame, on the other hand, cuts to the core. It makes a person feel inherently flawed and unworthy, and it leads to self-criticism and a sense of inadequacy. It causes parents to question not only their actions but if they are deserving of being welcomed back into their child's life. Estranged parents often feel deep shame, because their identity as a parent has been fractured. Society doesn't help. Friends or acquaintances may ask thoughtless questions like, *"What did you do to make your child cut you off?"* Even if no one says it out loud, parents often internalize the belief: *"I must be a bad parent."*

Let's clarify two types of guilt:

- **Appropriate Guilt:** You did something wrong, and you can make it right. *Example:* You forgot your daughter-in-law's birthday. Solution: Apologize, send a card, and move on.
- **Inappropriate Guilt:** You feel guilt for something you didn't do, couldn't control, or that isn't your responsibility.
Example: You are blamed for "not supporting your child's boundaries," even though the boundaries are weaponized and ever-changing.

How Guilt Is Used for Control in Estrangement

Narcissists and emotionally manipulative people thrive on guilt and shame, because they are powerful tools of control. Once a narcissist discovers what triggers your guilt, they will use it to their advantage, holding it over you with quiet satisfaction that they've found your weak spot. When they regurgitate the same old accusations, it's because they know those words once planted a seed of doubt in your mind. They'll keep playing that card as long as it works, until you learn to release the guilt for things you didn't do, couldn't control, and were never yours to carry in the first place. Here's how guilt and shame are used to control estranged parents:

Overcompensation:

Estrangement Example: A parent, consumed with (inappropriate) guilt, over-apologizes, over-gives, or agrees to unfair terms just to regain contact.

Impact: It gives the narcissist more control and teaches them that guilt works to keep you compliant.

Avoiding Necessary Conflict:

Estrangement Example: You walk on eggshells and avoid speaking up, fearful it will push your child further away.

Impact: You lose your voice and influence, and the manipulator gains full control of the narrative.

Emotionally Driven Decisions:

Estrangement Example: You agree to therapy with a biased provider, give money, or accept false blame, just to "keep the peace."

Impact: These actions validate the narcissist's claims and prolong your emotional pain.

You deserve to challenge the guilt and shame that don't belong to you. Ask yourself: "Is this guilt based on facts, or is it being fed to me by fear and manipulation?"

Healing begins when you stop carrying shame for something you didn't break and start reclaiming the truth about who you are: a loving, human, imperfect parent doing your best.

Healing the Need for Their Love

An eye-opening realization for estranged parents is that part of their healing may involve grieving not only the relationship they had with their child but also the deep-seated need for their child's love. That may sound harsh, but it's a powerful and compassionate shift. The need for your child's love can feel so instinctive, so intertwined with your identity as a parent, that losing it feels like a betrayal of your soul. Yet, when that love is withheld, conditional, or controlled by someone else, it becomes a source of profound suffering. Healing that need doesn't mean you stop loving your child; it means you stop making your emotional well-being dependent on their validation or their decision to return.

Letting go of the need for your child's love is an act of radical self-preservation. It creates space for your own identity, peace, and restoration. You can still hope for reconnection and love them deeply, but healing begins when you learn to love yourself enough not to tie your wholeness to the actions or inactions of someone else. This is not about giving up; it's about grounding your worth in something that can't be taken from you. When you free yourself from the need for their love, you pave the way for healing on your own terms.

Releasing Self-Blame and Finding Peace

Are you blaming yourself? It's completely natural for self-aware, loving parents to reflect and question their role; that's part of the painful cycle of rumination. Thoughts like *"What did I do wrong?"* or *"If only I had..."* can consume you. This relentless self-questioning, however, isn't coming from within; it's the result of emotional manipulation that's designed to make you doubt your worth.

Narcissistic individuals are skilled at shifting responsibility and rescripting the past in a way that places blame on the people they are actively trying to push away. For estranged parents, especially those trying to keep any fragile connection alive, this blame is not only shocking, it's paralyzing. The more you blame yourself, the more power they hold over you and as I often say, that's how you know their poison is working.

Common Ways Narcissists Manipulate Parents into Self-Blame:

- Rewriting history: *"You were never there for me,"* even if you were constantly present and supportive.
- Blaming boundaries: *"If you hadn't pushed back or questioned us, we'd still be in contact."*

- Using grandchildren as leverage: "*If you really loved us, you'd do [insert unreasonable demand] so you could be in their lives.*"
- Shaming for your reactions: "*You're too emotional / difficult / dramatic,*" whenever you try to express your pain or confusion.
- Weaponizing therapy language: "*You're toxic, you need therapy,*" as a way to shut you down rather than open up dialogue.
- Selective memory: Ignoring your sacrifices and love while magnifying one mistake you made years ago.

How to Begin Releasing Self-Blame

To begin healing, you must first recognize that being blamed doesn't mean you *are* to blame. The narcissist wants you to carry the weight of the relationship, so they don't have to. That's manipulation, not accountability.

Start reframing the narrative with simple truths:

- I made mistakes like any parent, but I also showed up, loved, and supported my child.
- Someone trying to erase all the good I've done is not being fair or truthful.
- I cannot control another adult's actions, decisions, or perceptions.

Write down the accusations you've internalized, then next to each one, write what you know to be true. This helps shift the emotional weight off your chest and brings clarity back to your heart. Blame should never be confused with love. If love is conditional on your blame, then it was never love at all.

You didn't cause this alone. You can't fix it alone. And you certainly don't need to carry the weight of the blame just to stay connected. Expect to be blamed, because it is their tool. Understand that when you expect it, it loses its shock. You can't be thrown off balance by what you've already prepared for. Expect it and reject it.

In my book on divorcing a narcissist, I included a chapter called *The Dumbass Theory*. It's my way of helping people stop being shocked by predictable narcissistic behavior. The premise is simple: expect them to do exactly what they've always done. When they pull the same tired stunts or manipulative moves, don't let it rattle you. Instead, laugh at how transparent they are. Just like those old V8 commercials, give yourself a little tap on the forehead and say, "Of course they're pulling this again… dumbass." That shift in mindset can be the very thing that keeps you grounded.

Overcoming Rejection and Betrayal in Estrangement

I know this emotional section is hard to read, but please know why I'm sharing it with you. Most estranged parents struggle with many—if not all—of these deeply painful emotions. Rejection, abandonment, and betrayal sit at the core of estrangement, and without giving these feelings language and validation, they fester. When we begin to understand that these emotions are not just reactions, but often *intentional outcomes* of a narcissist's manipulation, we can begin to regain control over our pain and stop blaming ourselves for it.

The Betrayal

One of the most heartbreaking wounds estranged parents face is betrayal, especially from their own child. The betrayal doesn't always come in a dramatic, single moment. It creeps in as your child aligns more and more with their narcissistic partner. At first, they might challenge the exaggerated stories or twisted versions of the truth. Over time, though, even when they *know* the truth, they stay silent. They don't correct the lies. They don't defend you. That silence *is* betrayal.

Here are a few common ways that betrayal presents:
- They stop standing up for you, even when they know you didn't do what you're being accused of.
- They sit silently while their partner speaks poorly of you, spreading falsehoods.
- They allow access to your grandchildren to be used as leverage.
- They pretend your relationship never had love, closeness, or history.
- They rewrite the narrative of their childhood in ways that invalidate your entire role as a parent or paint you as the abuser.

The Rejection

The rejection by your own child cuts deeper than almost any other kind. You may hear phrases like:

- *"I need space."*
- *"I'm doing what's best for my mental health."*
- *"You're toxic and I can't be around you."*
- *"I am reevaluating my childhood."*
- *"I love you, but don't think I can have you in my life right now."*

Often, these statements are not truly their own but are borrowed from the narcissistic playbook of their partner. Your child may be surviving in a relationship based on control, fear, and manipulation. Rejection becomes the price they pay to maintain peace at home. And you become the casualty.

How to Stay Grounded

When you are betrayed or rejected, your nervous system goes into survival mode. You question your worth, your memories, your role as a parent. Here is what I want you to hold onto:

- You are not alone. Many parents are facing this. You are not broken or unlovable.
- The love you gave was real. No one can take that away from you, not even your child's silence.
- This isn't about your worth, it's about control. Your family has become collateral damage in someone else's dysfunction.
- Stay rooted in your truth. Write it down. Speak it aloud. Return to it when doubt creeps in.

When betrayal and rejection feel overwhelming, remind yourself that the game is rigged, and you refuse to play. You deserve peace. You deserve love. One day, if your child awakens to the truth, you'll still be standing in yours.

The Fear of Never Reuniting with Your Child or Grandchildren and What to Do About It

Fear can paralyze you. Fear is self-amplifying. Fear is a liar. There is a saying, "fear is like the devil." This suggests that fear, like the devil, can be a powerful force that hinders growth and well-being, often used to instill doubt and negativity. Some religious and spiritual perspectives view fear as a tool used by the devil or a negative force to control and manipulate individuals.

Has your mind ever whispered, *"What if I never see them again?"* That haunting question doesn't just linger, it screams in the quiet moments, rattles through your mind at night, and replays like a film reel you can't shut off. And when grandchildren are involved, that fear cuts even deeper, touching a place in your heart that words can't reach.

We've talked about how narcissists rule with fear, and this is one of their most brutal tactics. They dangle your child and grandchild like a carrot on a string, knowing that the mere *threat* of permanent separation will keep you quiet, compliant, and full of shame. This is emotional terrorism masked as "boundaries."

Fear builds a story. When we live in that fear, the story becomes louder, scarier, and clearer in our minds. We catastrophize *I'll never see them again. They'll forget me. They'll believe I abandoned them.* But fear is a master storyteller, and it exaggerates. It pushes you to believe the worst possible ending. You might not even realize you are writing a scary fearful conclusion to a story that's still unfolding

Let's interrupt that narrative.

Instead of living in the shadow of what might never be, try anchoring yourself to what *was,* and to the truth of your love. Remember the laughter, the bedtime stories, the tiny arms that wrap around your neck. Those memories are real. They matter. And they live in your heart and your grandchild's heart, too, even if they've been told otherwise.

Many parents have found creative and quiet ways to stay connected to their grandchildren's memory. A trusted friend might be able to sneak a picture your way, or you may come across a school event photo online.

You don't have to erase yourself just because someone else has tried to. Your love didn't vanish when the door closed. It lives on. In fact, it can thrive. And if that door opens again, even just a crack, those memories will come flooding in like sunlight pouring through the window on a cloudless summer day.

The fear of never reuniting is real, but it's not prophecy. Let it exist, but don't let it write the ending.

Exercise: Leaving a Legacy of Love

I have a friend who is estranged from her grandchild, and instead of letting the silence consume her, she found a beautiful way to keep the connection alive. She began recording short, 10-minute videos on her phone, nothing polished or professional, just her, speaking from the heart. In these videos, she shares stories about her life, her family history, and what she experienced growing up. She tells sweet and funny memories about her daughter (the child's mother) when she was little - the kinds of stories that might otherwise be lost to time. Anecdotes told to grandchildren become the threads that stitch generations together, weaving memory into legacy. She hopes that one day hers will cherish her chronicles, even if it's not right now.

She also talks about her passion for baking, how she used to make beautiful birthday cakes for her daughter, with handmade sugar flowers and custom designs that took days to prepare. She shares her favorite recipes and the joy she felt seeing her family gathered around something she made with love. These memories are a way of bringing warmth and connection into a space where she's currently not allowed.

She even reads Christmas books aloud, sitting in front of her own decorated fireplace with a roaring fire, imagining her granddaughter sitting on the floor listening. These are moments full of love, comfort, and a grandmother's quiet hope. She's saving them all with the help of her other child, trusting that one day, maybe at 18 but hopefully sooner, her granddaughter might want to know her roots. These videos will be waiting.

Even though she fears being forgotten, she's building a legacy: a time capsule of love.

Now it's your turn.

What can *you* do to preserve your presence, your stories, your heart? Could you keep a journal? Write letters? Record memories or special messages. Create a scrapbook of your time together? Share a skill or passion through video or audio? These acts are not just for them; they're healing for *you* too. It's your love, still showing up, even in the silence.

Traversing Judgement from Others

An emotional resilience chapter wouldn't be complete without acknowledging another painful and isolating aspect of estrangement: *the judgment of others*. You're already navigating the heartbreak of losing a connection with your child or grandchild, and on top of that, you're met too frequently with unsolicited opinions, shallow assumptions, and patronizing advice.

Even well-meaning friends and extended family can become a burden in the emotional weight you carry. Maybe they don't understand estrangement at all; they assume *you* must have done something truly terrible for your child to walk away. To add insult to injury, they toss out simplistic advice like:

- "Just apologize."
- "Be the bigger person."
- "They'll come around, give it time."

Your friends and family are not intentionally cruel, but they are critically uninformed. These comments ignore the nuances, the emotional abuse, the narcissistic manipulation, and the years of minding your p's and q's. Worse, they can make you question your own instincts and retraumatize you when you're doing your best just to stay afloat.

Here's what I want you to remember:

People who haven't experienced estrangement rarely understand its complexity. They view it like a bad argument or a parenting misstep. They don't understand narcissistic dynamics or how false narratives can take root in your child's mind. They also don't see the behind-the-scenes manipulation you've endured. Take their advice for what it is: uninformed, uncomfortable filler from people who just don't get it.

Tips for Navigating Judgment:

Set boundaries with those who minimize your pain.

You don't owe anyone an explanation for what you're going through. A simple, "Thanks, but I'm working on this with support," is enough.

Know your truth.

Keep a journal of your memories, your efforts, and your truth. This is not about proving anything, it's about validating your experience.

Don't argue with ignorance.

You don't have to educate every person who doesn't understand. Save your energy for the ones who deserve it.

Use the Dumbass Theory.

Expect people to say dumb things, and instead of taking them personally say, "Oh right, *dumbass*." Humor can be a powerful tool for survival.

Estrangement is already an over-the-top emotional battlefield. Protect yourself from the extra arrows of judgment by strengthening your boundaries and staying rooted in your truth. You know your heart. You know your efforts. And you deserve compassion, not criticism.

SECTION 4
The Art Of Communication In Estrangement

"Most parents carry a quiet truth in their hearts seeing the control, the manipulation, the narcissism in their child's spouse. They long to speak it, to shake their child awake. But love makes them hesitate, and fear keeps them silent. They know that naming it could drive their child further away. So they swallow the truth, hoping that love will one day guide them back before the silence shatters them both."

CHAPTER 8
Understanding the Narcissist's Communication Style: The Eggshell Dance

One painful dynamic of an estranged parent-child relationship is the way communication becomes a minefield. This chapter explores what I call *The Eggshell Dance,* a pattern where every word, every silence, and every gesture feel like it could be wrong. The narcissist's communication style is often controlling, unpredictable, and emotionally manipulative. Whether they're overtly critical or passively withholding, the outcome is the same: the person on the receiving end lives in fear. Fear of doing it wrong. Fear of losing the relationship altogether. The worry that anything you do could make bad go to worse. When the narcissist has influenced your child, you begin to hear that same language echoed back, and it can feel like hearing the voice of a stranger in the mouth of your once-loving child. Parents often share, "I don't know who this is—it's like who we knew has completely disappeared."

Narcissistic communication is designed to destabilize. It moves the goalposts constantly: you're either too much, too little, too emotional, too cold, not sincere *enough*... it's like a rotating lock - just when you think you've found the key, it turns again. Even something as simple as blinking too many times or smiling at the wrong moment becomes evidence against you. I often tell my clients, "You're damned if you do, and damned if you don't." This is not a coincidence, it's control. One common tactic used in these exchanges is known as **DARVO**: *Deny, Attack, and Reverse Victim and Offender*. When you try to raise a concern, the narcissist denies your experience, attacks your character or intentions, and then flips the script to make themselves the victim and you the perpetrator. Understanding this pattern is the first step toward untangling yourself from it.

The Perpetual Victim: How the Narcissist Enlists Your Child

While DARVO is a powerful lens for understanding narcissistic communication, it's really only one piece of a larger puzzle. At the core of nearly every interaction with a narcissist is the deep-seated belief that they are the victim. *Always*. No matter the situation, no matter the facts, they manage to position themselves as the one who has been wronged.

To your child, this becomes their truth. The narcissistic in-law frames themselves as the misunderstood hero or wounded soul who has suffered deeply at the hands of others, especially you and your family. You become "the toxic parent," "the controlling mother," or "the emotionally unavailable father," whatever label fits the narcissist's narrative at the time. Your child's past is reconstructed to reflect a life of mistreatment and betrayal - those experiences are distorted, exaggerated, or entirely fabricated. In this new storyline, your child is cast in a starring role: *their protector*.

Narcissists are skilled actors. They know exactly when to pull out the charm, the vulnerability, and the well-timed tear. This performance is designed to evoke empathy and loyalty, and it's incredibly effective. Your child, who may have once loved your family traditions and laughed with you around the dinner table, is now being emotionally groomed to see you as dangerous, unsupportive, or a threat to their partner's well-being. The narcissist uses phrases like *"They've never accepted me,"* or *"Your family always treats me like an outsider,"* knowing these words will stir your child's sense of justice and protection.

Over time, your child may begin to echo this language. You'll hear them repeat the same stories, adopt the same tone of suspicion, or shut down when you try to connect. It can feel like watching a loved one slowly disappear into someone else's worldview, hearing your child speak with words that don't sound like their own, but instead like an echo of the narcissist whispering in their ear.

Am I Talking to My Child or the Narcissist?

Nearly every estranged parent I've worked with shares a similar heartbreak: the realization that communication from their child no longer feels like it's truly *from* their child. Gone are the easy, everyday messages, those simple *"How was your day?"* texts that once felt so natural. The frequency of interactions may dwindle, but what hurts most is the shift in tone. One day, something in their child's voice, whether spoken or written, just sounds *off.* It's colder, more formal, often laced with distance or tension. In that moment, the general consensus is: *Where did my child go?*

The words, the tone, the way they frame conversations all feel foreign. The warm, familiar language you once knew is replaced with cold, calculated phrases that sound rehearsed, almost scripted. Phrases like *"Our bond means the world to me, but I need space,"* or *"You've always been controlling,"* are often direct reflections of the narcissistic in-law's influence. It's as if you're not just conversing with your child, but with their spouse standing invisibly behind them, feeding them lines.

This shift can be disorienting and deeply hurtful. You may find yourself wondering, *Is this really what my child believes, or are they just repeating what they've been told?* The answer is both. Under the narcissist's manipulation, your child slowly began to adopt their partner's narrative, sometimes unknowingly. Over time, their writing style, emotional expression, and even conflict language can start to mirror the narcissist's patterns. This is why it's crucial to understand:

when you're communicating with your child, the narcissist is often reading, influencing, or even helping craft the message.

The narcissist often takes on the role of gatekeeper to your child, closely monitoring communication and controlling access. They may start crafting your child's texts or emails or even insist that all contact go through them, claiming you're too upsetting or unsafe for your child to speak to directly. This tactic mirrors the very narrative they've fed your child: that you are the problem. Now, they're turning that same script on you, using guilt and emotional manipulation to reinforce their control. It's a carefully orchestrated form of gaslighting, designed to convince both you and your child that all communication must pass through them. It's not about protection, it's about power.

When trust has been broken, both parent and child often approach communication with guarded care. The parent may feel intense anxiety about saying the wrong thing, afraid that one misstep could cause another rupture. Meanwhile, the adult child, especially if they've been heavily influenced by their partner, may carry deep fears of being pulled back into what they've been told is a manipulative or unhealthy dynamic. The emotional wall between you isn't just made of hurt; it's built on fear, confusion, and distorted beliefs.

This is why I urge parents to assume that *nothing is private anymore.* Emails, texts, even voice messages - anything you say will be shared, twisted, or used to further alienate you. It's vital to protect your heart and your intentions by being mindful of what you put in writing. Never bash the narcissistic in-law, no matter how justified it may feel. Instead, keep your tone neutral, kind, and calm. Think of your messages as if they were being read aloud, because in the court of emotional manipulation, they are. What you say should always reflect your values, not your frustration. This awareness won't solve the estrangement, but it will keep you from unknowingly fueling the fire.

Has this happened to you? Many parents begin by noticing a troubling pattern: before dialogue with their child was cut off, calls often happened when their child was alone in their car to and from work or when on a solo errand. Over time, however, something shifts. A sixth sense alerts parents that they're no longer speaking to their child alone. The pauses become longer, the tone changes, and eventually it becomes clear the partner is sitting nearby, possibly even coaching their responses. What once felt like a small step toward reconnection now feels filtered, controlled, and unsettlingly scripted.

Narc-Speak: Decode Their Communication and How to Respond

When parents receive a missive from their adult child filled with emotion, accusations, and unresolved pain, it can be overwhelming to know how (or even whether) to respond. I encourage my clients to begin by *printing the message:* this helps bring some emotional distance and allows for a more grounded, analytical approach. With a pen in hand, identify what's being repeated. Ask yourself: *Is this the same grievance I've already addressed? Is this a recycled narrative I've apologized for repeatedly?* If so, take note but remember, repetition doesn't necessarily require re-engagement.

Next, look for what, if anything, is actually being asked of you. Is your child making a specific request, or are they venting and unloading unresolved feelings? Not every statement needs a response. You do not have to defend yourself against every attack, justify every past decision, or engage in circular conversations that have historically gone nowhere. Instead, highlight the parts that are actionable or sincere. Is there a question being asked? A boundary being set? A moment of vulnerability, however small? Those are the areas where a thoughtful, calm response may be appropriate.

Finally, decide what aligns with your values and your emotional safety. I'll say it again: just because something is written doesn't mean it deserves a reply. Your goal is not to win an argument or convince your child of your worth; it's to communicate from a place of clarity, love, and strength. Respond only to what matters. You can acknowledge their pain without agreeing to every accusation. You can apologize again if it feels right to you but not if it's a performance demanded on cue. This process gives you back some control, allowing you to move from a place of reaction to one of intentional response.

Strategies to Prevent Conflict from Escalating - DARVO, BIFF, EAR, JAGGED

As I've covered earlier, DARVO (Deny, Attack, Reverse Victim and Offender) is often the narcissist's choice of articulation - it's their twisted love language. Thankfully, however, we have tools of our own. Bill Eddy, founder of the High Conflict Institute in California, created several defensive communication strategies for dealing with difficult people. One of his most effective is the acronym **BIFF**, which stands for **Brief, Informative, Friendly, and Firm**. This approach helps you express yourself clearly and respectfully, without getting pulled into emotional traps. Later, Eddy introduced **EAR, Empathy, Attention, and Respect,** to help guide interactions in a way that calms rather than escalates. Both of these approaches offer solid options when responding to a narcissistic in-law or navigating sensitive conversations with your adult child.

Introducing JAGGED – A New Tool for Estranged Parents

When emotions run high, it's easy to fall into patterns that unintentionally make things worse. That's why I created a new acronym to guide estranged parents in tough conversations: **JAGGED**. It's a simple yet powerful reminder of what ***not*** to do when communicating with your child—**Justify, Argue, Guilt, Gaslight, Explain, or Defend**. These reactions, often driven by pain or confusion, can deepen the divide and hand control back to a manipulative influence. Instead, pause. Breathe. Ask yourself: *Will this response bring clarity—or fuel more chaos?*

Things not to do in communication with an estranged child:
- **J** – Justify your actions or decisions
- **A** – Argue to prove your point or correct them
- **G** – Guilt them into reconnecting or complying
- **G** – Gaslight (minimize, deny, or reframe their experience)
- **E** – Explain in excessive detail to defend yourself
- **D** – Defend your character or past behavior

The power in these acronyms is that they help you stay grounded, protect your emotional energy, and resist the urge to prove yourself to someone who is committed to creating misunderstandings. In high-conflict dynamics, less is truly more, and sometimes thoughtful restraint becomes your best tool.

CHAPTER 9

Reaching Out to Your Child: Broaching the Situation

Should I Keep Reaching Out? Weigh the Pros and Cons

The list of agonizing questions estranged parents face is long, relentless, and often unanswerable - each one a dagger twisting with doubt: *What did I do wrong? Could I have stopped this? Should I keep trying? Will they ever come back?* These questions don't just visit - they haunt, echoing in quiet moments and sleepless nights alike. When every attempt is met with silence or cold distance, it's natural to question whether your outreach is helping or hurting. The truth is there's no one-size-fits-all answer. Every estrangement is unique, shaped by different histories, levels of contact, and outside influences. What feels like a lifeline to one child may feel like a boundary violation to another, especially if a narcissistic partner is shaping the narrative.

If you've been reaching out regularly and getting no response, your good intentions may eventually be used against you. Narcissistic in-laws tend to twist your efforts to stay connected as "proof" that you don't respect boundaries. They may tell your child, *"See? They don't listen. They're still trying to control you."* In this light, even a warm check-in or a photo of a family memory can be weaponized.

What Is Grey Rock?

Grey Rock is a term used to describe a communication style that is intentionally dull, unemotional, and unengaging—like talking to a grey rock. While often taught to victims of narcissistic abuse as a way to protect themselves from emotional manipulation, it is deeply painful when this tactic is used *against* you. If your child replies with short, indifferent texts, ignores your updates, or shows no concern even when you mention being unwell, this may be grey rock in action. They've likely been conditioned to view your vulnerability as manipulation - especially if the narcissistic in-law has influenced them to interpret your words as guilt-tripping. Also notice how little they share about their own life. This emotional flatness and the withholding of personal detail is another hallmark of grey rock. It's not that they don't care - it's that they've been trained not to show it.

That said, many experts agree it's okay to occasionally "ping" your child, gently and without expectation. A simple "thinking of you" message, a shared memory, or a photo from the past can serve as a quiet reminder that your love remains steady. Even if it goes unacknowledged, it may still touch something within them. These small, thoughtful gestures let your child know you're still here, still loving them, and not holding onto anger; they offer connection without pressure - a breadcrumb that says, *I'm still here, I care, and I'm not giving up on you.* In the best cases, it reminds your child that your love is unconditional, even in silence. It can soften the edges of estrangement when done with care and without expectation of a reply. The key is balance: be present without becoming oppressive. Again, when in doubt, remember less is often more, but don't underestimate the inaudible power of a heartfelt message sent at the right time. Just bear in mind, if those messages are unwelcome or become too frequent, they can and will be twisted by the narcissistic in-law as evidence against you. Even a well-meaning message can be seen as disrespectful.

This is the delicate dance of estrangement, and you may not know where the invisible line is until you accidentally step over it and find yourself suddenly in free-fall with your child slowly disappearing from your sight. Do it because it reflects who *you* are—not because you're hoping for an immediate change. Let the gesture be enough and allow it to stand on its own.

Finding the Right Moment and Tone for Communication

Reaching out to an estranged child can be tricky but above all, timing and tone are everything. Even the sincerest message can be misinterpreted or rejected if it arrives at the wrong moment or carries a dubious emotional weight. A calm, respectful attitude free of guilt, urgency, or emotional pressure is far more likely to be received with openness. This doesn't mean you should hide your feelings - it means expressing them gently, without upsetting the reader. When your child hears your voice through your words, let it be that of steady compassion and stability, not desperation or torment.

Equally important is finding the *right* moment to make contact. Avoid sending a message in the heat of agitation or during a major event in their life (such as a birthday, holiday, or big transition) unless it's purely a thoughtful, pressure-free gesture. If they've recently set a boundary or asked for space, it's important to honor that. Timing your outreach during a quiet, neutral period when there's less emotional intensity can make the difference in how your words are received. Trust your instincts. When in doubt, wait a few days and re-read your message with fresh eyes before hitting send.

When you do write, keep the timbre soft, non-defensive, and open-ended. Avoid phrases that sound like demands or attempts to force a response, such as *"I need to hear back from you,"* or *"You owe me a reply."* Instead, try language like, *"I just wanted to reach out and let you know I'm thinking of you,"* or *"If you ever feel ready to talk, I'm here."* These gentle approaches create security and show that you're willing to move at their pace. In estranged relationships, even small adjustments in tone and timing can build trust one message at a time.

This process can feel incredibly frustrating, and it should: you're trapped in a game with constantly shifting rules, oftentimes at a turtle's pace. You may find yourself holding back from saying what you truly feel, tiptoeing around the elephant in the room in fear of triggering attacks or being met with more false accusations. When narcissistic influence is at play, even honesty can be twisted and used against you. The truth becomes a weapon in their hands, not a path to resolution. This is why it's so important to proceed with caution and protect your peace while choosing your words with care.

Contacting Your Child: Common Letter Writing Mistakes to Avoid

Writing a letter to your estranged child can feel like pouring your heart onto paper - hopeful, vulnerable, and filled with passion. You may see it as a gesture of love, an olive branch, or a chance to be heard. However, if the letter isn't written carefully, it can unintentionally push your child further away. One of the most common mistakes is turning the letter into a defense of your actions or a platform to correct their version of events. Even if you feel the need to clarify misunderstandings or address false accusations, a written message is not the place to debate the past. If the tone comes across as defensive or accusatory, it will likely reinforce their belief that you still "don't get it."

Another pitfall is making the letter too sentimental or centered on yourself. While it's natural to want your child to understand how much you've hurt during the estrangement, overly emotional messages can feel like guilt-laden manipulation, especially if they are still in a protective or angry mindset. Phrases like *"I cry every day without you,"* or *"I can't live without you"* may be honest, but they shift the focus onto your needs rather than creating a space of safety for your child. Instead, express care and openness gently, without making them feel responsible for your healing.

It's also important to avoid placing expectations or conditions within the letter. Saying things like *"I hope this means we can be a family again,"* or *"I just want to meet my grandchildren"* might seem like heartfelt wishes in your mind, but they can come across as pressure-packed expectations on the other end. If your child feels pushed to respond, forgive, or reconnect before they're ready, they may retreat even further. A healthier approach would be to offer your love and presence without demanding a timeline or outcome. For example: *"I understand you need time, and I respect that. I just want you to know I'm here, if and when you're ever open to reconnecting."*

When I work with clients, there's a painfully candid truth I like to share, and while it usually gets a laugh, it always hits home. The writing style you're forced to adopt when communicating with a narcissistic in-law is so fake, so overly polite, so unnaturally filtered, it will make you want to *barf in your mouth*. You're bending over backward to avoid triggering them, carefully crafting every word to sidestep drama or retaliation. It doesn't feel like your voice—and that's because it isn't. It's survival language, not authentic expression. Unfortunately, it's often the only way to keep the door even slightly ajar.

Lastly, be conscientious not to over-apologize, especially for things you didn't do. Empty or excessive apologies can sound performative, and if your child is under the influence of a controlling partner, they may be seen through or used against you. Instead, acknowledge their feelings where you can, without confessing to false narratives. Keep your letter short, sincere, and calm. The goal is to create a sense of emotional safety, one that quietly says, *"You can reach out when you're ready. I'll be here."*

Navigating Manipulative Tactics in Communication

Navigating communication with a narcissist whether directly or indirectly through your child, often feels like walking through a field of emotional landmines. One of the most destabilizing tactics they use is gaslighting. This involves denying your reality, rewriting shared experiences, or making you question your memory and intentions. You may find yourself wondering, *Did I really say it that way?* or *Maybe I did overreact?* Gaslighting isn't always loud; it can be subtle, woven into passive-aggressive comments or casual contradictions that leave you feeling confused and unsteady. The more you try to clarify, the deeper into the bog you may sink.

Lying is another common tactic, whether it's outright fabrication or lies by omission. Narcissists lie to control the narrative, paint themselves as victims, or to sow mistrust between family members. These lies are often strategic, designed to isolate you or erode your credibility, especially with your child. They may claim you said things you didn't or that you behaved in ways that never happened, and once your child believes those lies, correcting the record can feel like an uphill battle in ten feet of snow. The more you try to explain or defend yourself, the easier it becomes for the narcissistic in-law to twist your words and portray *you* as the manipulative one.

A particularly hurtful form of manipulation is twisting the story or making things up entirely. Narcissists excel at taking partial truths and spinning them into a web of damaging accusations. Something as simple as setting a boundary or expressing a concern can be reframed as an attack, a betrayal, or proof of your supposed toxicity. This tactic puts you in a no-win situation: if you remain silent, you confirm their version of events; if you speak up, you're accused of being defensive or combative. Recognizing this course of action is critical, not only to protect your emotional well-being but also to help you choose your responses carefully and avoid falling into the traps set by manipulative communication.

For estranged parents, few things are more gut-wrenching than seeing these lies and distortions in writing from their child. The pain runs deep. It's not just that your words or intentions have been misrepresented; it's the disorienting shock of realizing your child actually believes these things. The confusion can be enormous as you search your memory, trying to pinpoint where things went so drastically wrong. There's grief in watching your truth be erased, replaced by a storyline shaped by manipulation. And there's heartbreak in recognizing that your child may now be the messenger of someone else's voice, carrying words that aren't theirs. It's a heartbreaking trauma that's paradoxical to describe - one that combines sadness, helplessness, and a longing to be seen and remembered for who you truly are. Be kind to yourself. This pain is real.

In the midst of pain and confusion, thoughts race. The following are some examples of what might run through an estranged parent's mind:

- *This is not how we raised you. What changed? Where did we go wrong?*
- *Who raised you to believe this is the way to handle things? I thought we were better than this.*
- *After all the love, sacrifices, and care we gave you, how could you turn on us like this?*
- *Who are you? I feel like I don't even recognize the child I raised.*
- *We used to have such a close relationship. We could always talk to each other. Why is it so different now?*
- *What did we do to make you feel this way? I wish I could understand.*
- *How can we fix this? I'm willing to do whatever it takes to make things right again.*
- *Why won't you talk to us and tell us what's wrong? We just want to understand.*
- *Do you ever miss us the way we miss you? It feels like there is a hole in our lives.*
- *Do you even know how much this hurts us? We love you more than you'll ever know.*

CHAPTER 10
They Called—Now What? Preparing for the Unexpected

Understanding Their Messages: Plan Your Response Effectively

When you receive a message from your child, it's natural to analyze every word, especially when you're longing for signs of reconnection. Maybe in the past they ended their messages with "I love you" or another small expression of warmth. But this time, it's missing. That absence can feel crushing.

It's also important to acknowledge that the frequency, tone, and warmth of their messages may not resemble the connection you once shared. You might feel heartbroken that their texts sound cold, transactional, or even distant. That difference can trigger grief all over again. But remember this shift is often a reflection of the influence they're under or their own unresolved emotions, not a measure of their love for you or your worth as a parent.

One of the first steps I guide my clients through is evaluating the tone of the communication. By stepping back and assessing the tone objectively, you can remove the emotional charge and gain a clearer perspective. This allows you to craft a thoughtful response rather than reacting out of frustration.

Not every message requires a reply, but by carefully reviewing it, you can determine the best way to respond, if at all. Identify the main points and clarify what actually needs to be addressed. Let's start by understanding how to analyze tone.

Analyzing Tone:

- **Highly angry and accusatory:** there is little room for constructive conversation.
- Blames the parent for past actions and perceived betrayals. *"You chose to side with them over me, and now you wonder why I don't trust you. Every time I needed you, you let me down."*
- Dismissive of any attempt at reconciliation, reinforcing a victim-perpetrator dynamic.
- Uses emotional manipulation by saying things like *"I guess I just have to accept whatever crumbs of a relationship you're willing to offer me."*
- Threatening undertones such as *"We've been patient long enough, but actions have consequences. If things don't change, we'll have no choice but to protect ourselves in ways you may not like."*
- No clear request for what the child wants from their parent, only continuous criticism.
- Contradictory: *"I really want us to have a close, healthy relationship, but how can I when you continue to choose everyone else over me? You have completely abandoned me, and yet you expect me to just accept your pathetic attempts at communication? You don't even realize how much you've hurt me, and honestly, I don't think you ever will. I'm doing my best to be close to you, but you make it impossible with your lies and betrayal."*
- Highly emotional and accusatory: The email is full of anger, blame, and resentment. It expresses deep frustration and a sense of betrayal. *"I can't

believe how easily you turned your back on me after everything I've been through. You chose to betray me, to side with people who have done nothing but hurt me, and now you expect me to just move on like nothing happened? You have no idea the pain you've caused, and yet you continue to act like the victim. I have given you chance after chance to do the right thing, and you've failed me every single time. Do you even care about the damage you've done, or are you just pretending this isn't your fault?"

- Victim mentality & justification of In-law's behavior: *"I never wanted things to be this way, but I had no choice after the way you treated me. If I've reacted strongly, it's only because I've been pushed to my limit. Anyone in my position would have done the same. You left me with no other option."*
- Lack of openness to reconciliation: While the child claims they want to stay connected, the overall message is rigid, conditional, and focused on past grievances.
- Pressure & control: *"If you really cared about me, you would stand up for me and cut ties with anyone who has treated me badly. The fact that you still speak to them shows where your true loyalties lie. I don't see how we can move forward unless you make it clear that you're on my side."* This manipulates the recipient into feeling guilty and coerces them into proving their loyalty by distancing themselves from others, reinforcing the in-law's control over family relationships.
- Manipulative language: Statements like *"You should appreciate that I've held back as much as I have if I really wanted to, I could have made things much worse for everyone. I've been more patient and forgiving than you deserve.".* Another example is using the grandchildren. *"I've been more than generous in letting you have a relationship with the kids, but that can change if I don't see real effort from you. If you truly cared about them, you'd prove it by respecting my boundaries and showing that you're on my side."*

Here's a list of possible common points an estranged parent might encounter in a message from their estranged child or in-law:

- You were never there for me growing up.
- I need space and you don't respect that.
- You only care about yourself and your feelings.
- You refuse to acknowledge the pain you caused me.
- I don't trust you to be around my children.
- You only reach out when you want something.
- I'm tired of the guilt trips and manipulation.
- You still defend [other parent/sibling] even after what they did to me.
- You always make yourself the victim.
- You ignored my boundaries, and now I have to protect myself.
- This relationship will never be the same again.
- I don't owe you a relationship just because we are related.
- Stop acting like you don't know why I cut you off.
- You only want access to my kids, not a real relationship with me.
- You never took my side when I needed you.
- I will decide if and when I'm ready to talk to you.
- You've shown no effort to change or acknowledge your mistakes.
- You are toxic, and I can't have you in my life.
- I have to do what's best for my family, and that means keeping my distance.
- You are passive aggressive or a narcissist

These types of statements can be emotionally charged and difficult to process but breaking them down into main points can help to form responses (if needed) with clarity and intention rather than reacting out of hurt.

What Needs a Response?

When developing a response to your estranged child or in-law, it's important to stay focused on what truly requires a response. Try to pause before you build a story around it. Avoid emotional reactions, over-explaining, or engaging in unproductive debates. Instead, center your response on the following key areas:

Do Not Justify, Validate Lies with a Response, or Over-Apologize:
If they make false accusations, avoid defending yourself extensively.

- Acknowledge their feelings without agreeing to distorted narratives.
- Do not apologize for things you didn't do just to appease them.

Boundaries & Allegations of Betrayal:
- If they accuse you of siding with others or betraying them, calmly clarify your position.
- Reinforce that respecting boundaries is not a sign of taking sides.
- Maintain your own boundaries regarding what behavior you will or won't accept.

Misinterpretation of Neutrality:
- If they assume neutrality means favoritism, gently correct this misconception.
- Reiterate that you are not choosing sides but respecting all parties' boundaries.

Repetitive Grievances:
- If the message revisits past conflicts that have been addressed, do not get caught in a cycle of rehashing them.
- Acknowledge past mistakes, if necessary, but focus on moving forward.

Affirm Love & Desire to Stay Connected:
- Regardless of the tension, express your love and hope for a healthy relationship.
- Keep your message open-ended to allow for future reconciliation.

Acknowledge Their Pain Without Fueling the Fire:
- Recognize their feelings without escalating the conflict.
- Use neutral language to prevent defensiveness.

Clarify the Parent's Position & Boundaries:
- Clearly define what you are willing to discuss and what is off-limits.
- Stand firm in your own needs while expressing willingness to communicate.

Avoid Engaging in Attacks Against Others:
- Do not get pulled into attacking their spouse, sibling, or other family members.
- Keep the conversation between you and your child.

Set Boundaries on the Conversation:
- If the communication is abusive or unproductive, state that you will only engage in respectful discussions.
- If needed, set limits on the format of communication (e.g., email only, meeting with a mediator, etc.).

Not every attack deserves a defense, and not every lie requires correction. When you receive a message from your child, especially a lengthy or emotionally charged one, it's important to push pause and evaluate what truly needs a response. A ten-page letter does not warrant a ten-page reply. Instead, look for what might be a true request or a moment where connection could be built, and focus your energy there.

Remember the tools we discussed in the communication chapter: **BIFF** (Brief, Informative, Friendly, Firm), **EAR** (Empathy, Attention, Respect), and **JAGGED** (Justify, Argue, Guilt, Gaslight, Explain, or Defend). These acronyms are your compass in navigating hostile or manipulative communication. The more emotion you inject into your reply, no matter how justified, the more likely it is to be twisted or used against you later. Narcissistic dynamics thrive on reaction. Your goal is to remain grounded, neutral, and clear.

Many estranged parents describe going back and rereading texts, searching for clues—wondering why one message felt warm while the next felt like a wall. This cycle of emotional interpretation can be exhausting. Instead, try to match their tone without attaching expectations, and acknowledge their effort without measuring it against the past.

Before sending any reply, reread your message through a critical lens. Scan it for any signs of guilt-laced language, defensiveness, sarcasm, or even subtle passive-aggressive undertones. These may be subconscious, especially when you're hurt or overwhelmed. This careful self-editing is what I call the *eggshell dance* of communication - every word can be misread, every tone misinterpreted. The best protection is clarity, calm, and control. Respond with grace, not because they deserve it, but because you do.

If you measure each exchange against what it used to be, discouragement can creep in. It's important to recognize these baby steps for what they truly are: movement. A response, however brief, is not the end of the story; it's part of the journey. Protect your emotional energy by staying present and remind yourself: this doesn't have to mean more than it does. By staying calm, focused, and intentional in your response, you can maintain your dignity and keep the door open for future healing while protecting yourself from unnecessary emotional turmoil. It's a step. And for today, that's enough.

Stop Being Blindsided: How to Plan Conversations and Responses

A painful aspect of communicating with an estranged child is constantly being blindsided by new accusations or twisted narratives. While it's impossible to prepare for every possible attack, you *can* plan for the most common or familiar ones. If you've been accused of specific things in the past, whether it's being controlling, emotionally unavailable, or never supportive, write them down. These recurring themes often reveal the emotional hooks that are being used to manipulate or guilt you. By identifying them, you can begin to take their sting away.

Once you've listed the accusations, reflect on each one honestly and gently. Think back to what happened, your version of the story... not to prove anyone wrong, but to ground yourself in your own truth. Plan out how you might respond if it comes up again. Instead of defending or correcting (which often escalates things), focus on language that speaks from your heart without sounding accusatory. For example, instead of saying, *"That's not what happened,"* you might say, *"That's not how I remember it, and I'm sorry it left you feeling that way."* This kind of response affirms your perspective while showing empathy, a powerful balance that can disarm tension and maintain your dignity.

Practicing these responses, even role-playing them with a therapist, partner, or trusted friend, can help you feel more confident when the moment arises. It builds emotional resilience so that when the conversation takes a turn, you're less likely to shut down or become reactive. This preparation isn't about control; it's about preserving your peace. Being mentally prepared for familiar attacks helps reduce the fear of the unknown ones. When you're no longer caught off guard, you gain a sense of strength and stability in conversations that once left you shaken.

The Cruel Lies: Maintain Composure in the Face of Attacks

Hearing cruel lies from your own child is gut-wrenching. The instinct to defend yourself, correct the story, or plead for understanding is completely natural. However, when you're up against someone who isn't open to hearing your truth, those reactions often only escalate the situation. This is why one of the most powerful skills you can develop is *emotional composure.* Preparing yourself to hear difficult, even outrageous falsities, without reacting impulsively, gives you the strength to stay in control of your own narrative, even if your child can't yet see it.

Start by grounding yourself in the knowledge that not every accusation needs a response. Some things are spoken to provoke, to bait you into reacting, or to reaffirm the narrative they've been told. Before going into a conversation where conflict may arise, remind yourself: *I don't have to prove anything. I only need to stay calm and aligned with who I am.* Practice taking slow breaths. Keep your posture relaxed. Imagine the lie passing by you instead of hitting you. You can silently note, *that's not true* in your own mind without saying it out loud. Holding your center in these moments will speak louder than any response you may have.

If you feel yourself getting emotionally flooded, have a plan to pause. You can say, *"I need a moment to take that in,"* or *"I hear you, and I'd like to take some time to reflect before I respond."* This protects your dignity and gives you time to gather your thoughts. The key is to avoid being pulled into a reactive place where you're saying things you'll later regret. Staying composed doesn't mean you're accepting their fiction, it simply means you're refusing to let them push your buttons. Your reaction is the supply the narcissist wants. That silent strength, over time, can become a powerful contrast to the chaos and distortion your child may be living in.

What's often labeled as "attempts to reconcile" can feel anything but healing. Parents may go into these calls expecting resolution, only to feel deeply disrespected, silenced, and dismissed when they're over. In a space that's supposed to feel safe, you may instead feel attacked, misrepresented, or even outright lied about. Beyond that, if you react like any human being would in that same circumstance, you risk being labeled as angry, abusive, or unstable. The very behavior that's provoked by their chaos is then used as evidence that you are exactly what they've said you are.

This is the impossible position many parents find themselves in: absorbing the emotional blows, staying composed under pressure, and tolerating painful distortions, all in the hope of preserving some connection with their child. The narcissist may have created the mayhem, but it's the parent who's expected to endure it quietly. For those who want to keep the door open, it can feel like the price of love is the willingness to be kicked when you're down but still stand tall, smiling with open arms.

Planning Your Next Steps: Learn to Stay Grounded in Reality

One unexpected day, that long-awaited phone call finally comes. Your heart may leap, but so will your anxiety and blood pressure. What should feel like a hopeful baby step can arrive wrapped in dread. Your body may brace for impact, anticipating another round of blame, accusations, or emotional ambush. And yet, your mind will feverishly hold onto hope that *this time* will be different. It's important, however, to go into the conversation with clarity. Before speaking, listen. Observe their tone, are they angry? Distant? Pleasant? As if nothing ever happened? Do they sound like your child or the puppet to whom you have become accustomed? Tone tells you more than the words themselves. Don't forget this is not the moment to dive into fixing the past. It's the moment to stay present and grounded.

One of the most powerful tools you can carry into this moment is JAGGED: **(Justify, Argue, Guilt, Gaslight, Explain, or Defend)**. These natural instincts can easily backfire in estranged communication, especially if a narcissistic partner is involved. Anything you say may be used against you at any time going forward. Rather than engaging, try to remain calm and neutral. You're not in a debate; you're trying to crack open the proverbial door without compromising your dignity or authenticity.

For clients who live in one-party consent states (in 2025, 37 states and the District of Columbia fall into this category which means a person can legally record a conversation if they are a participant or if one participant consents), I often recommend — *if it's legal* — to record conversations when meeting with their child and the in-law. This suggestion is not about catching someone in a lie or using the recording to confront them later. It's about protecting your mental clarity. Emotions will run high in these meetings, and it's incredibly easy to forget what was actually said—or to remember it differently after the fact based on how you were feeling in the moment. I've seen this happen even between spouses: one parent, desperate to reconcile, may overlook subtle jabs or veiled insults because they're clinging to a shred of hope, while the other—more attuned to manipulation—walks away focused solely on the red flags. Both remember what their heart was ready to hold.

This is where a private, legal recording can become a powerful personal tool. It gives you the ability to revisit the conversation with a clear head, free from emotional fog or internal bias. It also offers quiet protection by creating a record of what *you didn't say,* a critical safeguard in high-conflict, narcissistic dynamics where words are often twisted or weaponized afterward. The recording is never meant to be shared or used against your child or their partner; it's strictly for your own reference and peace of mind. In the presence of gaslighting, shifting narratives, and emotional overwhelm, having a factual audio record will help you stay rooted in reality, especially when everything around you feels unstable and distorted.

While some parents may feel uneasy about the idea of secretly recording, it's worth careful consideration. If you reside in a one-party consent state, remember—if you can legally record, *they* can, too. It's not advisable to ask for permission to record, as doing so may create distrust or derail the conversation altogether. *The purpose is not surveillance; it's personal grounding.*

I'll share a personal story that highlights the importance of this. Years ago, after ending a two-year relationship with a narcissist, I agreed to meet with him to get closure. What I didn't expect was an explosive outburst over a matter involving his ex-wife. Though I left immediately when asked, he called the police, falsely claiming I refused to leave. Unbeknownst to me, he had recorded our conversation and later manipulated the audio to match his fabricated police report. Even with expert analysis proving the recording had been edited, authorities blindly accepted his version. That experience left a lasting impact, and it taught me the hard lesson that without a record of your own, the truth can be revised by anyone who controls the narrative.

Recording discreetly is simple. You can place your phone in video mode and lay it face down or use a small legal audio recording device such as a recording pen. The goal isn't to trap anyone, but rather to give yourself a safe point of reference, a way to stay grounded, and the ability to reflect on the conversation retrospectively without relying solely on memory or emotion. In high-stakes conversations, protecting your peace sometimes means quietly protecting your truth.

CHAPTER 11
Planning To Meet Your Child In Person

Preparing for the First Meeting and Choosing a Neutral Location

Meeting with an estranged child after a long separation can be terrifying, and the uncertainty of what will be discussed only adds to the apprehension. One way to reduce tension and set the stage for a calm, constructive conversation is by choosing a neutral, private location. Meeting in either party's home can carry emotional weight, trigger past dynamics, or lead to unexpected conflict. Instead, consider a quiet restaurant with high booths for privacy, or even renting a small meeting room at a hotel or shared office space. An impartial environment can help create a sense of safety and equality as no one holds the "home court" advantage, and the structure of the setting may encourage a more respectful, balanced dialogue. A little planning can go a long way to help you stay grounded, present, and open to whatever the conversation brings. Consider these key steps to prepare:

Manage Expectations & Emotions
- Acknowledge your feelings – Fear, hope, guilt, or anxiety are natural. Take time to process them before the meeting.
- Let go of assumptions – Your child may want closure, to reconnect, or to express anger. Avoid expecting a specific outcome and be open to anything.
- Practice emotional regulation – Deep breathing, journaling, or therapy can help manage potential triggers.

Adopt a Listening Mindset
- Your role is to listen first – This is their moment to express whatever they need.
- Avoid defensiveness – Even if accusations arise, resist the urge to explain or justify.
- Use reflective listening – Repeat back their words to show understanding (*"I hear that you felt abandoned when I..."*).

Prepare for Difficult Topics
- Acknowledge past mistakes – If appropriate, a sincere apology without excuses can go a long way.
- Don't force forgiveness – Rebuilding trust takes time; focus on hearing their experience first.
- Stay calm if there's anger – They may need to express pain before moving forward.

Keep the Focus on Your Child
- Ask open-ended questions – *"How have you been?" "What would you like me to know?"*
- Respect their boundaries – If they don't want hugs or emotional intensity, honor that.
- Let them set the pace – They may need time before deciding what comes next.

Why It's Important Not to Show Fear When Meeting Your Child

Fear is the narcissist's strongest weapon. When a parent meets their adult child and the narcissistic in-law, showing any sign of hesitation or submissiveness only reinforces the narcissist's belief that they are in control. Narcissistic in-laws thrive on fear and control, but that does not mean parents have to live in constant anxiety. The moment they sense they can utilize manipulation; they will use it repeatedly to keep their target compliant. By recognizing the tactics at play and preparing for interactions with calm confidence, parents can reclaim their sense of self-worth and stability. While the narcissist may continue their attempts to instill fear, a parent who refuses to react will take away their power.

Standing firm without displaying fear is essential because:

- It prevents the narcissist from tightening their control.
- It shows the adult child that their parent is not easily manipulated.
- It lays the foundation for a healthier, more balanced dynamic.
- It reduces the power of future threats or ultimatums.

Examples of statements that show fear:

Fear-Based Guilt Responses:
- "I've already lost so much time with you; I can't bear to lose any more."
- "If you knew how much this is breaking my heart, you'd understand why I keep reaching out."
- "I don't know how to live without you in my life."
- "I raised you; I sacrificed everything for you—can't you see how much this hurts me?"

Fear-Based Desperation Responses:
- "Please, just give me one more chance, I promise I'll be different."
- "I'll accept any terms you set, just don't walk away forever."
- "I'll never forgive myself if I don't try to fix this. Can we please just talk?"

- *"I'm begging you, don't shut me out."*
- *"I just want to see my grandchildren. I'll stay quiet, I promise."*
- *"Please don't cut me off, I'll do whatever you need me to do."*
- *"I don't want to lose you, just tell me what I need to say to make this better."*

Fear-Based Defensiveness Responses:
- *"I don't even know what I did wrong—why are you punishing me like this?"*
- *"I was just trying to help, I don't understand why you're so upset."*
- *"I never meant to hurt you, so why are you treating me this way?"*
- *"I don't deserve this; I was a good parent."*

Fear-Based Attempts to Fast-Track Reconciliation Responses:
- *"Let's just put everything behind us and start over."*
- *"Do we really need to keep talking about the past? Can't we just move forward?"*
- *"You're my child, and I'm your parent, nothing should come between that."*
- *"I don't care about what happened, I just want us to be okay again."*

These responses stem from deep emotional pain, but they can unintentionally pressure or push away the adult child. Approaching reconciliation with patience, self-awareness, and respect for their feelings is often more effective.

How to Prepare for a Meeting Without Showing Fear

Shift Your Mindset – Remind yourself that you are not powerless. The narcissist may attempt to intimidate, but you are in control of your emotions and reactions.

Practice a Calm and Neutral Demeanor – Avoid appearing anxious or eager to please. Speak in a steady, composed tone, and maintain good posture.

Detach Emotionally – Enter the meeting with the mindset that this is a strategic interaction. Keep emotions in check and avoid overreacting to passive-aggressive comments or veiled threats.

PLANNING TO MEET YOUR CHILD IN PERSON

Prepare Responses in Advance – Anticipate potential manipulative remarks and have neutral, non-defensive responses ready. Examples:

- If they say, "*You always overstep boundaries,*" respond with, "*I hear that boundaries are important to you. I also want to make sure our relationship remains respectful on all sides.*"
- If they imply that you won't see your child or grandchildren unless you comply, respond with, "*I love my family, and I will always be here for them.*" (Do not beg or plead.)

Do Not Engage in Arguments – If the narcissist tries to provoke you, refuse to take the bait. Respond calmly or redirect the conversation to something unbiased.

Set and Maintain Your Own Boundaries – Boundaries are not just for them. You have the right to decide how much bad behavior you're willing to tolerate and what you will not allow. Common boundaries often requested by parents include no name-calling, no yelling, and, in some cases, no rehashing of the same past issues. However, be mindful — any attempts to block circular conversations or limit repeated discussions can trigger the narcissist's anger and escalate conflict. Choose your boundaries carefully and enforce them consistently, but with awareness of how certain limits may provoke pushbacks.

Manage Your Expectations – Understand that a narcissist will never suddenly become reasonable or fair. Go into the meeting with realistic expectations so you are not caught off guard or disappointed in the outcome.

Debrief After the Meeting – After the interaction, take time to process what happened. Journal your thoughts or talk with a trusted friend or therapist to reinforce your emotional resilience.

Above all, remember this: there is no need to prove yourself to the narcissist or even to your child. These meetings may leave you emotionally raw. You might walk away feeling deeply hurt, shaken by their words, their accusations, or the way they seem to align with distorted truths. You may not even recognize the person sitting across from you, and you might not like the version of them you're encountering. *That's okay.* What matters most is that you stay grounded in your truth. You love your child, even if right now, they are caught in what I call a *cult of one* a dynamic where influence, trepidation, and emotional control can replace logic, loyalty, and love. Hold onto your heart and know that you don't need to win them back in one moment you just need to protect your peace and preserve your hope.

Setting Boundaries: Will They Come Alone?

When planning an in-person meeting with your estranged child, one of the first and most helpful things you can do is find out *who will be attending*. Will it be your child alone, or will their partner also be present? Knowing ahead of time what to expect can significantly reduce anxiety and help you emotionally prepare. Walking into a meeting with unknown dynamics puts you at a disadvantage, especially when you're already bracing for negativity.

You have the right to ask some simple, respectful questions in advance, questions that aren't about control, but about emotional safety and preparedness. For example: *Who will be attending? Can we agree on a time limit for the meeting?* Many parents find comfort in setting a defined duration, such as an hour, to mirror the structure of a therapy session. You should also privately identify what you're not willing to tolerate. Clarifying your own boundaries ahead of time allows you to stay grounded, even if you don't voice them directly.

That said, it's important to recognize the fragility of these situations. Sometimes, simply asking for boundaries or clarity can be misinterpreted as controlling or demanding, especially because your child is being influenced by a narcissistic partner. In these cases, even a gentle inquiry might risk shutting down the meeting entirely. Only *you* know your child and the nuances of your relationship well enough to determine what can safely be asked. Planning your internal boundaries, even if you don't get to set external ones, is still an act of self-care and strength.

Understanding The Adult Child's Needs in an In-Person Meeting

When reconnecting with an estranged adult child, it's important to recognize that they may experience a wide range of emotions, some expected, and others surprising. How they present themselves during the meeting can offer valuable insight into what they may be needing or hoping for in that moment. Preparing yourself for different emotional responses whether it's anger, sadness, distance, or even warmth, can help you approach the conversation with greater patience, empathy, and emotional flexibility. In the sections below, I've outlined several common situations to help you understand what they might be seeking and how to respond in a way that supports meaningful connection.

Child Presents Scenario 1: The Child is Guarded and Distant

Child: "I don't really know why I even agreed to meet. I don't have much to say."

This child may be testing the waters, unsure if they can trust the conversation.

They may appear detached or emotionally shut down, needing reassurance that the discussion is safe and without pressure.

Child Presents Scenario 2: The Child Wants an Explanation

Child: *"I need to know why you did what you did (or why you didn't fight harder for me). I've spent years wondering if I even mattered to you."*

This child carries unresolved pain and is seeking clarity.

They may feel abandoned, overlooked, or confused about the past, and they want to hear your perspective before considering reconciliation.

Child Presents Scenario 3: The Child is Open but Hesitant

Child: *"I'm not sure where this is going, but I'm willing to hear what you have to say. What do you want from this?"*

This child is cautiously hopeful but wary of being hurt again.

They may be open to a conversation but need reassurance that your intentions are genuine and that you respect their boundaries.

Child Presents Scenario 4: The Child Expresses Pain but Also Interest in Reconnecting

Child: *"I've been hurt for a long time, but I don't want to stay stuck in the past. I just don't know how to move forward with you."*

This child is acknowledging their pain but also signaling a desire for healing.

They may need validation for their feelings and guidance on how to rebuild trust step by step.

Child Presents Scenario 5: The Child Seems Happy but Surface-Level

Child: *"Hey! So, how's life? What have you been up to?"*

This child may be keeping things light to avoid emotional depth.

They could be unsure about reopening old wounds or hesitant to fully engage in the reconciliation process.

Child Presents Scenario 6: The Child is Angry and Confrontational

Child: *"You think you can just show up now and everything will be fine? Do you even realize what you put me through?"*

This child is carrying deep resentment and may feel that past wounds have not been acknowledged.

They need space to express their emotions before they can consider moving forward.

Child Presents Scenario 7: The Child is Aggressive and Blames You

Child: *"This is all your fault. You ruined my life, and now you want to fix it? It's too late."*

This child is using anger as a shield for their pain.

They may be unwilling to listen at first, needing time and proof of your sincerity before they are willing to engage.

Child Presents Scenario 8: The Child is Emotional and Hurt

Child: *"I don't know how to feel about this. I've missed you, but I don't know if I can trust you again."*

This child is conflicted, balancing their love for you with fear of being hurt again.

They may need patience, reassurance, and consistent actions to rebuild the relationship.

How the Narcissistic In Law Can Present

Now that we've explored how your child may show up and what their emotional needs might be, it's equally important to consider the potential presence and influence of the narcissistic partner. Reconnecting with an estranged child is already a delicate and emotional process, but when a narcissistic in-law is involved, the dynamics become even more complex. Rather than supporting open and honest communication, they may step into the role of guardian, redirecting the conversation, inserting blame, or using guilt and manipulation to maintain control over the narrative.

Recognizing these patterns in advance can help you stay smartly grounded and avoid being drawn into conflict. The key is to keep the focus on your child, not the provocations. By preparing calm, thoughtful responses, and resisting the urge to defend or correct, you create the most stable environment possible for genuine connection. Planning for these challenges doesn't mean you expect the worst; it means you're empowering yourself to show up with clarity, grace, and purpose.

How to Defuse a Narcissistic In-Law's Control in Reconciliation Talks

When reconciling with an estranged child, a narcissistic in-law may attempt to control the conversation through guilt, manipulation, or interference. Here's how to recognize their tactics and respond effectively.

Narcissistic In-Law Scenario 1: The In-Law Controls Access to Your Child

The Offense: Your child is hesitant about reconnecting, making vague excuses about time and stress.

In-Law Says: "*They're really overwhelmed right now. This isn't a good time to bring up the past or stir things up.*"

How to Defuse: "*I completely understand that life gets busy. There's no pressure—I just want [Child's Name] to know that I'm always here whenever they're ready. I respect their timeline.*"

This response removes urgency and allows your child to decide for themselves while signaling that the door is open without interference.

Narcissistic In-Law Scenario 2: The In-Law Triangulates and Speaks for Your Child

The Offense: Your child's words feel scripted, and they seem to be echoing the in-law's language instead of speaking from their own emotions.

In-Law Says: "*We've already talked about this as a couple, and we both agree that it's not healthy to revisit the past.*"

How to Defuse: "*I respect that you both talk about things together, and I'd love to hear directly from [Child's Name] about how they feel. Our relationship is important to me, and I want to understand them in their own words.*"

This response keeps the focus on your child and challenges the in-law's attempt to control the conversation without direct confrontation.

Narcissistic In-Law Scenario 3: The In-Law Rewrites the Family History

The Offense: Your child presents a drastically different version of past events, likely influenced by the in-law.

In-Law Says: *"They've done a lot of reflecting and now realize how much harm was done in the past. It's important that you acknowledge that."*

How to Defuse: *"I hear that [Child's Name] has been reflecting, and I would love to have an open conversation about their feelings. I know we might see things differently, but my love for them has never changed."*

This validates your child's emotions without agreeing to a false or manipulated narrative, keeping the conversation open and balanced.

Narcissistic In-Law Scenario 4: The In-Law Creates a Crisis to Justify Distance

The Offense: Every time reconciliation seems possible, a new crisis appears, making your child feel like they can't handle reconnecting.

In-Law Says: *"This is just not the right time. We have so much going on, and the stress of this conversation is too much for them."*

How to Defuse: *"I don't want to add any stress to your lives. I just want [Child's Name] to know that I love them and am here whenever they feel ready. There's no pressure, just an open door."*

This removes any sense of obligation or burden, making it harder for the in-law to use stress as an excuse for continued distance.

Narcissistic In-Law Scenario 5: The In-Law Uses Guilt and Fear to Maintain Control

The Offense: Your child expresses concern that reconnecting will "cause problems" or create tension in their home.

In-Law Says: "*They don't want to upset anyone, and we've worked really hard to build a peaceful home. Digging into old wounds will just make things worse.*"

How to Defuse: "*I never want to cause problems, and I respect the life you've built. I only want [Child's Name] to know that I love them and support them, no matter what. A relationship with me should bring peace, not conflict.*"

This reassures your child that reconnecting doesn't have to be a source of tension, countering the in-law's fear-based control.

Narcissistic In-Law Scenario 6: Shifting the Focus to Other Family Conflicts

The Offense: When you attempt to reconcile, the narcissistic in-law redirects the conversation to past conflicts involving other family members—such as your child's sibling(s) or extended relatives. They try to shift the focus away from your relationship with your child and onto family drama you have no control over, creating unnecessary tension and distractions.

In-Law Says: "*Before we can even talk about you and [Child's Name], we need to address how [Sibling's Name] has treated us. How can we move forward when your other child has been so disrespectful?*"

How to Defuse: "*I understand that there may be issues between [Child's Name] and their sibling, but I'm not here to speak on anyone else's behalf. My goal today is to focus on my relationship with [Child's Name] and how we can move forward. I hope we can keep this conversation about that.*"

By setting this boundary, you keep the focus on your reconciliation efforts, rather than getting dragged into a conversation that you can't resolve. It also signals that you won't be manipulated into taking sides in sibling disputes.

By calmly defusing the in-law's control tactics, you keep the focus on your child, reinforcing love, patience, and an open door. The secret is learning to brace for impact, a cool head, and preparation.

Navigating a reconciliation conversation when a controlling in-law is involved requires patience, awareness, and a steady approach. The more you anticipate their tactics, the less likely you are to be caught off guard or react emotionally.

Understanding How Parents Present and How It May Be Interpreted

Just as adult children may present themselves in a certain way during in-person meetings, parents also bring their own emotional state into the mix. It's natural to feel hurt, sad, or even angry at times. It's how you're able to remain calm on the outside that will matter in this scenario.

I want to highlight common ways that loving, well-intentioned parents express themselves, and how those expressions may be misinterpreted by your child or their narcissistic spouse. I'll provide examples of typical statements that parents make in different emotional states and explore how those words might be perceived.

My goal is to help you recognize not just how you come across, but also how your tone, words, and emotions can be twisted, ultimately derailing communication and preventing progress in negotiations.

Parent Presents Scenario 1: The Defensive & Guilt-Tripping Parent (Worst Case Scenario)

How the Parent Sounds:

"After everything I've done for you, this is how you treat me?"
"I wasn't perfect, but I was a good parent! You have no idea how hard I had it."
"You act like I abandoned you, but I was doing the best I could! You should be grateful."
"You think I'm the bad guy? Maybe you should look at yourself and how you've treated me."
"I don't even recognize you anymore. We didn't raise you to be this selfish."

How the Child Feels:

Invalidated – Their pain is dismissed or minimized.
Frustrated – The conversation becomes about defending the parent rather than acknowledging the child's experiences.
Trapped – They feel pressured to either accept the guilt or walk away.
Hopeless – If the parent refuses to listen, reconciliation seems impossible.
Unloved – Feeling hopeless that you will never love them.

Parent Presents Scenario 2: The Angry & Combative Parent

How the Parent Sounds:

"You're blowing this way out of proportion. Stop acting like a victim."
"You think you had it bad? You have no idea what I went through growing up!"
"You're the one who cut me off! I should be the one who's mad, not you!"
"I don't need to sit here and listen to this nonsense. If you don't want me in your life, just say it."
"I gave you a roof over your head, food on the table, and this is how you repay me?"

How the Child Feels:

Attacked – Their emotions are met with aggression instead of understanding.
Unheard – The conversation turns into a fight rather than a chance to heal.
Defensive – They might shut down or lash out in response.
Unsafe – It confirms their decision to distance themselves from the parent.
Unloved – They feel attacked by your anger and give up hope that you will change.

Parent Presents Scenario 3: The Parent Who Wants to Fix Things but Still Struggles with Ego (hurt)

How the Parent Sounds:

"I didn't realize how much I hurt you, but I see it now. I just don't know how to make it right."
"I don't want to lose you, but I also don't know what you need from me."
"It's hard to hear you say these things, but I'm trying to listen."
"I never meant for you feel that way, but I guess my intentions don't matter if I hurt you."
"I just want to understand... even if it's painful."

How the Child Feels:

Hesitant but Hopeful – The parent still struggles, but they're making an effort.
Cautiously Open – They might be willing to continue the conversation.
Seen – Even if the parent isn't perfect, they're trying to acknowledge the child's pain.
Curious – They might wonder if healing is actually possible.
Loved – They see glimmers of the parent they remember.

Parent Presents Scenario 4: The Emotionally Mature & Accountable Parent (Best Case Scenario)

How the Parent Sounds:

"Thank you for meeting with me. I know this isn't easy for you."

"I want to start by saying I'm sorry. I see I hurt you, and I take full responsibility for that."

"I don't expect you to just forgive me or trust me right away. I know that has to be earned."

"I want to understand your pain, even if it's hard to hear. You deserve to be heard."

"I won't make excuses. If you're willing, I'd like to listen and learn what I can do to be better."

"You don't owe me anything, but I hope we can find a way forward at a pace that feels right for you."

How the Child Feels:

Validated – Their pain is acknowledged without being dismissed.

Respected – The parent isn't demanding forgiveness or rushing the process.

Safer – They feel more comfortable expressing their emotions.

Hopeful – The door to possible healing is open without pressure.

Empowered – They have control over how and when to rebuild the relationship.

This response creates space for the child's feelings while showing genuine accountability. It removes pressure, avoids guilt-trips, and focuses on rebuilding trust over time.

Preparing to Respond to Known Offenses

When I work with estranged parents, many receive a long list of grievances—like an endless Santa's naughty list detailing everything they've supposedly done wrong. Some of these accusations date back to childhood, while others focus on more recent events. If you haven't received such a list and are instead met with silence, I want to acknowledge that pain, too. This is, unfortunately, a common tactic used in some estrangements, particularly when narcissistic influence is involved.

Even if you don't know exactly what you're being accused of, this exercise will still help you. By understanding common scenarios and the types of responses that foster healing, you can prepare yourself for the day communication is possible again.

In this section, I'll walk you through different examples of offenses and how to respond in a way that increases the likelihood of meaningful dialogue. These are just guides—use them as a foundation to shape your own responses.

While you can't predict every new accusation, developing a thoughtful approach to the known ones will give you the confidence and tools to handle whatever comes next.

If you've ever watched my videos, listened to my podcasts, or met me on Zoom, you've likely heard me say this before, but it bears repeating. These suggested healthy responses may feel completely disingenuous. After all the pain your child and their narcissistic partner have put you through, saying these things will make your stomach turn. I also understand that the responses labeled as "Reactive Parent Response" are exactly what many of you *want* to say because, quite frankly, they reflect the truth. Brace yourself, expressing your true thoughts can trigger the narcissist's fragile ego, often leading to an even longer period of silence and punishment.

However, if you're one of those parents who would do *anything* to reconnect with your child or grandchildren, these strategies will increase your chances of reopening that door. Yes, you are appeasing the narcissist's ego to gain access to your child. There, I said it.

Parent Offense Scenario 1: You Didn't Respect the Child's Boundaries (Unintentionally)

Failing to respect boundaries is one of the most frequent accusations parents face in estrangement, and it can take many forms. In reality, the narcissist in the equation often enforces what I call "invisible boundaries," rules that were never clearly communicated yet are held against the parent without warning. Parents are frequently accused of violating these so-called boundaries and are often punished with silence or complete cut-off, without any opportunity for discussion or clarification. Nearly every case of estrangement I've encountered includes this claim. The following are common accusations parents face regarding boundary violations, along with examples of unhealthy responses that can create further conflict as well as healthier alternatives that foster understanding and respect.

> **Accusation Example**: *"You always showed up at my house unannounced, even when I asked you to call first."*
>
> **Reactive Parent Response:** *"Oh, come on! I'm your parent, I shouldn't have to make an appointment to see my own child. You're being overly sensitive."*
>
> **Constructive Parent Response:** *"I hear you, and I'm truly sorry for not respecting your request. That was never my intention, I just wanted to see you, but I now realize that my actions may have made you feel unheard or disrespected. I understand how important your space and boundaries are, and I will absolutely respect them moving forward."*

> **Accusation Example**: *"I told you I didn't want to discuss my personal life, but you kept pushing for details and giving advice I didn't ask for."*
>
> **Reactive Parent Response:** *"I was just trying to help! If you don't want my advice, fine, but don't act like I did something wrong by caring about you."*
>
> **Constructive Parent Response:** *"You're right, I didn't respect your wishes, and I'm sorry. As a parent, I've always wanted to be involved in your life and offer support, but I now see that my approach may have felt intrusive. I will work on stepping back and only offering advice when asked for it."*

> **Accusation Example**: *"You never respected my boundaries! Even if you didn't know, you still crossed the line."*
>
> **Reactive Parent Response:** *"How was I supposed to know? You never told me! Now you're just looking for reasons to be mad at me."*
>
> **Constructive Parent Response:** *"I hear you and even if I didn't realize it at the time, that doesn't excuse it. I'm sorry for not being more aware and for any hurt I caused. I want to understand what boundaries are important to you now so I can honor them moving forward."*

These types of responses show accountability, validate the child's feelings, and express a willingness to change—key elements in repairing strained relationships.

Parent Offense Scenario 2: You Did Something Inappropriate While Babysitting

For parents with grandchildren, estrangement comes with an extra layer of pain. In many cases, grandparents are initially welcomed into their grandchild's new life, helping financially, setting up trusts, babysitting, and supporting their growing family. You're part of the new beginning.

But just like any love bombing phase, the cycle eventually shifts. The devaluation stage begins, and suddenly, everything you do (or don't do) is picked apart and becomes a problem. Your role as a trusted, valued grandparent starts to fade, replaced by criticism and control. Finding faults in your grandparenting becomes the justification for limiting or cutting off your access. It feels like they reeled you in, only to discard you when it was convenient. It's heartbreaking.

Inevitably, you'll be accused of something inappropriate, because that's how the game is played. I'll share some common accusations, along with examples of unhealthy, reactive responses versus healthier, intentional responses. Use these as a guide to adjust your tone and messaging and learn from the bad examples to refine how you engage.

Accusation Example: *"You went against my rules when you babysat my child. It doesn't matter if it was 'just' a sweet, it was about respect."*

Reactive Parent Response: *"Oh, come on! It was just one little candy. You're overreacting. I raised you just fine, and a treat every now and then isn't going to hurt them!"*

Constructive Parent Response: *"You're absolutely right. I didn't think about how that would feel like a violation of your trust, and I should have. I'm really sorry for not following your wishes, and I will be more mindful and respectful moving forward."*

Accusation Example: *"You posted pictures of our child on social media after we told you not to. You never respect our boundaries and privacy!"*

Reactive Parent Response: *"That's ridiculous! Everyone posts pictures of their grandkids. You're just being overly sensitive. I'm their grandparent, and I should be able to share how proud I am!"*

Constructive Parent Response: *"I hear you, and I regret that I didn't fully consider how important this was to you. I wasn't thinking about it from your perspective, and I can see now that it felt like I disregarded your wishes. I respect your choices as a parent and will be more mindful in the future."*

Accusation Example: *"You bought my child a gift I specifically asked you not to get. You always go behind my back!"*

Reactive Parent Response: *"I don't see what the harm is! You're being way too controlling. It's my money, and I'll buy my grandchild whatever I want!"*

Constructive Parent Response: *"I hear you, and I see how that could feel like I didn't respect your wishes. That wasn't my intention, I just wanted to make them happy. I understand now that respecting your decisions as a parent is more important than any gift, and I will be sure to check with you first in the future."*

Note: Acknowledge the impact, not just the action, and commit to change.

Parent Offense Scenario 3: You Disrespected Their Spouse

Accusation Example: *"You've never treated my spouse with respect. You're so critical. How can I trust you when you can't even be kind to my partner?"*

Reactive Parent Response: *"I'm just being honest; she was rude to us and we do not deserve to be treated like that! How can you allow her to talk to us that way? If you weren't so sensitive, you'd realize I'm only trying to help. You deserve better anyway."*

Constructive Parent Response: *"I'm sorry if my words came across as critical. That was not my intention. I respect your choice in a partner, and I will make an effort to be more supportive moving forward."*

Accusation Example: *"You refuse to acknowledge my spouse as part of our family."*

Reactive Parent Response: *"I just don't feel the need to pretend to like someone who doesn't fit in with us. If they made more of an effort, maybe I'd feel differently."*

Constructive Parent Response: *"I hear you, and I regret if I've made your spouse feel excluded. They are important to you, and that means they are important to me. I'll make more of an effort to include them."*

Accusation Example: *"You interfere in our marriage by offering unwanted advice or taking sides in our disagreements."*

Reactive Parent Response: *"I'm only telling you this because I care. You do too much and it isn't normal. If you don't listen to me, you'll regret it later. I know more about relationships than you do."*

Constructive Parent Response: *"I respect that your marriage is between you and your spouse. I'll step back and only offer advice if you ask for it. My goal is to support you, not interfere."*

Parent Offense Scenario 4: You Chose Their Sibling Over Them

One thing we know about narcissists is that they are fueled by jealousy. If your child has a close bond with their sibling, the narcissistic spouse will see that connection as a threat and work to destroy it.

A common maneuver is to twist and distort their relationship, planting seeds of doubt to convince your child that their sibling is the real problem. At first, the narcissist may appear supportive, just as they did with you. But once they've secured your child's loyalty, the devaluation begins. The sibling is suddenly painted as toxic, and false accusations start to surface. Eventually, when the sibling reacts to manipulation their response is reframed as *abuse*.

This is where parental estrangement often comes into play. The narcissist uses this division to accuse you of *choosing* the other sibling over them, one of the oldest triangulation tricks in the book.

Now, let's go over some common accusations, followed by examples of both unhealthy and healthy responses.

> **Accusation Example:** *"Your parents always favored your sister. They gave her more attention, support, and love while treating you like an afterthought."*
>
> **Reactive Parent Response:** *"That's ridiculous! I treated you both the same. I can't believe you're falling for this nonsense!"*
>
> **Constructive Parent Response:** *"I'm so sorry if you ever felt that way. That was never my intention, and I would love to understand what made you feel like this. Our relationship is important to me."*

> **Accusation Example:** *"Your parents drop everything for your sibling, but they never go out of their way for you. They clearly don't care about you as much."*
>
> **Reactive Parent Response:** *"That's not true! I've done plenty for you, and it's unfair for you to accuse me of this."*

> **Constructive Parent Response:** *"I never meant to make you feel less important. If I've given that impression, I regret it. Please help me understand what I can do to show you how much you mean to me."*

> **Accusation Example:** *"Your brother is obviously the golden child. Your parents always defend him and never take your side. You're just the scapegoat."*
>
> **Reactive Parent Response:** *"That's not true! You're just making up reasons to be upset. Your sibling has had struggles too!"*
>
> **Constructive Parent Response:** *"I hear you, and I'm really sorry if you've felt overlooked or unsupported. That was never my intention, and I'd like to talk about how we can move forward in a way that feels better for you."*

By responding with validation and openness rather than defensiveness, you can create opportunities for healing and possibly counteract the narcissist's manipulation.

Parent Offense Scenario 5: You Were Too Controlling or Overbearing

A narcissistic in-law who is working to estrange your adult child will often frame your past parenting as controlling or overbearing to justify cutting you out of their life. They twist normal parental concerns and guidance into evidence of toxic behavior, reinforcing the idea that the child needs to escape your influence.

The following are three common accusations they might plant in your child's mind:

> **Accusation Example:** *"You never let you make my own choices. You always had to have control over everything I did."*
>
> **Reactive Parent Response:** *"That's not true! I was just trying to protect you and make sure you didn't make bad decisions!"*
>
> **Constructive Parent Response:** *"I can see how you might have felt that way. My intentions were always to support you, but I understand now that you may have*

needed more independence. I'd love to hear more about how I can respect your boundaries moving forward."

Accusation Example: *"You never respected my privacy. You always had to know everything about my life and never let me have any space."*

Reactive Parent Response: *"That's ridiculous! I was just trying to be involved in your life because I love you!"*

Constructive Parent Response: *"I never wanted to make you feel like I was invading your privacy. If there were times I overstepped, I sincerely regret that. I respect your independence and want to build a relationship that feels comfortable for you."*

Accusation Example: *"You always want to do things around our house but when we do need something, you're never available to help. You are interfering and trying to control us."*

Reactive Parent Response: *"That's not true! We try to always be there for you when you ask for help. You should be grateful that we help like we do instead of accusing us of something so ridiculous!"*

Constructive Parent Response: *"I see how our efforts to help may have come across as interfering. That was never our intention. We only ever want to be supportive, but we respect your space and won't step in unless you ask us to."*

The Importance of Role Playing

One of the best ways to prepare for any tough situation is through role-playing with a trusted family member or friend. Practicing different scenarios will help you refine your responses, stay calm under pressure, and ensure that your message remains focused on love and understanding. As the saying goes, *"If you are aware, you can prepare."* By going into the conversation with clarity and confidence, you increase the chances of breaking through the in-law's interference and reconnecting with your child on your own terms.

The purpose of this exercise is to show how the emotional state of everyone involved shapes the conversation. By walking through these examples, you'll see common pitfalls to avoid and gain insight into more effective responses.

If you've made mistakes along the way, remember, you're human. Every parent does until they realize they're dealing with a narcissistic in-law, where the usual relationship rules simply don't apply.

EXAMPLES:

Role Playing #1 - Wounded Parent Ego

This version reflects a parent whose ego is hurt, leading them to react emotionally rather than thoughtfully. Instead of focusing on listening, they take the child's feelings as a personal attack, guilt-trip them, and express disbelief at their behavior.

Scene: Meeting at a Café

(The child arrives, sits down, arms crossed, hesitant.)

Child: *"So... why did you want to meet?"*

Parent: *"Well, I miss you and I guess I just wanted to see my child again. Honestly, after everything I've done for you, I never thought I'd have to beg for a conversation."*

Child: *"Miss me? Now you miss me? Where was that when I actually needed you? You can't just show up now and expect everything to be okay."*

Parent: *"I was always there for you! Maybe not in the way you wanted, but don't act like I just abandoned you. Do you have any idea what I was going through? You weren't the only one with problems!"*

Child: *"That doesn't matter. I was a kid and I was left to figure everything out on my own. Do you even know what that was like for me?"*

Parent: *"You're acting like I was a horrible mother! I did the best I could! And this, this is how you repay me? By cutting me out and treating me like a stranger?"*

Child: *"I don't even know where to start. There were so many times I needed you, and you just weren't there. When I was struggling, when I needed advice, when I felt like no one else cared... and you were gone."*

Parent: *"That is NOT fair. I gave you everything! A roof over your head, food on the table... you had it way better than I did growing up! Now you sit here and act like I was a monster?"*

Child: *"That doesn't change anything. You weren't there. You can't just fix things with words. Why should I believe you will ever be different?"*

Parent: *"You don't! And you know what? Maybe I don't need to prove anything to you. You're the one who walked away! Do you even care what this has done to me? You think you're the only one in pain?"*

Child: *"I don't know if I can ever trust you again. You've let me down too many times. How can I just forget all of that?"*

Parent: *"Well, I guess that's up to you, isn't it? But if you expect me to sit here and grovel, you're wrong. I have feelings too! I never thought my own child would turn into someone who could be this cruel to me."*

Child: *"It's impossible to see how anything would be different. I've been hurt for so long, and I don't know if I'm ready to open up to you again."*

Parent: *"Well, I hope you realize one day how much you're throwing away. Family is supposed to mean something. I just don't even recognize you anymore."*

Child: *"I don't even know what I want from you. I don't know if I want to try again or if I want you to just leave me alone."*

Parent: *"Unbelievable. After everything I've done, this is what I get? Fine. If you want to throw me away, go ahead. But mark my words, one day you're going to regret this."*

Child: *"Maybe but I need time to think. I'm not sure when I'll be ready, but I'll let you know."*

Parent: *"Yeah, well, don't take too long. I'm not going to wait around forever."*

What This Parent Does Wrong:
- Makes It About Themselves – Instead of acknowledging the child's pain, they focus on their own hurt.
- Guilt-Tripping – They manipulate the child by making them feel ungrateful.
- Defensive & Dismissive – They refuse to accept any responsibility and try to justify past actions.
- No Respect for Boundaries – They pressure the child instead of allowing space for healing.

This kind of response will push the child further away rather than fostering any real reconciliation. The parent's hurt is understandable, but instead of expressing vulnerability in a healthy way, they lash out, making it impossible for the child to feel safe reconnecting.

Role Playing #2 – Fearful & Defensive Parent Conversation

In this example, the parent is deeply afraid of saying the wrong thing and longs to reconnect with their child but struggles with how to approach the conversation. This is a common response for parents who haven't had guidance on navigating estrangement. If you've found yourself reacting in a similar way, know that you are not alone. Parents often respond from a place of deep emotion, whether it's pain, sadness, or even anger, without realizing how it may impact the conversation. Recognizing these patterns is the first step toward healing and rebuilding the relationship.

PLANNING TO MEET YOUR CHILD IN PERSON

Scene: Meeting at restaurant

(Your child arrives, sits down, and looks at you with crossed arms.)

Child: *"So... why did you want to meet?"*

Parent: *"I wanted to see you. I've missed you, and I know I've hurt you. I don't expect this to fix anything right away, but I want to start by listening."*

Child: *"Miss me? Now you miss me? Where were you when I actually needed you? You can't just show up now and expect everything to be okay."*

Parent: *"I know it seems sudden, but I've been thinking about this for a long time. I didn't know how to reach out. I was dealing with my own demons, but I know that doesn't make up for what you went through. I was afraid I'd say the wrong thing or make things worse. I never wanted to hurt you."*

Child: *"Sorry, that doesn't change anything. You weren't there, and I had to figure everything out on my own. Do you even know what that was like for me?"*

Parent: *"I can only imagine. I never wanted you to feel alone. There were things going on in my life that made it hard for me to be there the way you needed me to be. I thought I was doing my best at the time, but looking back, I can see that it wasn't enough."*

Child: *"I don't even know where to start. There were so many times I needed you, and you weren't there. When I was struggling, when I needed advice, when I felt like no one else cared... and you were just gone."*

Parent: *"That's hard to hear, but I need to hear it. I was caught up in my own life, and I didn't realize how much I was letting you down. I should have been there. I should have made sure you never felt alone. I don't want you to think I didn't care, I always cared, even if I didn't show it the right way."*

Child: *"That doesn't change anything. You weren't there, and now it feels like you're just trying to fix things with words. How do I know this time will be different?"*

Parent: *"I get why you feel that way. I know I've let you down before, and I don't expect one conversation to change everything. I just want the chance to show you that I mean it this time. I don't know how to prove it, but I'm willing to do whatever it takes. I know there aren't enough words. I can tell you I've changed, but I need to show you. That's on your terms, not mine. If you ever feel ready to give me that chance, I'll be here."*

Child: *"I don't know if I can ever trust you again. You've let me down too many times. How can I just forget all of that?"*

Parent: *"I'm not asking you to forget. I don't think you should. You have every right to feel the way you do. Trust isn't something I can demand—it's something I have to earn over time, if you decide you want that."*

Child: *"I guess... but it's still hard to see how anything will be different. I've been hurt for so long, and I don't know if I'm ready to open up to you again."*

Parent: *"That makes sense. You don't have to decide right now. I don't want to pressure you. I just want you to know that I'm here, whenever that time comes."*

Child: *"I don't even know what I want from you. I don't know if I want to try again or if I want you to just leave me alone."*

Parent: *"If you decide you need space, I'll respect that. If you ever want to try, I'll be here. No expectations, no pressure."*

Child: *"Maybe. I just need some time to think. I'm not sure when I'll be ready, but I'll let you know."*

Parent: *"That's okay. Take all the time you need. I just appreciate you sitting down with me today. That means more than you probably realize."*

Child: *"Yeah... okay. I'll think about it."*

Why This Approach Works Better:
- Stronger Validation – The parent acknowledges the child's feelings instead of explaining them away.
- Less Defensiveness – The parent doesn't justify their absence; only recognizes the impact it had.
- No Pressure – They leave the door open but let the child set the pace.
- Subtle Explanation – They acknowledge their struggles without making excuses.

This version allows the child to feel heard while giving them space to process their emotions. The parent still struggles with fear but that doesn't stop them from being open and present.

Final Thoughts: Meeting with Your Estranged Child and Their Narcissistic Spouse

Reuniting with your estranged child, especially in the presence of a narcissistic spouse, requires careful planning, emotional regulation, and strategic communication. This meeting is not just about reconnecting; it's about demonstrating that you are a safe and non-threatening presence in their lives. Key considerations to help set the stage for the best possible outcome:

Never Call Out the Narcissist

No matter how clear the dynamics are to you, never tell your child (or their spouse) that you believe they are dealing with a narcissist. Doing so will only trigger defensiveness, push them further away, and reinforce the narcissist's narrative that you are the problem. Focus on your relationship with your child, not diagnosing their partner.

Choose a Neutral, Private Location

The setting matters. A neutral, private location can help reduce power imbalances and distractions. Some parents have successfully used:

- A rented conference room at a hotel or shared office space for a few hours.

- A quiet café or restaurant with private booths (avoid noisy or crowded places).
- A public park with seating where interruptions are minimal. Avoid meeting at their home or yours, as either place may feel like an advantage or disadvantage to one party or hold bad memories.

Set Clear Boundaries for the Discussion
- Decide in advance what topics you are willing or unwilling to discuss.
- If you sense the conversation turning into an attack, redirect calmly or state that you want to focus on the present and future, not past grievances.
- Be prepared for manipulation or blame-shifting, but don't engage emotionally, stick to your calm, measured approach.

Handle Physical Contact with Caution
- Don't initiate a hug unless they show interest. If the meeting goes well, you can ask at the end, *"Would it be okay if I give you a hug?"*
- If they allow it, keep it brief and respectful lingering too long may feel overwhelming.
- If they refuse a hug, don't take it personally. It doesn't necessarily mean rejection; they may just need more time.

Control Your Emotional Reactions
- Expect criticism, rewriting of history, or blame. Stay calm and non-defensive, this isn't the time to argue or "set the record straight."
- Don't react emotionally to provocations, guilt-tripping, or attempts to push your buttons.
- Practice active listening by repeating back their concerns to show you understand, even if you don't agree.

Keep Expectations in Check
- One meeting will not fix everything. This is a small step toward rebuilding trust.

- Even if they remain distant or cold, don't push for immediate closeness—that will take time.
- Be prepared for possible rejection and remind yourself that their decision isn't always about you, it's more likely about the influence of the narcissist.

End on a Positive Note
- Before leaving, thank them for meeting with you, no matter how it went.
- If the conversation was productive, ask if they'd be open to another meeting in the future.
- Let them know that you love them without pressuring them to respond in kind.

This meeting is about planting a seed, not forcing an outcome. Stay calm, patient, and strategic, and remember—you are being tested. Handle yourself with grace, and you improve your chances of keeping the door open for future interactions.

Have a Self-Care Plan After the Meeting

Meeting your child will undoubtedly introduce intense emotions. Plan time for reflection, support (a trusted friend or therapist), and self-care afterward. This is a tough time in your life, and you deserve to be treated well – even if it is by yourself.

Bracing for Impact: Prepare for Potential Attacks

When the day comes to finally sit across from your estranged child, it's natural to feel a mix of hope, fear, and anxiety. For many parents, that moment is clouded by uncertainty. *Will this be a step toward healing, or a platform for more blame and accusations?* A powerful way to reduce that anxiety is to prepare emotionally and mentally for what may be said. This doesn't mean expecting the worst; it means equipping yourself to stay calm if old wounds are reopened. As I previously mentioned, I often recommend parents create a private list of the most common or painful accusations they've heard in the past or anticipate may come up. These are your "known offenses," the stories or narratives that have been used to define you, fairly or unfairly.

Once you've written them down, go one by one and reflect: *What is my truth in this situation? What actually happened?* Then practice how you might respond if it's brought up again. This would be similar to role-playing but different – you are looking for answers to specific things rather than how the entire conversation may go. Your goal is never to defend yourself into exhaustion or to convince your child you're right but rather to stay emotionally grounded. Prepare responses that acknowledge the pain without feeding the fire. For example, instead of saying, *"That's not what happened!"* you might say, *"I remember that differently, but I can see it still hurts, and I'm willing to hear more."* This keeps you present and calm, even if your child is emotional or harsh. Practicing this ahead of time can make a huge difference.

The more emotionally prepared you are for what might be said, the less likely you are to be thrown off course. Remember, you don't have to respond to everything. Some attacks are meant to provoke or test others are echoes of someone else's narrative. Your job is to stay in your lane: be calm, open, and respectful. Bracing for impact doesn't mean shutting down your heart; it means strengthening it, so you can show up as the version of yourself you'll be proud of, no matter how the conversation unfolds.

> "By failing to prepare you are preparing to fail."
> ~ Benjamin Franklin

Planning Your Next Steps: Know When It's Safe to Ask

What happens next? Parents look to find some sign of progress with optimism that this won't be the only conversation. It's natural to want to ask, *"Where do we go from here?"* or *"Can we talk again soon?"* But knowing *when* to ask is just as important as *what* to ask. These meetings are emotionally charged and draining, and timing can make all the difference. Asking about the next steps too soon, especially if the conversation has been tense or unresolved, can cause your child to shut down or feel pressured. Reading the room is essential.

Pay attention to the emotional tone of the meeting. Signs your child may be open to future contact include they maintain eye contact, their tone softens as the conversation progresses, they seem willing to reflect rather than just accuse, or they bring up memories or hopes from the past. If your child shows curiosity, asks you a question about your life, or lingers at the end of the meeting, these are also good indicators that there's some openness. Even a small smile, a sigh of relief, or a simple *"Thanks for coming"* might signal a willingness to continue engaging.

On the other hand, if your child remains guarded, defensive, or emotionally shut down - if the entire conversation feels like you were walking along the edge of a cliff - it may be wise to hold off on asking for more. Instead, you can lay the groundwork by gently saying something like, *"I'd be open to meeting again sometime if that ever feels right for you."* This allows them to feel in control while still knowing the door is open. The truth is emotional safety needs to be rebuilt over time. For now, let your calm presence, respectful tone, and non-reactive energy speak louder than any request. Sometimes the most powerful next step... is simply not closing the door.

Planning the Conversation: Key Lessons Learned

When you finally sit down with your estranged child, you may not have much control over the direction of the conversation but that doesn't mean you're powerless. One of the most important tools you can bring to the table is *awareness*. By reviewing past interactions, whether it's emails, texts, or previous conversations, you can start to identify patterns. What topics have consistently triggered strong emotional reactions? For example, maybe every time you've mentioned their partner, things have quickly escalated. Or perhaps when you try to share your own feelings, they shut down or accuse you of making it all about yourself. These are valuable cues. They may feel unfair but recognizing them helps you prepare and avoid accidentally steering the conversation into emotionally dangerous territory.

Equally important is paying attention to what *hasn't* caused conflict. Look for the moments when your child didn't react with anger or retreat. Were there times when a neutral "thinking of you" message wasn't met with hostility? Have they ever acknowledged something you said or responded calmly when you simply listened? These are your "green light" zone topics or approaches that may feel emotionally safe to return to. For example, they may be okay with you asking about their job but not their partner, or they may appreciate a brief expression of care but not a deep emotional statement about your pain.

Reading the room in real time is just as important as reviewing the past. Even if you're curious or desperate to ask about the grandchildren you've never met, doing so too soon may feel intrusive or manipulative from their perspective. Instead, go in with the intention to *listen more than speak*. Let your child guide the flow, and observe their tone, body language, and energy. Use your "lessons learned" as a quiet internal guide to navigate what feels safe, what feels risky, and where there may be space to gently build connection. Write them down if it helps. Preparation won't guarantee the outcome, but it can help you stay grounded, respectful, and ready for whatever unfolds.

Managing Emotional Anxiety Before the Talk

Meeting with your child for the first time since the estrangement began is an emotionally intense experience. While there's a flicker of hope that *maybe this is the beginning of reconciliation,* that dream is usually tangled with deep fear. Fear of saying the wrong thing, of unintentionally triggering them, or of being met with a tidal wave of blame and false accusations. The passionate buildup can be overwhelming, and it's crucial to prepare not only for what might be said, but also for how to steady yourself in the midst of it.

A powerful tool you can bring to the conversation is *emotional containment*. Your job isn't to fix everything in one meeting, it's to remain calm, grounded, and centered, even if the conversation turns painful. Plan ahead: visualize yourself sitting through the meeting, voice soft, posture open, and your words few, but steady. If you're going into a setting like a coffee shop or a neutral location where you won't have a professional there to mediate or stop an onslaught of personal attacks, *you* become the stabilizing force. You can't control your child's emotions, but you *can* control your response.

A simple but effective resource I often suggest parents bring is a small object to help manage the physical symptoms of anxiety. A smooth stone, a small stress ball, or even a hair tie wrapped around your wrist can serve as a tactile anchor. When you feel the emotional heat rising, the words coming fast, and the attacks feel relentless, you can quietly squeeze the object in your hand or snap the band around your wrist. It may sound meritless, but this simple act can help regulate your nervous system and prevent reactions out of pain or panic. Think of it as your silent reminder: *You are safe. You are grounded. You will get through this moment with grace.*

Rebuilding Trust: Small Steps Forward

Rebuilding trust with your estranged child doesn't happen through a single conversation; it's a slow, delicate process made up of countless small moments. In that initial meeting, it's important to remember that your child may be coming in with walls up and expectations low. They may be waiting to see if you'll respond with defensiveness, guilt-tripping, or blame all things that, even if unintentional, can reinforce the reasons they pulled away. Trust begins with *emotional safety*. The more you can demonstrate consistency, calmness, and a willingness to listen without correcting or controlling, the more likely they are to begin softening, even just a little.

The key is to focus on showing, not telling. Rather than saying, *"You can trust me,"* show it through your inflection, your body language, and your emotional restraint. Let them lead the conversation where they feel safe going. Validate what you can without sacrificing your truth. This isn't about taking blame for things you didn't do but about acknowledging their feelings without arguing about their experience. Don't ask for too much, push for resolution, or attempt to "fix" everything in one meeting. Rebuilding trust happens in *thousands* of small, trustworthy moments where you are calm when it would be easier to react, kind when it would be easier to defend, and open when it would be easier to shut down.

What should you avoid? Don't press for explanations or apologies. Don't try to correct their version of the past. And definitely don't lay your pain at their feet expecting comfort. They may not be ready or capable of holding space for your grief yet. Instead, think of this meeting as laying a single brick - one small act of showing up in a way that is different from whatever story they've been told or come to believe. In time, enough bricks can build a bridge. But for now, just focus on the one in your hand.

Celebrating Small Wins: Progress Over Perfection

When you're longing for a connection with your estranged child, it's easy to set your heart on a big, emotional breakthrough: a full reconciliation, an apology, a return to how things used to be. The fact is, healing rarely happens in one sweeping moment. It unfolds through tiny, unglamorous steps that don't always feel like "wins" at the time. Your child agreeing to a meeting, responding to a message, or even simply not reacting with anger - these are the truly meaningful moments. They're the slow, quiet signs that the embers are still alive. They're worth acknowledging. And celebrating.

Celebrating the small wins means shifting your focus from the pursuit of perfection to the value of improvement. It's about recognizing that trust, respect, and connection are rebuilt gradually, in brief moments of safety and shared humanity. It's resisting the urge to label a meeting as a failure just because it didn't end in hugs or resolutions. Was there less tension than last time? Did your child stay a little longer? Did they share something, even small, that gave you insight into their world? Those are signs of movement. When you notice them, even silently, it helps you stay hopeful and steady for the long road ahead.

Give yourself permission to honor these moments. You don't need confetti or fanfare, just a quiet, private acknowledgment that *this mattered*. Progress isn't always linear, and it's almost never perfect. But each step forward, no matter how small, is part of the foundation you're laying for a new kind of relationship: one built on patience, resilience, and unconditional love.

CHAPTER 12
Going to Therapy with Your Estranged Child

Choosing the Right Therapist: Yours, Theirs, or Neutral?

Therapy may feel like the baby step you've been hoping for.

When your estranged child finally agrees to go to therapy with you, it can feel like a breakthrough, a long-awaited door cracking open...an opening—perhaps small, but significant. It's a chance to sit across from them in a space that, ideally, promotes understanding and healing. While this doesn't guarantee immediate progress, it signals that there's still room for hope.

Almost immediately, however, a crucial question will arise: *Who should the therapist be?* In many cases, the adult child suggests their own therapist, someone they've already been working with and who "understands the situation." On the surface, this may seem logical, even comforting. For parents, however, this can quickly become a source of concern because that therapist has only heard *one side* of the story. Whether intentional or not, they may already hold unconscious bias based on what your child (and potentially their partner) has shared.

This puts parents in a difficult position. You're relieved your child is finally open to therapy that it feels unthinkable to raise concerns without sounding resistant or accusatory. *But this is a legitimate concern.* If the goal of therapy is to repair and rebuild, neutrality is essential. Without it, sessions can turn into emotional trials rather than safe spaces for healing. So, *yes,* you absolutely have the right to suggest working with a neutral therapist, someone new, someone who hasn't already formed impressions or alliances. How you raise the issue is everything.

The key is in your tone and framing. You might say, *"I'm so grateful we're taking this step. I'd love for us to find someone new, someone who can get to know us both from a fresh, balanced perspective."* This shifts the focus away from blaming their therapist and toward building something new together. It won't always be easy, and it may not always be accepted, but your voice matters in this process. You deserve a space where your story can be heard, too.

How to ask your child - example 1: The Collaborative Approach
"I'm really thankful you're open to doing therapy together, it means a lot to me. Since this is new territory for both of us, maybe we should find someone who's new to both of us, someone who can get to know us equally and help guide the process from a neutral perspective?"

How to ask your child - example 2: The Fresh Start Frame
"I'd really like this to feel like a fresh start for both of us. How would you feel about choosing a therapist together, someone who doesn't already know either side, so we both feel equally heard and supported?"

Navigating Therapy – What to Expect

Parents trying to reconnect with estranged children are sometimes asked to participate in therapy sessions, and while this sounds like a step toward healing, it can also be a powder keg waiting to blow. The controlling influence and attacks of the narcissistic in-law can make these sessions feel less like reconciliation and more like confrontation.

Stepping into this uncharted territory, it's not uncommon for the parent to feel hopeful *and* terrified simultaneously; hopeful that this might lead to healing, and terrified that it might become a stage for blame or pain. The first thing to understand is that therapy will likely be uncomfortable at times. Your child may bring up past hurts with raw emotion, and you may hear accusations that feel unfair or untrue. Expect a flood of feelings, from grief to guilt to defensiveness, but also moments of possible connection and insight. Therapy is a container for emotions that were never safely expressed before, and it often gets harder before it gets better.

Preparation is key to navigating these sessions with grace. It's essential to approach the meeting with careful organization, clear goals, and a plan for your emotional resilience. Go in with a mindset of *listening to understand*, not to defend. Before each session, take time to regulate yourself emotionally. Practice grounding techniques, deep breathing, journaling, or visualizing a calm, non-reactive version of yourself in the room. It can be helpful to set a quiet internal intention, such as *"I am here to listen with compassion,"* or *"I will stay steady, even when the conversation is hard."* If you think it would help, bring a small item like a smooth pebble or stress ball to hold during tense moments. Most importantly, show yourself compassion. These sessions are not about perfection, they're about presence. Each time you show up calm, open, and willing, you're placing a stone in the foundation toward potential reconciliation.

Prepare with intention. Ask open-hearted questions. Gently explore what they need to feel emotionally safe: *"What do you need from me to feel safe again?"* or *"How can I earn your trust back?"* The goal is not to defend yourself, but to genuinely understand their experience—particularly how they've interpreted past events. Empathize with their pain. Show humility. Therapy can provide a safe space for this dialogue, but it's most effective when approached with patience and emotional composure.

Understand the Dynamics at Play

Estrangement involving a narcissistic in-law typically goes hand in hand with a distorted narrative. The narcissist has planted defamatory statements, manipulated your child's perspective, and created an "us vs. them" dynamic which is what drives the entire estrangement. Therapy in this context may not always feel neutral; it may actually feel like you're on trial headed to the firing squad. Knowing this in advance can help you avoid being blindsided.

Your child may enter the session deeply influenced by the narcissist's portrayal, so the therapist will likely hear a one-sided version of events. Be prepared for the possibility that the session could feel unbalanced initially, as the focus may lean heavily on addressing your child's grievances.

Prepare Your Goals and Objectives

Before stepping into therapy, it's crucial to define what you hope to achieve. Write down your goals for the session, such as:

- Gaining insight into your child's feelings and perspective.
- Reaffirming your love and desire to rebuild the relationship.
- Setting healthy boundaries that protect your emotional well-being.

Having clear objectives will keep you focused and help you avoid getting derailed by emotional accusations or arguments.

Anticipate False Allegations and Attacks

One of the most difficult moments for parents in therapy with their estranged child is hearing lies or false allegations presented as reality. Hold steady, even when it hurts. You may be accused, blamed, or confronted with stories that feel wildly distorted. If the narcissistic partner is present, they may try to provoke or discredit you. Stay calm.

Your child will be watching—not just your words, but your body language, your tone, and your ability to remain grounded in the face of pain. Some accusations may stem from real, unresolved emotions your child has carried—feelings of being unheard, unloved, or dismissed. Even if the narrative isn't entirely accurate, their emotions are valid. If your goal is to rebuild trust and reconnect, you'll need to show a willingness to listen without becoming reactive. It may be one of the hardest tests you face, but also one of the most important. The goal in therapy isn't to litigate the past, but to begin rebuilding emotional safety, so choose your responses with care.

Below is a list of common accusations that estranged parents often face from their adult children. Many of these reflect distorted narratives shaped by narcissistic partners, past misunderstandings, or unresolved emotional pain. These accusations can be particularly confusing and triggering, especially when they feel inaccurate or misrepresented:

Parenting & Emotional Support
- *"You were never there for me growing up."*
- *"You were emotionally unavailable."*
- *"You never loved me for who I am."*
- *"You always made me feel like I wasn't enough."*
- *"You invalidated my feelings."*
- *"You only cared about appearances."*

Control, Enmeshment, and Identity
- *"You were too controlling growing up."*
- *"You were too involved in my life."*
- *"You were too enmeshed with me."*
- *"You never let me have my own identity."*
- *"You always had to be right."*

Boundaries & Autonomy
- *"You ignored my boundaries."*
- *"You never respected my boundaries."*

- *"You don't respect my need for space."*
- *"I will decide if and when I'm ready to talk to you."*
- *"I don't owe you a relationship just because we are related."*

Perception of You as a Parent
- *"You always made yourself the victim."*
- *"You made everything about you."*
- *"You manipulated me."*
- *"You only reach out when you want something."*
- *"You never took my side when I needed you."*
- *"You still defend [other parent/sibling] even after what they did to me."*

Toxicity and Accusations
- *"You are toxic, and I can't have you in my life."*
- *"You are passive-aggressive."*
- *"You gaslit me."*
- *"You're the narcissist."*

Trust & Safety
- *"I don't trust you to be around my children."*
- *"You've shown no effort to change or acknowledge your mistakes."*
- *"You never took accountability."*
- *"I need to protect myself and my family."*
- *"I'm tired of the guilt trips and manipulation."*

Relationship Reality Check
- *"This relationship will never be the same again."*
- *"Stop acting like you don't know why I cut you off."*
- *"You only want access to my kids, not a real relationship with me."*
- *"I must do what's best for my family, and that means keeping my distance."*

Accusations of Not Accepting the Narcissistic In-Law
- *"You never accepted my [wife/husband/partner]."*
- *"You were never kind to them."*
- *"You judged them from the beginning."*
- *"You made them feel unwelcome."*
- *"You never gave them a chance."*
- *"You always sided with [someone else] over them."*
- *"You talked about them behind their back."*
- *"You never respected our relationship."*
- *"You always undermined their role in my life."*
- *"You didn't support our marriage."*
- *"You made our wedding all about you."*
- *"You refused to include them in family traditions."*
- *"You act like they aren't part of the family."*
- *"You embarrassed me in front of them."*
- *"You forced me to choose between you and them."*
- *"You never stood up for them when your friends or family disrespected them."*
- *"You made everything harder for us as a couple."*
- *"You tried to turn me against them."*
- *"You made them feel like an outsider."*
- *"You tried to control our relationship."*

These types of statements can be emotionally charged and difficult to process but breaking them down into Main Points can help parents respond (if needed) with clarity and intention rather than reacting out of hurt.

Some accusations that feel outrageous or deeply unfair may resurface during therapy but responding defensively can backfire. Instead:

- Pause before responding: Give yourself a moment to absorb the accusation without reacting impulsively.

- Use neutral language: For example, instead of saying, *"That's a lie!"* try, *"That's not how I remember it, but I'd like to understand your perspective."*
- Stick to facts: Don't get pulled into a debate. Calmly offer clarification if needed but avoid trying to "prove" your innocence—it can come across as defensive.

If you feel attacked, rather than immediately denying or defending, focus on staying steady and grounded. Remind yourself of JAGGED: don't Justify, Argue, Guilt, Gaslight, Explain, or Defend. You are not there to win an argument, but to create space for your child to feel seen and heard. That doesn't mean you have to agree with every version of the story, but it means resisting the urge to correct or debate in the moment. If something untrue is said, it's okay to pause, breathe, and respond with something like, *"That's not how I remember it, but I can see it had a big impact on you,"* *"That's hard to hear, and I'd be open to talking about it more when we're ready,"* or *"I didn't realize you felt that way, and I want to understand."* These kinds of statements can keep the conversation from spiraling and show that you are committed to growth, even if the road is bumpy. They also hold space for their emotion without confirming the false narrative. Remember, you can always clarify or correct in later sessions when trust is stronger. In the beginning, emotional containment is key. Expecting these moments, and planning for how to navigate them, helps you protect your own peace while still showing up as the calm, loving parent your child needs to see, even if they don't yet recognize it.

Communicate with Compassion

When speaking to your child, prioritize compassion and understanding. Use phrases like:

- *"I hear how much pain this has caused you."*
- *"I didn't realize how my actions affected you, and I want to do better."*
- *"Rebuilding our relationship means the world to me, and I'm willing to do the work."*

Acknowledging Their Pain and Experience
- "I can't imagine how much this has hurt you, and I want to understand better."
- "Your feelings are valid, and I regret not acknowledging them sooner."
- "I understand that you've been carrying a lot, and I want to be here to listen."
- "I'm so sorry that my actions hurt you. That was never my intention, but I understand now how it made you feel."
- "I can see that you've been carrying this pain for a long time, and I want to better understand your experience."
- "Thank you for being honest about how you feel. It takes courage, and I want to listen."

Taking Responsibility Without Defensiveness
- "Looking back, I can see that my actions hurt you, and I'm deeply sorry."
- "I know I wasn't perfect, and I want to take responsibility for the mistakes I made."

Acknowledging Their Perspective
- "I can see now how my choices may have impacted you, and I truly regret that."
- "I want to better understand how you're feeling because your emotions matter to me."
- "I didn't realize how my words/actions came across at the time, but I want to listen and do better."

Apologizing Without Justifying
- "I'm so sorry for the pain I caused, even if it wasn't my intention."
- "I wish I had handled things differently, and I'm committed to learning from this."
- "I regret not being more aware of how my actions affected you, and I take responsibility for that."

Validating Their Experience
- *"I hear you, and I can tell how much this situation has hurt you."*
- *"I understand that you've been holding onto a lot of pain, and I want to give you the space to express it."*
- *"I never wanted to hurt you, but I understand now that I did, and I want to make it right."*

Expressing Love and Commitment
- *"You've always been so important to me, and I want to show you that."*
- *"I want to rebuild our connection because I love you and miss you deeply."*
- *"You mean so much to me, and I'm here to do the work needed to heal our relationship."*

Focusing on Moving Forward
- *"I can't change the past, but I want to focus on creating a better future for us."*
- *"I'm open to hearing what you need from me to feel safe in this relationship again."*
- *"Please let me know how I can support you as we work toward healing."*

Addressing Their Concerns
- *"If I said or did things that made you feel judged, I'm truly sorry. That was never my intention."*
- *"I hear that you feel I didn't support you the way you needed, and I regret not being more present."*
- *"I understand if trust feels broken, but I'm willing to take steps to rebuild it."*

Avoid Common Mistakes
Estranged parents often unknowingly make missteps during therapy that can harm their chances of reconciliation. Here are some things to avoid:

- Defending every accusation: This can make you seem unwilling to listen and validate their feelings.

- Over-apologizing: While apologizing for specific mistakes is important, apologizing excessively for things you didn't do can reinforce false narratives.
- Blaming the narcissistic in-law: While you may recognize the in-law's toxic influence, blaming them outright can make your child feel like you're dismissing their agency. Focus on your relationship with your child instead.

Avoid statements that come across as accusatory or judgmental, such as *"You've been brainwashed"* or *"You've let [name] ruin our family."* While these may be expressions of deep pain and frustration, they often trigger defensiveness and reinforce emotional distance. Instead, focus on language that reflects emotional maturity, phrases that center on listening, personal responsibility, and genuine care. This kind of communication lays the groundwork for a more open, compassionate dialogue and helps maintain the possibility of connection, even in the face of estrangement.

Preparing for the Role of the Therapist

Not all therapists are trained or equipped to understand the complexities of narcissistic abuse or family estrangement. Agreeing to attend sessions with your child's therapist can be risky, especially if the therapist has only heard your child's perspective. In many cases, the therapist may unintentionally take sides, aligning with their client rather than facilitating a neutral or mediating role. I've heard many stories from parents who walked into those sessions hopeful for reconciliation, only to feel blindsided, criticized, or even attacked, further deepening the wound instead of helping to heal it.

If the therapist appears biased during the session, it can feel deeply frustrating and invalidating, especially when you've worked hard to prepare for the conversation. However, reacting defensively or arguing can escalate tension and make it harder for your perspective to be fairly considered. Instead, focus on maintaining your composure and using clarifying questions to redirect the conversation and ensure your voice is heard.

Suggestions for how to handle this situation:
- Stay calm: If the therapist appears biased, finish the session with that knowledge. Creating a scene by sharing your thoughts will not help.
- Present your side thoughtfully: If given the chance, share your perspective in a way that is calm, factual, and empathetic. Avoid using inflammatory language.
- Evaluate the therapist's fit: If the therapist seems unwilling to address your side or the narcissistic influence, it may not be the right environment for productive healing.

Here are examples of how to approach these situations constructively:

Scenario 1: The Therapist Dismisses Your Feelings

If the therapist seems to minimize your emotions or brushes off your perspective, you can reframe the situation by asking a clarifying question that brings your feelings into focus. Example:

- **Therapist:** *"Your child feels that you've never respected their boundaries."*
- **Your response:** *"I understand that boundaries are very important to them, and I'd like to work on respecting those. Could we explore specific examples where they've felt this way? I want to fully understand what I can do differently."*

This response acknowledges the concern but also gives you the opportunity to ask for concrete details that may not have been fully explored.

Scenario 2: The Therapist Leans Toward Your Child's Perspective

Sometimes therapists unintentionally align with the one side's narrative, particularly if they've been influenced by a narcissist. You can gently redirect the conversation to ensure a balanced discussion. Example:

- **Therapist:** *"It sounds like your child has been carrying a lot of pain from the way they feel they were treated growing up."*

- **Your response:** *"I hear that, and it's difficult to know I caused pain, even if unintentionally. Could we also discuss how my child's withdrawal has affected me? I think understanding both sides could help us move forward."*

This shows empathy while asserting your need for your experiences to be part of the conversation.

Scenario 3: The Therapist Focuses Exclusively on the Past

If the therapist keeps steering the discussion toward past grievances without addressing future goals, use clarifying questions to pivot the conversation toward solutions. Example:

- **Therapist:** *"Let's talk more about the conflicts from years ago that led to the estrangement."*
- **Your response:** *"I think it's important to acknowledge the past, and I'm open to hearing those concerns. Could we also explore ways we can start rebuilding trust moving forward? I'd like to understand what steps I can take now to improve our relationship."*

This approach balances accountability for the past with a focus on actionable steps for reconciliation.

Scenario 4: The Therapist Overgeneralizes

If the therapist makes sweeping statements that don't reflect the nuances of your situation, clarify to ensure your unique perspective is considered. Example:

- **Therapist:** *"Parents often struggle to understand how their actions impact their children."*
- **Your response:** *"That's very true, and I want to better understand how my actions might have contributed here. I'd also appreciate discussing the specific dynamics of our situation because there may be additional factors at play."*

This gently challenges overgeneralization while reinforcing your willingness to engage in self-reflection.

Scenario 5: The Therapist Misunderstands Your Intentions

If the therapist interprets your words or actions in a way that doesn't align with your intentions, take the opportunity to clarify. Example:

- **Therapist:** *"It seems like you're trying to control the situation by reaching out so frequently."*
- **Your response:** *"I can see how it might come across that way. My intention wasn't to control but to show that I care and want to reconnect. How can I communicate that in a way that feels less overwhelming to my child?"*

This reframes the narrative while demonstrating your openness to change.

Why This Approach Works

Clarifying Questions Encourage Nuance: By asking for specifics, you ensure that your perspective isn't lost in broad statements or assumptions.

Empathy Diffuses Tension: Acknowledging your child's feelings, even when they seem unfair—helps prevent escalation and keeps the focus on reconciliation.

Self-Advocacy Without Defensiveness: These examples show how to assert your needs without sounding combative, which fosters a more balanced dialogue.

Approaching biased moments in therapy with thoughtful questions and a calm demeanor increases the likelihood that your voice will be heard, and the session will remain productive. Remember, the goal is not to "win" but to move closer to understanding and healing.

Focus on Long-Term Healing

Therapy is just one step in the reconciliation process, and it may not resolve everything in one session, or even several. Use therapy as an opportunity to set the stage for future growth.

CHAPTER 13
Hostage Letters and Demands

Apology Demands – Why Does It Feel Like Santa's Naughty List?

An overwhelming moment for estranged parents is being presented with a long, detailed list of offenses, each one requiring an apology before the relationship can move forward. I often refer to this as *Santa's Naughty List* because it truly feels like they've been keeping track of every word, action, and perceived slight over the years. Whether it's a comment you made ten years ago, a misunderstood look across the dinner table, or how you handled a situation with your grandchild, everything is remembered, exaggerated, and repackaged as proof of your failures. What makes it even harder is that many of these so-called offenses are twisted: things taken out of context or complete fabrications shaped by the narcissistic partner's mind.

When these lists come from a narcissist, or from your child under the narcissist's influence, they rarely reflect a true desire for resolution. Instead, they function as tools of control. You may find yourself expected to apologize for things you didn't say, didn't mean, or simply didn't do. Either way, the expectation is clear: *apologize or else.* The "or else" can be heartbreaking because you know what it means: no further contact, no access to your child, and no relationship with your grandchildren. These demands begin to feel less like attempts at healing and more like emotional blackmail. You're not being asked to repair a moment of hurt, you're being asked to confess to a rewritten version of your entire past.

In the face of such pressure, it's important to protect your integrity while also navigating these demands with care. Not every item on the list requires an apology, especially if it's based on distortion or manipulation. However, if there's anything on that list, even small, that you *can* sincerely acknowledge, consider doing so in a way that expresses empathy without surrendering your authenticity. Saying something like, *"I'm truly sorry that made you feel hurt,"* allows you to show compassion without validating their falsehoods. You are not required to carry guilt for things you didn't do, but your strength lies in responding with clarity, calm, and care, even when you're being asked to make peace with a version of yourself that never existed.

Let's be clear: offering apologies, even heartfelt ones, won't necessarily bring your child back into your life. In fact, I've seen many parents offer an olive branch for the unsaid and the undone, simply in the desperate hope of reconnecting, and it backfires. Dramatically. When the concession is offered, the narcissistic partner may seize it as validation, saying, *"See? I told you they were the problem all along."* Instead of softening the situation, the apology becomes more fuel for the fire that you are entirely to blame. Tread lightly.

Apologies can be a powerful step toward healing when they're mutual, genuine, and part of an open-hearted dialogue. In high-conflict circumstances, especially those influenced by a narcissistic partner, they are often warped, rejected, or deemed not good enough. I've seen parents pour their heart into an amends, only to be told it lacked sincerity, depth, or accountability. The truth is, when control is the driving force, no acknowledgment will ever be enough. There is nothing you could do or say that would fulfill their wishes.

This is why it's critical not to place all your hope in a single apology as the fix for this heartbreaking situation. If you choose to offer one, do it from a place of integrity, not desperation. Say what's true for you, not what you're pressured to say. Always understand that the real power of making amends lies not in changing their mind, but in showing your own growth, clarity, and strength regardless of how it's received.

If you choose to respond to a false allegation, it's possible to acknowledge your child's feelings without taking responsibility for something you didn't do. This is a powerful way to maintain both empathy and integrity. For example, instead of saying, *"I'm sorry I did that,"* you might say, *"I'm truly sorry that you felt hurt by what happened. That was never my intention."* This kind of statement validates their emotional experience without admitting to an action or intent that wasn't true. It allows you to meet them with compassion while still standing in your truth, an essential balance when dealing with distorted narratives or manipulation.

The Apology Barrier: Why They Won't Accept It

For many estranged parents, an apology feels like the key to reconciliation. If you could just find the right words, take responsibility, and show your child how much you love them, surely they would forgive you... right?

But what happens when your heartfelt admission is met with silence, or worse, rejection? Why won't your child accept the genuine words you've offered?

It's necessary to accept the fact that since the narcissist has influenced your child, your apology may never be enough. Not because you haven't tried, but because accepting it would break the narcissist's control over them.

Why a Narcissist Doesn't Want Your Child to Accept Your Apology

A narcissist thrives on dominance, division, and rewriting history to serve their own agenda. If they have turned your child against you, it's not about the facts, it's about power. Here's why they make sure your child refuses to accept your apology:

Your Forgiveness Threatens Their Narrative

The narcissist has likely convinced your child that you are toxic, abusive, or unsafe. If your child accepts your apology, they have to question that story, something the narcissist can't allow. Letting you back into the fold will forever unbalance the control that they need.

Keeping You the "Villain" Keeps Them the "Hero"

Narcissists need a black-and-white world where they are the savior, and you are the enemy. If your child forgives you, the narcissist loses their grip on the story, and on your child.

Apologies Require Independent Thinking

A genuine apology invites reflection. If your child is under the narcissist's influence, they have been trained to see you as bad. Period. Accepting your apology would require them to think critically, which the narcissist has likely discouraged.

Forgiveness Would Weaken Their Loyalty to the Narcissist

Many children in these situations feel like they have to "choose" between their parent and the narcissist. Accepting your apology could be seen as betraying the person who has manipulated them into cutting you off.

Estrangement Gives the Narcissist Power

If your child remains estranged, the narcissist gets to control them, manage their emotions, and keep them dependent. Forgiveness would be an act of independence, and narcissists can't tolerate that.

What Does This Mean for You?

It's easy to believe that if your child won't accept your apology, it means you've failed. Not true. This has never been about the words you say or the sincerity of your heart. It's about the walls the narcissist has built between you - walls that can't be broken by one (or multiple) heartfelt message(s).

What Can You Do?

- Let go of the need for immediate reconciliation - Your healing can't be tied to their response. An apology is about taking responsibility, not forcing a resolution.
- Continue being a safe, loving presence - If your child ever starts to see through the manipulation, they need to know they can turn to you without shame or fear.
- Stop playing the game - If the narcissist is involved in the estrangement, nothing you do will ever be "enough." Step back and refuse to chase the carrot.
- Focus on your own healing - You can't control your child's choices, but you can control how much of your life you allow this pain to consume. Find peace, even in the waiting.

Your apology isn't the problem. The real issue is the narcissist's hold over your child's perception. In time, many estranged children begin to see the manipulation for what it is, but they have to come to that realization on their own.

Crafting an Apology Letter - Sample Letters

How to Write an Apology Letter to Your Estranged Child: A Guide to Rebuilding Trust

Reaching out to an estranged child can feel overwhelming, especially when you're not sure what to say or how your words will be received. If you're considering writing an apology letter, it's important to approach it with humility, sincerity, and a deep understanding that reconciliation takes time. Your goal isn't to fix everything in one letter but to show your child that you acknowledge their pain, take responsibility, and are willing to listen without pressure or expectation.

When writing an apology letter to an estranged child, it's essential to strike the right balance—take accountability for past actions without over-explaining, justifying, or defending yourself. A well-crafted apology acknowledges their feelings, expresses regret, and leaves the light on in the window for future communication.

Below is a step-by-step guide to help you craft a meaningful and heartfelt apology letter.

Begin with Warmth and Love

Start your letter with a gentle and warm opening that reassures your child that your intentions are rooted in love. Avoid diving straight into apologies or explanations. Instead, set a tone of care and sincerity.

Example:
"Dear [Child's Name],
I hope this letter finds you well. I've been thinking about you so much, and I want to reach out with love in my heart."

Acknowledge Estrangement Without Blame

Your child may have chosen distance for a reason. Acknowledge the estrangement without shifting blame or making them feel guilty for their choices. This shows that you respect their feelings and autonomy.

Example:
"I understand that there is distance between us right now, and I want to acknowledge that without pushing you for anything you're not ready for."

Take Responsibility Without Defensiveness

This is the most important part of your letter. Your child likely needs to hear you take accountability for your actions without excuses. Avoid phrases like "I'm sorry if you felt that way" or "I never meant to hurt you," as they can feel dismissive. Instead, acknowledge their pain and validate their experience.

Example:
"I realize now that my actions (or words) may have hurt you, and I deeply regret that. Looking back, I can see how I may not have fully understood your feelings or how my behavior impacted you. I take full responsibility for that, and I am truly sorry."

Avoid Justifications or "But" Statements

One of the biggest mistakes in apology letters is following an apology with an explanation that minimizes the hurt. Phrases like "I was only trying to help" or "I didn't mean it that way" can make your child feel unheard. Let your apology stand on its own.

Avoid:
"I'm sorry you felt hurt, but I was just doing my best."

Better:
"I am sorry for my actions; I can see now that they caused pain. That was never my intention. I understand that intention doesn't erase the hurt."

Express a Willingness to Listen and Learn

Your child may or may not be ready to reconnect but letting them know you are open to hearing them is crucial. Make it clear that you are willing to listen without judgment or defensiveness.

Example:
"If you ever feel comfortable sharing your feelings with me, I am ready to listen with an open heart. I want to understand your perspective because your feelings truly matter to me."

Offer Reassurance Without Pressure

Let your child know that you are here for them, but don't pressure them for a response. Pushing for reconciliation on your timeline can make them feel unheard. Instead, reassure them that your love is unconditional.

Example:
"I don't expect an immediate response, and I understand that healing takes time. Please know that no matter what, I love you and always will."

End with Love and Openness

Close your letter with warmth and a gentle reminder that you are always here. Keep it short, kind, and pressure-free.

Example:
"With love, always,
[Your Name]"

What to Avoid:

Justification or Defensiveness – "I only did that because…" can make the apology seem insincere.

Blaming or Shifting Responsibility – Even if you believe their perspective is unfair, an apology is not the place to argue your case.

Over-Apologizing – Apologizing excessively can seem like begging rather than a touching attempt to mend the relationship.

Writing an apology letter to an estranged child is an emotional process, but it's also an opportunity to plant the seeds of healing. Whether or not your child responds, taking responsibility and expressing unconditional love can be a meaningful step toward rebuilding trust. Even if they don't respond, they will feel the sentiment.

Reconciliation takes time—if it doesn't happen, you can find peace in knowing that you have taken a step toward healing with an open heart.

Sample Letters Using These Guidelines

An apology letter is not a magic fix. Many estranged parents have apologized multiple times with little to no response. However, in most cases, not apologizing at all ensures continued silence because the lack of acknowledgment gets used as further justification for estrangement. The goal is to extend an olive branch while maintaining your dignity and boundaries.

I've put together 14 sample letters addressing the most common demands estranged adult children make of their parents. While there are countless reasons you may be asked to apologize, these examples are designed to provide guidance on tone and direction. My hope is that they help you craft an apology that is heard and, ultimately, opens the door to reconnection.

Sample Letter: Acknowledging Their Pain and Seeking Understanding

Dear [Child's Name],

I hope this letter finds you well. I want to start by saying that I love you, and I think about you often. No matter how much time has passed or what has come between us, my love for you has never changed.

I also want to acknowledge the distance between us. I don't want to assume I understand all the reasons why, but I do know that somewhere along the way, I caused you pain. For that, I am truly sorry. I regret any words or actions that made you feel unheard, unimportant, or unvalued. That was never my intention, but I now understand that intention doesn't erase the hurt.

Looking back, I can see that there were times I may not have truly listened to you or respected your feelings in the way you needed. If there are specific things I have done that you would like me to take accountability for, I am open and willing to hear you without judgment or defensiveness. More than anything, I want to understand your perspective because your feelings matter to me.

I don't expect this letter to fix everything, and I know healing takes time. Please know that I am here whenever you are ready, in whatever way feels comfortable for you. There is no pressure—only a deep desire to show up better for you if given the chance.

No matter what, I love you and always will.

With love, always,
[Your Name]

Sample Letter: Apologizing for Not Respecting Boundaries

Dear [Child's Name],

I want to start by saying that I respect your need for space, and I am sorry if I have ever overstepped your boundaries. Looking back, I now realize that there were times I may have pushed too hard, expected too much, or didn't give you the room you needed. That wasn't fair to you.

I understand now that boundaries are not about rejection; they are about safety and self-care. If I made you feel like your boundaries weren't valid or important, I regret that deeply. You have every right to protect your peace, and I should have honored that from the start.

Please know that I will not push or demand anything from you. Instead, I want you to know that I am here, with no expectations, whenever you are ready if that time ever comes.

With love and respect,
[Your Name]

Sample Letter: Acknowledging Dismissed Feelings and Unintentional Harm

Dear [Child's Name],

I have been thinking a lot about our relationship and the times you tried to express your feelings to me. I am deeply sorry if I ever dismissed your pain, invalidated your experiences, or made you feel like your emotions didn't matter. That was never my intention, but I now understand that my intentions don't change how you felt.

I can see now that you needed to be heard, and I failed to give you that. You deserved validation and understanding, and I wish I had done a better job of offering that to you.

I am not writing to ask for anything I just want you to know that I see where I went wrong, and if you ever want to share more, I will listen without defense, without excuses, and without trying to change how you feel.

I love you, and I respect whatever decision you make about our relationship. I am here if and when you are ready.

With all my heart,
[Your Name]

Sample Letter: Owning Up to Past Control or Criticism

Dear [Child's name],

I have been reflecting on the way I parented and the ways I may have unintentionally hurt you. I now realize that there were times when I was too controlling, too critical, or too focused on what I thought was right instead of allowing you to be fully yourself. For that, I am truly sorry.

I see now that what I thought was helping may have actually made you feel judged, stifled, or even unloved. That breaks my heart because I have always loved you. If my actions made you feel otherwise, I regret that more than I can express.

I cannot change the past, but I can acknowledge it. I want you to know that I see my mistakes, and I am committed to being someone who listens, respects, and supports you for who you are, not who I thought you should be.

Please know that I will always be here, whenever and however you might need me.

With love,
[Your Name]

Sample Letter: Expressing Love Without Pressure

Dear [Child's name],

I just want you to know that I love you. No expectations, no pressure, just love.

I know that our relationship is complicated and that you needed space. I respect that, even though I miss you every day. More than anything, I want you to be happy and at peace. If being apart from me is part of that, I accept it.

That doesn't mean my heart isn't open to you. It always will be. If the time ever comes when you want to reconnect, even in the smallest way, I will be here with no judgment and no demands.

Until then, I will hold you in my heart and wish you nothing but love and happiness.

Always,
[Your Name]

Sample Letter: Acknowledging Hurt and Taking Responsibility

Dear [Child's name],

I have been doing a lot of reflection. I now realize that some of my actions and words may have caused you pain, and I want to take a moment to say that I am truly sorry. I deeply regret that. I never wanted to hurt you, but I understand now that my intentions don't erase the impact.

I hear you. I may not have fully understood what you were feeling before, but I want you to know that your experiences and emotions are valid. If I dismissed your feelings in the past, I was wrong to do so. You deserved to feel heard and supported, and I am sorry if I failed to provide that.

I am not writing to ask for anything in return; I simply want you to know that I take responsibility for my part in our relationship and that I am open to listening if you ever want to share more. Your boundaries matter to me, and I will respect whatever space you need.

I love you, and I will always be here if and when you are ready.

With love,
[Your Name]

Sample Letter: Apologizing Without Pressure

Dear [Child's name],

I want to start by saying I am sorry. I recognize now that my actions, words, or the way I handled things may have hurt you. Whether it was things I said, things I didn't say, or things I didn't fully understand at the time, I take responsibility for that.

I realize now that you made the difficult decision to step away for a reason. I don't want to argue or justify my past actions; I just want to acknowledge that I respect your feelings, and I am sorry if I ever made you feel unheard.

You do not owe me a relationship, and I don't want to pressure you in any way. I only hope that you know I love you, and I will always be here if you ever want to talk. I will respect your boundaries, and I will do my best to truly listen if you ever decide to reach out.

No matter what, I want you to know that I love you. Always.

With an open heart,
[Your Name]

HOSTAGE LETTERS AND DEMANDS

Sample Letter: Recognizing the Past and Expressing Readiness to Change

Dear [Child's name],

I have spent a lot of time thinking about our relationship and the ways I may have hurt you. I never wanted to cause you pain, but I realize now that my actions or my failure to act may have done just that. For that, I am truly sorry.

Looking back, I can see moments where I may not have listened as well as I should have, or where I may have been defensive instead of understanding. I deeply regret that. You deserved to feel safe and heard, and if I didn't provide that, I want you to know that I take responsibility.

I also understand that your boundaries are important, and I will respect whatever you need, whether that means space, time, or limited contact. Please know that I will not pressure you, but if there ever comes a time when you want to talk, I am here with an open heart and a willingness to listen.

No matter what, I will always love you.

With love,
[Your Name]

Sample Letter: Apologizing for Failing to Validate Their Experience

Subject: I Hear You Now

Dear [Child's Name],

I've spent a lot of time reflecting on our past, and I realize that there were times when I didn't fully acknowledge or validate your feelings. If you ever felt dismissed, unheard, or like your experiences didn't matter to me, I am truly sorry.

I now understand that my intentions didn't always match my impact. I never wanted you to feel like your emotions weren't important, but I see now that I didn't always listen in the way you needed. I am working on this, and I want to do better.

No pressure to respond—just know that I love you, and I'm open to hearing anything you ever want to share.

With love,
[Your Name]

Sample Letter: Apologizing for Not Protecting Them from Family Dysfunction

Subject: I Regret Not Doing More

Dear [Child's Name],

Looking back, I see now that there were times when I should have done more to protect you from the dysfunction within our family. Whether it was unhealthy dynamics, emotional pain, or toxic situations, I regret not stepping in more or recognizing the impact it had on you.

If you ever felt unprotected, unheard, or forced to navigate situations that weren't fair to you, I am deeply sorry. I wish I had seen things more clearly at the time. Please know that if you ever want to talk about your experiences, I am here to listen without defensiveness or justification.

I love you, and I always will.

Sincerely,
[Your Name]

Sample Letter: Apologizing for Emotional Reactivity or Conflict

Subject: I Regret How I Handled Things

Dear [Child's Name],

I want to acknowledge that there were times when my emotions got the best of me, and I reacted in ways that may have hurt or frustrated you. I deeply regret any times when I was reactive, defensive, or made things harder instead of easier for you.

I now understand that my own pain sometimes clouded my ability to show up in the way you needed. That was not fair to you. I am working on becoming a better listener and responding with more patience and understanding.

You don't have to respond, but I just wanted to say that I love you and I am committed to growing as a person, no matter what the future holds for us.

With love,
[Your Name]

Sample Letter: Apologizing for Not Accepting Your Spouse Sooner

Subject: I Regret How I Handled Things

Dear [Child's Name],

I've been reflecting on the past, and I realize that I didn't embrace [Spouse's Name] as quickly or as openly as I should have. Looking back, I can see how that must have hurt you, and I deeply regret it.

Please know that my hesitation was never about not wanting you to be happy. I see now that my own feelings and expectations got in the way of showing you the support and acceptance you deserved. If my actions or words made you feel like I wasn't respecting your choices or your relationship, I am truly sorry. That was never my intention.

What matters most to me is your happiness, and I want you to know that I respect and honor your life choices. I hope to move forward with a more open heart and the opportunity to truly get to know [Spouse's Name] as the person who means so much to you.

No pressure to respond—just know that I love you, and I am always here.

With love,
[Your Name]

Sample Letter: Apologizing for Perceived Favoritism

Subject: I Never Meant to Make You Feel Less Loved

Dear [Child's Name],

I've spent a lot of time reflecting on our past, and I want to acknowledge something that I now realize may have hurt you deeply. If you ever felt like I favored [Sibling's Name] over you or that you were less important, I am truly sorry. The last thing I ever wanted was for you to feel unseen, less valued, or like you had to compete for my love.

Looking back, I can see how my actions—or even the way I handled certain situations—may have given you that impression. That was never my intention, but I fully recognize that intent doesn't erase the pain it may have caused.

You have always been just as important to me as [Sibling's Name], and I regret any ways in which I may not have shown that clearly enough. If you're ever open to talking, I want to hear your feelings and understand your experience better, without defensiveness. What matters to me most is that you know how much I love you and that your feelings truly matter to me.

No pressure to respond, but please know that I am here, and I always will be.

With love,
[Your Name]

Sample Letter: Acknowledging Their Pain and Seeking Understanding

> **Subject:** I Want to Understand and Make Things Right
>
> Dear [Child's Name],
>
> I know that something in our past has hurt you, and I want you to know that your feelings matter to me. I may not fully understand what I did or how my actions affected you, but that doesn't mean I don't take your pain seriously. If I have caused you harm, even unknowingly, I am truly sorry.
>
> More than anything, I want to listen. I don't want to make excuses, defend myself, or dismiss your experience—I just want to understand. If and when you're ever open to sharing, I am ready to hear you with an open heart.
>
> I know that healing takes time, and I respect whatever space you need. Please just know that my love for you has never changed, and it never will.
>
> With love,
> [Your Name]

Normal vs. Narcissistic Expectations: Understanding the Difference

When writing to an estranged child, especially one who may be under the influence of a narcissistic partner or is themselves displaying narcissistic traits, it's critical for parents to adjust their expectations. In healthy relationships, apologies and heartfelt communication are often received with openness, reflection, and a desire to move forward. However, in relationships influenced by narcissism, those same efforts may be distorted, rejected, or even used against you. A thoughtful act of contrition that might bring healing in a normal relationship may be deemed "manipulative" or "not good enough" in this one. That's why managing desires is not just helpful, it's essential to protect your heart.

With narcissists, control and power take precedence over connection. Instead of receiving your words as a gesture of peace, they may dissect every sentence looking for hidden motives, imagined insults, or opportunities to shame or punish you further. Rather than softening the relationship, your vulnerability may be seen as weakness. This doesn't mean you should avoid expressing care or making amends; it simply means you need to do so from a place of strength and self-respect, *without expecting validation in return*. You need to do it for yourself only.

Writing an apology note in this context is more about your integrity than their reaction. It's an act of clarity, not control. You're showing up in a way that reflects who *you* are, even if they aren't capable of meeting you in the same space. Let your intention be about lighting the spark, not controlling the flame. You may not get a response or if you do, it may be hurtful or dismissive. Prepare for it. That doesn't mean you failed. It means you're navigating a complex dynamic with wisdom and dignity, rather than fantasy and hope alone.

By understanding the difference between healthy relational responses and those that are narcissistic, you'll be better prepared emotionally. Keep your letter brief, kind, and unentangled. Don't plead, overcompensate, or try to convince them of your worth. Your job is to speak your certainty, not to script their response. When you manage your expectations, you protect your peace because the letter is not a test of their love, but a reflection of yours.

Learn To Analyze Your Child Or In-Laws Texts Or Emails

When you receive a message from your child, it's natural for emotions to rise, especially when their words feel disrespectful or hurtful. One of the first steps I guide my clients through is evaluating the tone of a communication. By stepping back and objectively assessing it, you can remove the emotional charge and gain a clearer perspective. This allows you to craft a thoughtful response rather than react out of frustration. Don't let your heart set your efforts back.

Not every message requires a reply, but by carefully reviewing it, you can determine the best way to respond, if at all. The next step is to identify their main points, followed by clarifying what actually needs a response. Let's start by understanding how to analyze tone.

Highly angry and accusatory: there is little room for constructive conversation.

Blames the parent for past actions and perceived betrayals: *"You chose to side with them over me, and now you wonder why I don't trust you. Every time I needed you, you let me down."*

Dismissive of any attempt at reconciliation: Reinforcing a victim-perpetrator dynamic.

Uses emotional manipulation by saying things like *"I guess I just have to accept whatever crumbs of a relationship you're willing to offer me."*

Threatening undertones: *"We've been patient long enough, but actions have consequences. If things don't change, we'll have no choice but to protect ourselves in ways you may not like."*

No clear request for what is wanted from the parent, only continuous criticism.

Contradictory: *"I really want us to have a close, healthy relationship, but how can I when you continue to choose everyone else over me? You have completely abandoned me, and yet you expect me to just accept your pathetic attempts at communication? You don't even realize how much you've hurt me, and honestly, I don't think you ever will. I'm doing my best to be close to you, but you make it impossible with your lies and betrayal."*

Highly emotional and accusatory: The email is full of anger, blame, and resentment. It expresses deep frustration and a sense of betrayal. *"I can't believe how easily you turned your back on me after everything I've been through. You chose to betray me, to side with people who have done nothing but hurt me, and now you expect me to just move on like nothing happened? You have no idea the pain you've caused, and yet you continue to act like the victim. I have given you chance after* *chance to do the right thing, and you've failed me every single time. Do you even care about the damage you've done, or are you just pretending this isn't your fault?"*

Victim mentality & justification of In-law's behavior: *"I never wanted things to be this way but I had no choice after the way you treated me. If I've reacted strongly, it's only because I've been pushed to my limit. Anyone in my position would have done the same. You left me no other option."*

Lack of openness to reconciliation: While the words say she wants to stay connected with her parent, the overall message is rigid, conditional, and focused on past grievances.

Pressure & control: *"If you really cared about me, you would stand up for me and cut ties with anyone who has treated me badly. The fact that you still speak to them shows where your true loyalties lie. I don't see how we can move forward unless you make it clear that you're on my side."* This manipulates the recipient into feeling guilty and coerces them into proving their loyalty by distancing themselves from others, reinforcing the in-law's control over family relationships.

Manipulative language: Statements like *"You should appreciate that I've held back as much as I have—if I really wanted to, I could have made things much worse for everyone. I've been more patient and forgiving than you deserve.".* Another example is using the grandchildren: *"I've been more than generous in letting you have a relationship with the kids, but that can change if I don't see real effort from you. If you truly cared about them, you'd prove it by respecting my boundaries and showing that you're on my side."*

Evaluating What Needs a Response

When crafting a response to your estranged child or in-law, it's important to stay focused on what truly requires a response. Avoid emotional reactions, over-explaining, or engaging in unproductive debates. Instead, center your response on the following key areas:

HOSTAGE LETTERS AND DEMANDS

Do Not Justify, Validate Lies with a Response, or Grovel:
- If they make false accusations, avoid defending yourself extensively.
- Acknowledge their feelings without agreeing to distorted narratives.
- Do not apologize for things you didn't do just to appease them.

Boundaries & Allegations of Betrayal:
- If they accuse you of siding with others or betraying them, calmly clarify your position.
- Reinforce that respecting boundaries is not a sign of taking sides.
- Maintain your own boundaries regarding what behavior you will or won't engage with.

Misinterpretation of Neutrality:
- If they assume neutrality means favoritism, gently correct this misconception.
- Reiterate that you are not choosing sides but respecting all parties' boundaries.

Repetitive Grievances:
- If the message revisits past conflicts that have been addressed, do not get caught in a cycle of rehashing them.
- Acknowledge past mistakes, if necessary, but focus on moving forward.

Affirm Love & Desire to Stay Connected:
- Regardless of the tension, express your love and hope for a healthy relationship.
- Keep your message open-ended to allow for future reconciliation.

Acknowledge Their Pain Without Fueling the Fire:
- Recognize their feelings without escalating the conflict.
- Use neutral language to prevent defensiveness.

Clarify the Parent's Position & Boundaries:
- Clearly define what you are willing to discuss and what is off-limits.
- Stand firm in your own needs while expressing willingness to communicate.

Avoid Engaging in Attacks Against Others:
- Do not get pulled into attacking their spouse, sibling, or other family members.
- Keep the conversation between you and your child.

Set Boundaries on the Conversation:
- If the communication is abusive or unproductive, state that you will only engage in respectful discussions.
- If needed, set limits on the format of communication (e.g., email only, meeting with a mediator, etc.).

By staying relaxed, focused, and intentional in your response, you can maintain your dignity and keep the door open for future healing—while protecting yourself from unnecessary emotional turmoil.

When Things Go Wrong: Unraveling the Breakdown

Not every apology attempt will go as planned and that's okay. When you're reaching out to an estranged child - especially in the emotionally charged landscape of family estrangement that involves a narcissist - the situation can unravel quickly. You might receive silence, a cold response, or an angry reaction that leaves you questioning why you tried at all. These moments can feel devastating, but they aren't necessarily defeats. Instead, take them for what they really are: valuable learning opportunities to slow down, reflect, and understand what worked, what didn't, and what you might do differently next time.

One of the most grounding things you can do after a communication setback is to talk it through with someone you trust—perhaps your spouse, a sibling, or a friend who understands the complexities of your situation. Processing it out loud can help you release the emotional weight and gain perspective. Ask yourself: *Did I say too much? Was my tone too emotional or not emotional enough? Did I touch on a topic they've asked me to avoid?* This isn't about blaming yourself, it's about being curious and honest so you can keep growing and adjusting your approach from a place of calm and strength.

It might also be helpful to write down what felt right and what you'd change for future efforts. Was there a phrase that felt sincere and landed well? Was there a moment where your intention may have been misunderstood? Each attempt to connect, even those that don't go as planned, gives you more insight into how your child receives communication—and what their emotional tolerance is right now. The goal isn't perfection, it's progress. With each step, you're becoming more prepared, more emotionally steady, and more aware of how to communicate in a way that's both respectful of them *and* protective of yourself.

CHAPTER 14
Explaining Estrangement to Those Who Don't Understand

Explaining Estrangement: Protecting Your Story and Your Heart

Opening up about estrangement for the first time can unleash a flood of emotions - shame, self-doubt, guilt, and fear, to name a few. For many parents, saying the words 'my child doesn't want me in their life' is so horrifying that silence feels safer. When the relationship once felt close and loving, sharing this painful reality with friends or family can be nearly impossible. Too often, those first brave attempts to open up are met with insensitive questions like, "What did you do to make them walk away?" Responses like these can retraumatize an already fragile heart, reinforcing the very fears you've been holding onto — *What did I do?*

The truth is, many estranged parents are left trying to make sense of a situation they don't fully understand. It's hard to imagine you can make things right when you're not even sure what went wrong. And when you begin to suspect that a narcissistic son- or daughter-in-law may be influencing the estrangement, the story shifts direction and becomes even more difficult to explain. Narcissistic abuse is invisible to those who haven't lived it. Using words like gaslighting, smear campaign, or flying monkeys can lead others to dismiss your experience or label you as overly dramatic. What's meant to help you name the abuse can become yet another hurdle to being believed.

"Estranged parents feel like they can't do anything right because they don't even know what they did wrong."

If you are in this position, a hard lesson is realizing that not everyone is a safe place for your story. Sharing too much too soon can open the floodgates of emotion - or cause even more harm if the response lacks empathy. For that reason, a clear strategy is essential. In my book, *Divorcing Your Narcissist: You Can't Make This Shit Up*, I introduced what I coined *The Three-Bucket Strategy*—and it's just as helpful here.

The Three-Bucket Strategy for Estrangement Conversations

Step 1: Sort your relationships.

Think of everyone in your life as belonging to one of three buckets:

- **High Bucket (Trusted Inner Circle):** These are your safest people—your best friend, your therapist, a trusted family member, or coach. They get the whole story, because you know they can handle it and hold it with care. They believe you, support you, and don't offer empty platitudes or judgment.
- **Medium Bucket (Cautious Sharing):** These are people who care about you but may not fully understand the depth of what you're going through. You can test the waters here with limited, carefully worded statements. If they respond with empathy, you may continue. If they minimize your pain or defend your child, it's a sign to protect your heart and downgrade them.

- **Low Bucket (Need-to-Know Only):** These are acquaintances, neighbors, coworkers, or distant friends. You owe them nothing beyond a polite one-liner. "We don't see them as often as we'd like" or "They've been really busy" is enough. These statements are emotionally neutral and keep your story safe from gossip.

Step 2: Script your stories.

Craft a version of your story that fits each bucket. With your trusted circle, be vulnerable and honest. With medium-bucket folks, frame your words with care: *"It's been complicated, and we're still working through it."* With the low bucket, the goal isn't to lie, but to keep the conversation from harming you.

Composing a short, intentional version of your story - almost like an elevator pitch - can help ease the anxiety of sharing something so deeply personal. It gives you a sense of control in conversations that might otherwise leave you feeling exposed or emotionally overwhelmed.

When constructing your perspective, consider what follow-up questions someone might ask. The more details you share, the more likely you are to field unexpected or unsettling questions. It's important to set limits - not just on what you say, but on how much emotional space you're willing to give in that moment. Protecting your heart starts with preparation.

This approach empowers you to shield yourself emotionally and manage your triggers. It gives you structure when the anguish feels unpredictable. Most importantly, it helps you hold onto your truth while avoiding further wounds. You don't owe the world an explanation, but you do owe yourself the peace that comes from choosing how, when, and with whom you share your experience.

When a parent shares that their child has chosen estrangement, friends may respond with various questions, some well-intentioned, others inadvertently painful. To help parents prepare for such interactions, here are common questions they might encounter, along with considerations for thoughtful responses:

Common Questions Friends Might Ask

"What happened between you two?"

> Consideration: This question can feel intrusive. A parent might choose to respond with, "It's a complex situation, and I'm still processing it. I appreciate your concern."

"Do you think they'll come back around?"

> Consideration: Speculating about the future can be challenging. A possible response is, "I hold hope, but I'm focusing on healing and respecting their space right now."

"Have you tried reaching out?"

> Consideration: This may imply the parent hasn't made efforts. A gentle reply could be, "Yes, I've reached out in ways I felt were appropriate, but I also want to honor their boundaries."

"What about the holidays or birthdays?"

> Consideration: Such occasions can be particularly painful. A parent might say, "Those times are hard, and I try to find new ways to find meaning during them."

"Do they have kids? Are you in touch with your grandchildren?"

> Consideration: This touches on additional layers of loss. A response could be, "I'm not involved in their lives currently, which is difficult, but I respect their decisions."

"Do you think their spouse or partner influenced this?"

> Consideration: Assigning blame can be unhelpful. A parent might respond, "Relationships are complex, and I prefer not to speculate on their personal choices."

"Have you considered therapy or counseling?"

> Consideration: This can be a supportive suggestion. A parent could reply, "Yes, I'm seeking support to navigate this challenging time."

"Do you talk to your other children about this?"

> Consideration: Family dynamics vary. A possible answer is, "I try to maintain open communication while respecting each person's perspective."

"Do you regret anything?"

> Consideration: This question may evoke guilt. A thoughtful reply might be, "Like many parents, I reflect on past choices, but I'm focusing on growth and understanding now."

"Why don't you just apologize?"

> Consideration: Apologies may have been made or may not be the sole issue. A parent might say, "I've expressed my feelings and am open to dialogue when they're ready."

Preparing for These Conversations

- Set Boundaries: It's okay to decline discussing certain topics. Phrases like, "I appreciate your concern, but I'd prefer not to delve into this right now," can be helpful.
- Seek Support: Engaging with support groups or counseling can provide coping strategies and a sense of community.
- Educating Friends: Sharing resources about estrangement can help friends understand the complexity of the situation.

Remember, every family's situation is unique, and it's important to approach these conversations with compassion—for oneself and from others.

SECTION 5
What Now?

"As parents, we ache to fix what's broken but when our children choose a narcissistic partner, the hardest truth is knowing we can't save them. They must walk their own path, make their own mistakes, and learn the lessons their hearts are ready to hear."

CHAPTER 15
What To Expect Going Forward

Managing the 'Missing Them' Triggers

Estrangement begins with counting the days, days that turn into weeks, weeks that become months, and months that stretch into years.

Estranged parents count so many things:
They count the last time they saw their child or heard their voice.
They count the last time they held their grandchildren.
They count each attempt to reach out, and each painful rejection.
They count the outlandish lies told about them.
They count the family members affected by the rift.
They count the ways their child has changed.
They count the accusations that cut deep.
They count the prayers and bargains made with God and the promises whispered to do whatever it takes.
They count the apologies offered, and those never accepted.

They count the ultimatums that felt like ransom demands.

They count the times they reread every message before sending, careful not to make things worse.

They count the sleepless nights spent replaying every moment of their life.

They count the friends and family who shared their tears, shocked by this painful reality.

They count each missed birthday, for their child, their grandchildren, and their own.

They count the holidays spent with empty seats, without their child and grandchildren.

Because parents ruminate over these milestones, each one becomes a new sharp stab in the heart, a fresh reminder of the absence, the longing, the powerlessness. These are the 'missing them' triggers, and they don't need a special event to appear; it can be a scent, a memory, a place you used to go together, or just the quiet of an ordinary day. Even time itself can become the trigger, hinting about what used to be and reminding you of what's no longer there.

We expect the obvious ones: Mother's Day, Father's Day, holidays, birthdays, and anniversaries… any affair with their empty seat brings grief bubbling to the surface. These days will hurt, no matter how far out from the estrangement you are. Of course, you miss your child and grandchildren. Of course, your heart aches. Instead of pretending we can avoid that sorrow, let's plan how we'll carry it.

Planning for triggers is an act of self-compassion. Ask yourself: *What will I need on that day?* Some people choose solitude. Others fill their day with distractions or create new rituals. There is no right or wrong approach; what matters is that you are choosing how to move through it gracefully, rather than letting the day hijack your emotions. Neither hiding nor powering through will erase your suffering but having a plan will soften the blow and help you stay grounded.

If this is your first year, survival may be your only goal, and *that's okay*. However, if you're years in, you may start to realize something powerful: each time you cancel a gathering, skip a tradition, or stay home out of grief, you are still allowing the narcissist dominance over your life. *And they're not even there*! There comes a moment when it's time to take those days back - not because the sting is gone, but because you're finally ready to reclaim your joy, even with all that still lingers.

So yes, expect the triggers, but don't fear them. Make a game plan. Feel what you need to feel but guard your peace. That is strength.

Be Mindful of What to Expect

One of the first lessons I teach the parents I work with is this: *you must learn to manage your expectations.* Why? Expectations, especially in the chaos of estrangement, will set you up for a let down. Every damn time. They create a fragile sense of certainty, a script for how you hope things will unfold, only to leave you disappointed when reality takes a different turn. Disappointment can feel quietly tragic — not because of what happens, but because of what doesn't. It's the silent unraveling of hope, the slow realization that something you longed for may never come to pass. Unlike sudden loss, disappointment creeps in subtly, built on expectations, trust, and belief. What makes it tragic is not just the outcome, but the emotional investment that came before — the dreams you allowed yourself to imagine, the effort you gave, the vulnerability you offered. It's the heartbreak of possibility turned hollow.

In families where a narcissist has influence over or is controlling your child, anticipations become even more dangerous. You might believe that if you say the right thing, apologize one more time, or show unconditional love, by using a 180-degree shift in approach, the door for real conversation will open. That turn in direction, you're sure, must transform conflict into connection. True in most cases ... except when a narcissist is driving the narrative. They hold the power, not you. Managing your expectations isn't about giving up hope, it's about protecting your heart from the emotional collapse that comes from holding onto what isn't grounded in reality. Let's explore a few situations where adjusting your outlook can support your well-being.

Let Go of What You Can't Control: When dealing with a narcissistic in-law, it's crucial to remember that you can't change their behavior or force your child to see things from your perspective. The more you try to "rescue" your child (that will be seen as interference), the more entrenched the narcissistic spouse may become in their control. Focus on what you *can* control: your emotions, your reactions, and how you choose to process the strain of estrangement. Acceptance is key: accept that you cannot force a reconnection and that your child's decisions are their own and may not align with your wishes.

Adjust Your Expectations: It's natural to want a close relationship with your child and grandchildren, but when a narcissist is involved, it probably won't look like the idyllic family you've envisioned. Adjusting your expectations involves letting go of the eagerness for immediate reconciliation or a "normal" family relationship. Instead, set boundaries for your own mental health and assume interactions (if they happen) will be different than they were before. This accommodation doesn't mean you're giving up hope for the future, but it does mean you're wise enough to safeguard yourself against the constant frustration of unfulfilled desires.

Practice Compassion for Your Child: Estrangement often feels deeply personal but don't forget that your child may also be struggling internally. If they're in an abusive relationship, they may feel isolated, fearful, or unable to break free from the control of their narcissistic partner. Practicing compassion and empathy for your child's situation can help you manage your own emotional responses. Even though the distance between you feels like a breath-taking chasm, maintaining a sense of understanding for your child's predicament can offer some solace and help you avoid bitterness.

Build Your Own Support System: Isolation is a significant danger for parents dealing with estrangement. It's easy to spiral into feelings of guilt, shame, or loneliness. Find a support system, whether through friends, a therapist, or join one of my estranged parents groups, where you can share your feelings without judgment. A solid support network can help you process your thoughts, manage expectations, and stay focused on your own healing. Surround yourself with people who uplift and validate your experiences.

WHAT TO EXPECT GOING FORWARD

Create Space for Hope But Focus on Healing: It's healthy to leave space for the possibility of future reconciliation, but don't put your life on hold waiting for it. Use this time to focus on your own healing, whether that's through therapy, self-care, or engaging in activities that bring you joy. By shifting your attention away from estrangement and toward your own growth, you reduce the power that this harrowing situation holds over your life.

Establish Boundaries: If your child and their narcissistic partner do reach out, it's important to have clear boundaries for yourself in place. Narcissistic individuals thrive on drama and conflict, so by setting firm guidelines, you are able to buffer yourself from further damage. Define what kind of communication and behavior you will and will not tolerate. Boundaries are not meant to be punitive but are a form of self-care that ensures you can engage with your child (if possible) without being pulled back into toxic dynamics. Many parents live in deep fear that setting a boundary will provoke the narcissist and make the estrangement even worse, and that is a valid concern. Narcissists are notorious for resisting boundaries as they thrive on control and emotional access but there comes a point when the cost to your emotional well-being becomes too high. If you're being verbally abused, threatened, or consistently disrespected, it may be time to create a shield by setting a boundary against this type of communication. Only you can assess your plight and determine what's safe and appropriate but know that honoring your own limits is not an act of aggression, it's an act of self-respect. You must come first in this situation.

Acknowledge Your Grief: Estrangement involves a profound sense of loss, not just of the relationship with your child, but often with your grandchildren and extended family connections. It's important to give yourself permission to grieve this loss. You're not overreacting or being dramatic; this is a real and life-altering problem that must be processed with the gravity it deserves.

Managing your expectations during an estrangement is difficult, but adjusting them, practicing compassion, and focusing on your own well-being can help navigate this challenging time with strength and resilience. Remember that your emotional health is just as important as your desire for reconciliation, and investing in your own healing may be the best gift you can give yourself during this difficult period.

Managing Your Expectations: Things to Consider

If you are aware, you can prepare.

To better manage your expectations about seeing your child or grandchildren again, it can be incredibly valuable to ask yourself thoughtful and reflective questions. The following prompts are designed to foster self-awareness, acknowledge the uncertainties of estrangement, and guide you toward setting realistic, grounded goals. Take your time, journal your thoughts, talk with your partner, or explore them with your coach. This kind of deliberation can gently shift your focus from what you *wish* would happen to what you can realistically *prepare* for.

Understanding Hopes and Expectations
- What are your hopes for reconnecting with your child?
- Are there specific expectations you have for how and when reconciliation might happen?
- What would help you feel fulfilled or at peace, even if the relationship doesn't return to what it once was?
- What would an ideal outcome look like for you?

Exploring Past Interactions
- Have there been previous attempts to reconnect? What felt positive or challenging about those experiences?
- What lessons have you learned from any past interactions with your child that could guide your expectations moving forward?
- What actions have you taken in the past that were ineffective? How could you modify them to become beneficial in the future?

Self-Compassion and Acceptance

- How do you manage your feelings of disappointment or grief? If reconnection doesn't happen soon (or at all), will these same actions continue to offer reassurance in the future? If not, how can you adapt them so they do?
- What helps you feel grounded and whole, regardless of the state of your relationship with your child?
- In what ways do you extend kindness and compassion to yourself, especially during this waiting period? Are there any other comforting practices or ideas you've considered that might bring you even a little more peace?

Focusing on Your Personal Growth

- What have you been working on or learning about yourself during this time of estrangement?
- How can you continue your healing journey in ways that don't depend on your child's response?
- Are there personal goals or interests you could focus on that bring you joy and fulfillment?

Setting Realistic Goals for Reconnection

- If your child were to reach out, what are some small, realistic steps you could take to rebuild trust without rushing?
- What boundaries could you establish to protect your emotional well-being while still being open to reconnection?
- What are ways you could express your love or support for your child, even if they're not receptive right now?

Preparing for Different Outcomes

- How would you cope with different outcomes, whether it's a slow reconnection, a limited relationship, or no contact at all?

- Are there ways you can make peace with not knowing when or if reconciliation will happen?
- What would help you feel that you've done what you can to foster reconnection, regardless of the outcome?

These questions encourage you to reflect on your progression, consider possible outcomes, and find ways to nurture your well-being, whether or not reconciliation happens. This approach can help you foster a healthier mindset and help you navigate the complexity of your journey. Journal or simply reflect on these thoughts. Take them at your own pace.

It all begins with a single thought, and over time, some of the fear may ease as you work through the challenges in your mind. While this can be difficult, taking steps to soothe your fears will also help calm your nervous system.

Rebuilding Trust After Estrangement

Estrangement from an adult child is an agonizing and confusing experience for a parent. Even when contact is reestablished, the road to rebuilding trust is rarely smooth; both the parent and the adult child carry emotional wounds from the time apart. Reconnecting may bring hope, but it also brings new fears, unspoken doubts, and the weight of past misunderstandings.

Trust takes years to build, seconds to break, and forever to repair.
~ A.D. Ryan

The first instinct of many parents I work with is that "of course they will" trust their child again. However, with time and reflection, they often realize it's not that simple: it's not their child they're unsure about - it's the influence and control of the narcissistic partner pulling the strings behind the scenes who is the concern. The more honest question becomes: *Can I trust the narcissist?* And the answer, in every case, is a resounding no. That clarity is essential when deciding how and when to establish trust again. When your child is still potentially enmeshed and not yet fully autonomous in their choices, this is an especially precarious decision to make.

In my workshop on rebuilding trust, I always begin with this truth: *before we can trust anyone else, we must learn to trust ourselves, our instincts, our boundaries, and our inner wisdom*. When considering how much trust you have to give, these guiding questions can help:

- Can they take accountability, or do they always blame others?
- Do they show self-awareness and emotional maturity?
- Do they want a relationship built on mutual respect and equality?
- When you set a boundary, do they honor it or react with anger?
- Do they engage in healthy conflict resolution?
- Are they willing to work together to solve problems?
- Can they accept your feelings without judgment?
- Are they able to let go of unimportant issues?
- Are they consistently honest and truthful?
- Do they follow through on their word?
- Can they admit when they're wrong?
- Do they show compassion or criticism toward you and your family?

These are not insignificant questions as each one reflects qualities that are, at their core, incompatible with narcissistic behavior. Trust cannot grow where these traits are absent, and unfortunately, these are the very things a narcissist struggles with or outright refuses to do. They are the foundation for safe, mutual trust. Rebuilding confidence in someone doesn't happen at once - it's earned over time, through consistent, healthy behavior. It's best to move slowly. You're not only putting faith in your child, but you're also believing that they are emotionally free to show up as themselves. Until that's clear, proceed gently and protect your heart.

Relearning how to trust your adult child after estrangement is a delicate process that requires time, patience, and mutual effort. Here are some considerations and strategies to help navigate this path:

Acknowledge the Emotional Impact of Estrangement: Estrangement often leaves emotional wounds on both sides. For parents, feelings of betrayal, grief, and loss can cloud attempts to reconnect. Acknowledge these emotions and understand that they may affect your ability to trust fully, even if the relationship is improving. Estranged adult children may also carry unresolved feelings of hurt or anger, which can manifest as guarded behavior or inconsistent communication. Recognizing that both parties are healing from a deep trauma can help set a realistic outlook.

Understand the Reasons Behind the Estrangement: A crucial step in rebuilding trust is understanding what first led to the estrangement. Whether the separation was influenced by personal conflicts, external factors (such as a controlling narcissistic partner), or misunderstandings, taking accountability where necessary can help pave the way for honest dialogue. Without understanding the root causes, trust can remain fragile, as unresolved issues may resurface and strain the relationship further.

Accept That a Readiness to Trust May Be Uneven: It's common for one party to be more open to trust than the other. For example:

- The parent may feel cautious about whether the reconciliation will last.
- The adult child may still harbor doubts about the parent's intentions or willingness to respect their boundaries.
- Trust doesn't return all at once; it grows through consistent actions and positive interactions over time.

Establish Boundaries and Expectations: One of the most important aspects of rebuilding trust is setting clear boundaries and expectations. Openly discussing what each person needs for the relationship to feel safe can prevent misunderstandings and reduce tension. For example:

- The adult child may request that certain topics not be discussed or ask for space to process their emotions.

- The parent may express a desire for more consistent communication or shared time together.

Respecting these boundaries shows that both parties are committed to creating a healthier dynamic.

Be Patient with the Process: Rebuilding trust is a slow process, especially after a period of estrangement. It's important to remain patient and avoid rushing or forcing the relationship to progress faster than it would organically. Celebrate small milestones, such as a meaningful conversation, a shared meal, or an open discussion about feelings. These moments are the building blocks of a stronger relationship.

Address Fears of Being Hurt Again: For parents, one of the biggest challenges in trusting an estranged child is the fear of being hurt again. Reopening your heart makes you vulnerable, and the prospect of facing another period of silence or rejection can be terrifying. It's important to acknowledge these fears and share them in a way that invites understanding rather than placing blame. For example:

- *"I'm so happy we're reconnecting, but I hope you can understand why I feel nervous about losing contact again."*

Expressing vulnerability can help nurture empathy and deepen the connection.

Focus on Actions, Not Just Words: Rebuilding trust is as much about actions as it is about words. Look for consistency in your child's behavior rather than relying solely on promises or apologies. Similarly, demonstrate your own commitment to change through consistent actions, such as respecting their boundaries or showing up when they need support.

Embrace the Present, Release the Past: It's natural to revisit the pain of the past, but dwelling on it can hinder progress. While it's important to learn from past experiences, focusing on the present and future allows for mutual growth and understanding. All voices should be heard but instead of revisiting old conflicts, work on creating new, positive memories that strengthen your bond.

Allow Trust to Evolve: Trust after estrangement doesn't look the same as it did before. It evolves into something new, shaped by the lessons learned and the growth both parties have experienced. Accepting that the relationship will look different allows you to embrace what is possible rather than clinging to what was lost.

Rebuilding trust with an adult child after estrangement is an odyssey filled with adversities, but it also offers the possibility of mending and evolving. By approaching the process with patience, understanding, and a desire to adapt, you can begin to repair the connection and create a stronger, more resilient relationship.

Remember, trust isn't rebuilt overnight, but with consistent effort and mutual respect, it can flourish again.

Setting Boundaries for Your Mental Health

Am I allowed to even ask for a boundary? That's a prominent question estranged parents always ask. It's a fair concern, especially when every attempt at honesty or self-protection in the past has been met with anger, shutdowns, or further distance. When a narcissist is influencing your child, the simple act of setting a boundary can feel dangerous or impossible. But here's the truth: *yes, you can ask.* You *should* ask. Boundaries aren't demands; they are healthy limits that protect your emotional well-being. They are not meant to control others, but to define what is and isn't okay for you. In estrangement, where the emotional terrain is so unpredictable, boundaries become a lifeline.

What does a boundary look like? "I want to have a relationship with you, but I need our conversations to be respectful and free from criticism or hostility." Or "I'm open to reconnecting, but I need us to avoid rehashing the past unless we're both willing to do it in a calm and constructive way." Boundaries may also be set around your availability, your emotional safety, or how you're spoken to. Setting a boundary doesn't guarantee they'll accept or honor it, but it does allow you to regain a sense of agency and shelter your heart from further harm. If a boundary is crossed, you have the right to enforce it possibly by calmly ending the conversation, stepping away, or giving yourself space to reset.

Many parents fear that setting boundaries—no matter how respectful or necessary—will only push their child further away. That fear is real and valid, especially when you've already lost so much. The idea of losing even the faintest thread of contact can feel unbearable. But here's the risk you need to understand without boundaries, you may find yourself accepting mistreatment, enduring manipulation, or absorbing repeated emotional blows that erode your sense of self. Boundaries may not repair the relationship overnight—in fact, they may be met with resistance—but they create a foundation of self-respect and emotional protection. You are not obligated to tolerate cruelty in the name of staying connected. In truth, relationships built on fear, obligation, or silence are not healthy reconnections. Boundaries are not the cause of estrangement; they are tools for surviving it with dignity.

Equally important is respecting their boundaries, even when it's hard. If your child says they need time or space, comply with that request. It may feel like rejection but allowing them room to breathe may create a greater sense of trust in the long run. In estrangement, every interaction feels fragile. Boundaries help bring clarity, reduce harm, and build a structure where healing, even if it's slow, can start to take shape.

Practicing Self-Compassion

Practicing self-compassion is not just a luxury during estrangement, it's a necessity. When you're navigating the grief, confusion, and helplessness that comes from being cut off from your child or grandchildren, your emotional and physical reserves can be depleted quickly. This is why self-compassion must begin with the basics: eat nourishing meals, get enough sleep, hydrate, and move your body in gentle ways. These small but vital acts of care remind your body that it is safe and supported, even when your heart feels empty.

Self-compassion also means softening the way you speak to yourself. It's common for estranged parents to ruminate on past conversations, condemn themselves, or replay memories while wondering what they could have done differently. This cycle of self-blame and "what-ifs" deepens your suffering. Being gentler with yourself in these moments means pausing to say, *"I'm doing the best I can,"* or *"I didn't deserve this, even if I made mistakes."* Use affirming language as you would with a dear friend because you deserve the same forgiveness and grace you offer others.

Lastly, self-compassion can come from creating new small pockets of joy and peace in your life. Whether it's taking a walk in nature, dinner with a friend, unlocking your inner artist, window shopping, journaling your feelings, or allowing yourself to laugh at a funny movie - these moments matter. They do not erase the hurt of estrangement, but they *do* remind you that life is still happening and that you are worthy of beauty and light, even in the midst of sorrow. When the world feels cold and uncertain, let your daily acts of self-kindness become the warmth to keep you going.

Winning the Game You Never Wanted to Play

When Appeasement Becomes Strategy: A Way Back to Your Child

Sucking up to the narcissist - or more gently put, strategically appeasing them - is not about validating their behavior. It's about understanding their psychology. Narcissists are driven by ego, control, and a constant need for admiration. When you mirror those needs back to them - by showing deference, offering praise, or including them in ways that boost their image - they feel powerful. And when a narcissist feels powerful, they're less likely to see you as a threat, which can reduce their urge to eliminate you from the picture entirely.

This doesn't mean you must sacrifice your dignity, or integrity – it means choosing your goals wisely. If your primary goal is to rebuild a connection with your child or regain access to your grandchildren, you may need to temporarily set aside your pride. Narcissists thrive on being seen as superior, so when you stop trying to expose them or challenge their false narrative - and instead offer carefully curated praise or attention - you begin to disarm their defenses.

That could look like thanking them (yes, really!) for being such a committed partner to your child or complimenting them on how well they're doing as a parent. It might mean sending a birthday gift just for them - not just for your child or grandkids. Small things, when viewed through the lens of their ego, become significant. You're feeding their identity and while that may feel wrong, manipulative, or even unjust, it can be a calculated move in service of a higher goal: staying in your child's life.

Of course, you must weigh this carefully. Consider your boundaries, your mental health, and whether this kind of psychological dance is sustainable for you. Some parents find it degrading; others find it empowering because it's strategic. You are not doing this to befriend the narcissist - you're doing it to reduce resistance, calm the waters, and open a door, however narrow, that your child might be able to walk through.

For many parents, this can feel like a bridge too far. The pain, betrayal, and deep sense of injustice make it nearly impossible to imagine extending kindness—or even civility—to the very person who seems to be tearing their family apart. If that's how you feel, I truly understand. I'm including this section not to invalidate your experience, but to offer an option for those parents who are willing to try anything — those who are searching for one more strategy that *might* help reopen the door to their child.

While this approach is not universally effective, many of the estranged parents I've worked with who *have* reconciled with their child have used this very strategy—at least in the beginning. It didn't mean they agreed with the narcissist or forgot the pain, but they recognized that disarming the gatekeeper was often the only path back to their child. By offering strategic gestures of respect or flattery, they reduced conflict and gradually rebuilt trust, not with the narcissist, but with their child, who may have been watching to see if the environment felt safe enough to reengage. This method isn't guaranteed, and it won't work in every case, but in many, it has shifted the power dynamics just enough to let healing begin.

Just remember, this is not forever. This is a tactical season, and like many seasons, it can serve a purpose, pass with time, and maybe - just maybe - make way for healing.

How to Stop Playing the Game Without Giving Up

When do I stop? When do I stop trying, reaching out, or hoping for a different outcome?

Parents often describe the estrangement experience as an emotional game they never agreed to play, filled with silence, rejection, or constant attacks. Whether it's being met with cruel messages or no response at all, the pattern becomes exhausting and torturous. It can feel like a never-ending vicious cycle. Many parents ask, *"Is there a sign? How do I know when it's time to stop playing along?"* The answer isn't simple, but what's clear is that protecting your heart doesn't mean giving up on your child; it only means stepping back with intention and self-respect.

For many estranged parents, stepping back feels like giving up. The fear is real: if you stop reaching out, will your child think you no longer love them? Will the narcissist use your silence as further proof that you don't care? If you stop defending yourself, will the narcissist's lies become their truth?

> *If a tree falls in a forest and no one is around to hear it, does it make a sound?*
> ~ George Berkely

But here's the hard reality: If you play the game, the narcissist rules supreme. The more you react, defend, explain, or chase, the more power they hold over you and your child.

Ending the game isn't giving up on your child; it's stopping the manipulation. It's refusing to fuel the toxic cycle that keeps you stuck. Paradoxically, it's often the only way to leave the door open for true reconnection in the future.

How to Stop Playing the Game

Accept That You Can't "Win" Against a Narcissist
- Narcissists don't play fair. They move the goalposts, twist your words, and manipulate emotions.
- Trying to prove your worth, defend yourself, or correct the narrative only strengthens their control.
- Instead of engaging ... disengage. Let go of the need to convince anyone of the truth.

Stop Defending Yourself
- When your child repeats the narcissist's accusations, the automatic instinct is to defend, explain, or plead your case.
- Understand that your child is trapped in a false reality where you are the villain, and the narcissist is the hero.
- Instead of arguing, respond with love and neutrality:
    - *"I'm sorry you feel that way. I love you, and I'm here if you ever want to talk."*
    - *"I won't debate the past with you, but I will always care about you."*

Set Boundaries Around Toxic Communication
- If every conversation leads to blame, criticism, or manipulation, it's okay to step back.
- Let your child know what kind of communication you're open to:
    - *"I'm happy to have a respectful conversation, but I won't engage in attacks."*
    - *"I'll always be here for you, but I won't participate in arguments."*
    - If necessary, take a break from messages or calls that only bring pain.

Stop Begging for Their Love
- The more you chase, the more the narcissist convinces them that you're desperate, controlling, or toxic. And when you beg, the narcissist holds all the power, it confirms their narrative and fuels their control. Your desperation becomes their weapon, twisting your love into "proof" that *you're* the problem.
- Your worth is not defined by your child's ability to see the truth. Stand strong in your love, even if from a distance.

Focus on Your Own Healing
- Obsessing over the estrangement only deepens the wound. Shift the focus to your own well-being.
- Reinvest in your own life, happiness, and purpose. This is not the end of your story.

Trust That Time and Truth Have Power
- Many children who are manipulated into estrangement eventually see the truth, but they must do it in their own time.
- The less you engage in the drama, the more space they have to question the narcissist's narrative.
- Your steadiness, not your arguments, will be what eventually helps them see reality.

There comes a point when parents simply reach their limit. The pretending, the constant tension, the emotional whiplash - it all becomes too much. Eventually, some parents make the painful choice to step back. They say, "I'm done—for now." This doesn't always mean forever. It's a boundary, not a goodbye. It's a conscious decision to no longer bow to the manipulation, to stop playing a game where the rules keep changing. It's not just ego or pride; it's the culmination of frustration, heartbreak, and deep sorrow. But in that moment of choosing peace, the parent begins to reclaim their power. They hold space for their child to awaken or for the narcissist's grip to loosen. And in the meantime, they start to move forward not because they've stopped loving, but because they've started healing.

Letting Go Is Not Giving Up

Terminating your participation in the game doesn't mean your love for your child is gone. It's the exact opposite. It means refusing to be a pawn in a toxic system that keeps you hurting and your child trapped. You are not abandoning them, you are choosing peace, strength, and the hope that one day, they will find their way back on their own.

Navigating the Silence: How Journaling Can Bring Peace

Journaling is a powerful tool for navigating the pain of estrangement. When your heart is aching from unanswered questions, overwhelming fear, or the deafening silence of a relationship once full of love, use journaling as your safe place to release what you can't always say out loud. In the stillness of night, when the world is asleep and your thoughts race with what-ifs and memories, your journal will always meet you with open pages, a quiet eagerness to absorb your darkest thoughts, and, most importantly, no judgment. There, you're allowed to speak freely, cry through your pen, and let your deepest anguish rise to the surface, so it no longer stays buried inside. Let it heal your suffering and mend your wounds.

Journaling is more than just venting; it's a restorative practice that can bring clarity and peace. Begin by writing what you're feeling in the moment, such as anger, confusion, or grief. Then, ask yourself deeper questions: *What part of this hurts the most today? What do I need right now to feel safe or supported? What truth do I need to be reminded of?* You might write letters to your child that you'll never send or record good and bad memories, not to live in the past, but to gently release it. You don't need perfect words, just honest ones. The goal isn't to fix everything, but to face what hurts so you don't have to carry the weight in your body and mind.

Over time, journaling will do multiple things: it'll reveal patterns in your thoughts, show you in black and white how far you've come, and offer a calming perspective on your healing. It becomes a timeline of your growth and resilience. When practiced regularly, it grounds you in your truth and helps you reconnect with your own voice, especially when the noise of estrangement has silenced so much. Whether it's five minutes a day or five pages at 2 a.m., journaling gives your emotions a place to land and your heart a place to rest.

Journal Prompts for Healing Through Estrangement

Journaling can be a powerful companion on your path to liberation. All you need is a notebook and a readiness to put your thoughts into words. These reflective prompts are designed to help you process the complex emotions of estrangement grief, confusion, anger, and hope. Think of your journal as a private, daily therapy session where your opinions are safe, your truth is honored, and your healing begins.

- Write a letter to your child that you will never send. Pour out everything you've been holding inside—the anger, the heartbreak, the longing, the confusion. Write the letter that screams, the one that weeps, the one that simply whispers, *"I miss you."* Let your words be raw and real, not polished or censored. This isn't for them, it's for *you*. Write a letter each day if it helps. Say the things you used to be able to say freely. Share memories, express your grief, or ask the questions that haunt you. Use this practice to release the emotional weight you've been carrying. When you're done, pause, take a breath, and say to yourself, *"I got that out. Now I can move forward with my day."* Feel how your emotional burden has been lifted. Let your journal be the space where your pain is witnessed, and your healing begins.
- What do you miss most about your child or grandchildren, and what does that loss feel like in your body?
- What unanswered questions keep repeating in your mind? Write them out even if there are no answers yet.

WHAT TO EXPECT GOING FORWARD

- What was the moment you realized your relationship had changed? Describe it without judgment.
- If you could speak freely to your child without fear of rejection, what would you want them to know?
- How has estrangement changed your sense of identity as a parent or grandparent?
- What have you blamed yourself for, and is that blame rooted in truth or in pain?
- What parts of your story do you feel like no one else understands? Let them be seen here.
- What does "hope" look like for you? Is it helpful or harmful right now?
- What emotions are you afraid of feeling or expressing about this estrangement? Why?
- When you think of setting a boundary, what fears come up? What do you need to feel safe?
- What have you learned about yourself through this experience? What surprised you?
- What would you say to another parent going through this, if you could comfort them today?
- What do you need more of in your life right now, emotionally, physically, and spiritually?
- Are there moments of peace or clarity you've experienced amid this pain? What helped create them?
- What would healing, not reconciliation, look like for you today? Can you plan a baby step to get there?
- Who are you beyond being a parent? What other roles or passions do you want to reclaim?
- What forgiveness (for yourself or others) feels impossible right now and why?
- If you were to imagine a healthier future version of yourself, what would that version be doing differently today?
- What are you proud of surviving, even if no one else sees it?

Legacy Ideas to Keep You Busy

Silence can make time feel like it's standing still. When you're estranged from your child or grandchildren, life becomes emotional purgatory - you're unable to be the parent or grandparent you've always been yet still bear the full weight of that love. If you're like most estranged parents, you've tried everything to fix it. You've reached out, apologized, waited patiently - all with no success. It's heartbreaking. The question becomes: *what can you do with all this love, time, and hope?*

One way to reclaim your sense of purpose is to create a legacy for your child or grandchildren, even if they aren't actively in your life right now. Earlier, we shared the story of a grandmother who records short videos reading children's books, sharing memories of her daughter growing up, and telling family stories. With no knowledge of whether the videos will ever be seen, she is determined to build something. She's staying connected through intention. This creative outlet has not only comforted her, but it has also brought peace knowing her voice, her heart, and her truth are being offered on her terms.

Another meaningful idea might be to go through photo albums and write or record the stories behind each image. You could write letters to go with certain photos, or even design a memory book filled with captions, reflections, and lessons learned. These could become treasured gifts in the future or simply a way for *you* to make sense of the hand you've been dealt. Some record audio messages or write journal entries addressed to their grandchildren. Even if these remain unread, they offer a profound outlet for the love that continues to live on inside you.

One mother found renewal through crafting wooden hearts - a quiet tribute to the son she no longer sees. She began using items he had left behind, like old marbles in a coffee can that sat forgotten on a garage shelf. Now, those marbles are lovingly glued onto wooden hearts - each piece telling a story, each design holding a memory. What started as a way to process her heartache transformed his old bedroom into a gallery of love and loss, with over 60 handmade hearts adorning the walls. Through this creative expression, grief is released and the ache channeled into something beautiful. The approach became a form of therapy that didn't require words or permission. Now, she dreams of sharing these hearts with the world, offering them as symbols of hope, resilience, and the enduring love of a parent who continues to show up, even in the silence.

Other ideas include making a family recipe book filled with stories behind each meal or starting a YouTube journal of life lessons and wisdom you wish to pass on. Curate a playlist of songs that represent important moments in your family history and include a note about why each one matters. Plant a garden and map it out, with each flower or tree symbolizing a hope or prayer for the future. The possibilities are endless but no matter what, they are beneficial beyond words. These acts of legacy-building give purpose to the waiting and offer an outlet to pour love into that would otherwise have nowhere to land.

Legacy work is healthy work. It grounds you in your role as a parent or grandparent even if you're currently uninvited from those roles. It allows you to keep showing up, not just for them, but for yourself. One day, should the silence break, you'll have something meaningful to share. Even if that day never comes, your legacy will remain: a testament of unconditional love that refused to vanish, even in the face of absence and adversity.

CHAPTER 16
Financial and Legal Considerations

Protecting Your Child from Financial Abuse and Manipulation

One of the most insidious forms of abuse narcissists wield is financial control. It's common for a narcissistic partner to slowly drain the financial resources of their spouse, maintaining a sense of entitlement not only to their spouse's money, but to yours as well. In many cases, I've seen the narcissist convince the adult child to cut financial ties with their parents - while subtly beginning to control their spending, manage their accounts, or even use their credit cards. Over time, your child may become financially dependent on and completely manipulated by the narcissist, often without even realizing it.

The powerlessness to stop this is real, but there are still ways to quietly protect your child. If you have established savings accounts, trust funds, or other financial resources for your child, review them with an estate planner. You can explore options to set up protective trusts that limit access or specify use only for your child and grandchildren. excluding spouses. If you currently help your adult child financially, consider shifting from direct support (cash) to more controlled methods like gift cards, covering specific bills, or making payments directly to institutions (like tuition or medical bills). While this may cause friction between you and your child and/or their partner, it minimizes the risk of the narcissist accessing or misusing the funds.

If your child is under the influence of a narcissist, be cautious with joint accounts, co-signing on loans, or imparting sensitive financial information with them. They may innocently share with their partner or feel pressured to use it for their spouse's benefit. Unfortunately, when a narcissist senses financial opportunity, they tend to push for access in both low-key and aggressive ways.

Remember: while you can't control your child's choices, you *can* control what protections you put in place today. These efforts are not acts of punishment or revenge, they are acts of love and wisdom, meant to protect your child and grandchildren from long-term financial harm.

Planning Your Estate in Estranged Family Situations

As the years of estrangement drag on, many parents find themselves facing difficult decisions about their estate and how to handle the inclusion or exclusion of an estranged child and grandchildren. If you are concerned about the future, take proactive steps to protect your estate and legacy now. This section is designed to guide you through estate planning strategies that can prevent the narcissist from benefiting financially after you're gone.

Estate planning is always personal, but when relationships have fractured, those decisions take on new weight. It's not just about dividing assets; it's about protecting your wishes, your heritage, and sometimes your remaining sense of peace.

One of the first areas to review is who holds legal authority in your existing documents. If your estranged child is currently listed as your Medical Power of Attorney (MPOA) or Healthcare Proxy, ask yourself: *Would they show up if you were sick? Would they honor your wishes, or could their partner influence them?* For some estranged parents, especially those who are single or have no other children, these questions generate immense anxiety. Estate planning isn't just about distributing wealth; it's about deciding who you trust with your well-being and your footprint when you no longer have a voice.

One story that haunts me to this day comes from early in my work supporting victims of narcissistic abuse. It involved a woman going through a contentious divorce. Her husband was originally listed as her Medical Power of Attorney (MPOA), but as the emotional abuse escalated, she wisely updated her documents, assigning her trusted adult son as her new MPOA. Legally, she did everything right, but when a sudden health crisis landed her in the ICU, her estranged husband stepped in, and things quickly spiraled.

Even though she had created a new, legally binding MPOA, the not-quite-ex-husband convinced the hospital that his older document was still valid. He used his charm and manipulation, something narcissists often do expertly to assert their authority, and had the hospital ban her son from visiting or making any medical decisions on her behalf. The son worked tirelessly, fighting to prove his legal authority, but by then, valuable time had been lost, and his mother's care was being actively mismanaged. The narcissistic husband went so far as to refuse medically necessary treatments simply out of spite.

Eventually, the son was able to obtain a court order to override his father's control, but not before precious time, energy, and emotional stability had been drained from an already traumatic situation. Let this story be a clear warning: who you name in your medical and legal documents holds real power, especially if you're a single parent or are navigating estrangement. Review your estate and healthcare plan regularly - don't wait until it's too late. Abuse doesn't stop when someone falls ill. In fact, for a narcissist, it can become one more opportunity to control, punish, or erase.

A Reminder On Trust: There's a difference between trusting your child and trusting the influence of the narcissist who controls them. While your love for your child remains strong, it's important to recognize when their words and actions are no longer entirely their own. In narcissistic dynamics, your child may be operating under manipulation, fear, or emotional dependence and that means their choices may not reflect their true self. Consider this when assigning your various powers of attorney.

You can hold space in your heart for your child but never place your trust in the control the narcissist has over them. That control is rooted in self-interest, not love, and it can turn your child into a messenger or enforcer of someone else's agenda. Protect your heart and your body.

I've worked with many parents who opt to shift their child's inheritance into a trust, adding legal protection to ensure the money doesn't fall into the hands of the narcissistic in-law. If you're concerned that your assets are viewed as a future payday, you're not alone. Narcissists tragically manipulate their spouses and play the long game waiting out family ties until the windfall arrives so they can walk away. Develop a trust with clear boundaries, stipulations, and a neutral trustee to provide for your child or grandchildren without enabling exploitation.

For those who still wish to leave something to their grandchildren but fear it will be mismanaged or withheld by the adult child or narcissist, consider setting up a separate trust solely for the grandchildren. With careful planning, you can include clear rules about how and when those funds are accessed and ensure that a trustworthy person of your choosing oversees the distribution.

Unfortunately, in narcissistic dynamics, theft even from their own children is not uncommon. Establish these safeguards as a loving act of protection, not punishment.

A Caution When Revising Your Estate Plan

If you've decided to remove your estranged adult child from your will or estate, there's an important risk to consider especially if you have other children who will now receive a greater share. I've witnessed heartbreaking cases where a narcissistic son- or daughter-in-law fuels conflict between siblings after a parent's passing, triggering prolonged court battles. Narcissists often thrive in chaos and, as we say in the divorce world, they'd rather pay attorneys than see someone else receive anything easily. Even if they gain nothing, their goal is often to cause financial and emotional harm to others—just because they can.

To protect your other children, speak openly with your estate attorney about these dynamics. Some of my clients have worked with their lawyers to add specific language to the estate documents clarifying that the estranged child was intentionally disinherited—not overlooked by accident. An attorney friend of mine always reminds clients that this clarity is essential. A simple statement like *"this decision is intentional and not a clerical error"* can help limit the risk of costly, emotionally draining legal challenges. In some states, your attorney may also be able to include language that makes the decision legally unchallengeable or significantly harder to contest.

Even if you decide to leave your estate to your grandchildren instead, it's still crucial to protect those funds from manipulation. I've seen too many cases where a narcissistic in-law tries to access grandchildren's money through coercion or legal pressure. One powerful safeguard is placing the funds in a trust managed by a neutral third-party trustee, someone who can ensure the money is used exactly as you intended.

This is about more than money, it's about protecting your legacy and shielding the next generation from further emotional harm. A carefully crafted, narcissist-proof estate plan can offer tremendous peace of mind, allowing you to leave behind love and support rather than conflict and confusion.

You've already endured enough. Let your estate plan be a form of protection, closure, and thoughtful care for the ones you love.

Finally, reflect on your own financial boundaries. Some parents choose to continue supporting their estranged child out of guilt or a desperate hope that it will reopen the relationship. Others make the hard decision to remove them from the will entirely, based on the belief that love and respect should not come with a price tag. Neither path is wrong - it's your endowment and your choice. Just make sure it's a decision made from your truth, not your fear. A professional in the field can help walk you through the logistics but only *you* can decide what feels right in your heart.

Grandparent's Rights: What You Need to Know

When estrangement extends beyond your adult child and rips away access to your grandchildren, the emotional toll is profound. Many estranged parents say, "*I could learn to live without my child, but losing my grandchildren is unbearable.*" The innocent children, whom you once rocked, read to, and loved without limits, are suddenly gone. When a narcissistic in-law is involved, the pain is intensified because you're not just cut off, you're vilified and portrayed as the problem. In these moments, many grandparents begin to wonder: *Do I have any rights?*

Grandparents' rights vary greatly depending on the state or country you live in. In the U.S., only some states have formal legal provisions that allow grandparents to petition for visitation. However, even in those states, the process is far from easy. Courts tend to prioritize the rights of fit parents, and unless there has been a divorce, death, or proven unfitness, your chances of being granted court-ordered visitation are slim. Most states will only entertain grandparents' visitation if it's clearly in the best interest of the child, and you must often demonstrate a pre-existing, meaningful relationship with your grandchild that is being harmed by the cutoff.

Even if you meet those standards, pursuing grandparent's rights through the court system is often long, expensive, and emotionally grueling. Families end up in prolonged legal battles, only to lose in the end because unless there's something extreme, like abuse or neglect involved, judges are reluctant to interfere with a parent's right to decide who their child interacts with. Sadly, in narcissistic family systems, your attempt to legally assert your rights can be spun as further proof of your toxic or controlling behavior. Be very mindful of how this path might be used against you. Another serious risk is that taking legal action may be the nail in the coffin for ever seeing your child again. For some estranged children, especially those heavily influenced by a narcissistic partner, the moment legal pressure is introduced, the door slams shut permanently. You must weigh this possibility carefully before proceeding.

There's also a darker risk that few people talk about. In an effort to avoid court battles or the threat of visitation orders, a narcissistic in-law may move your grandchildren out of state or even out of the country without your knowledge. Once they disappear, pursuing any kind of legal recourse becomes nearly impossible. If they can't be located, court proceedings may stall or end entirely. This is a devastating reality that some grandparents have faced, where one moment they're in court fighting for visitation, and the next, their grandchildren are simply... gone.

Before taking legal action, consult with a family law attorney who specializes in grandparent's rights in your state. Weigh the emotional and financial cost and consider all possible outcomes. For some, filing is a way to fight for what's right and hold on to hope for a relationship with their grandchildren. For others, the risk of further alienation or retaliation outweighs the benefit. There is no one-size-fits-all answer but being informed will help you make the best choice for your heart, your sanity, your family, and your legacy.

SECTION 6
Conclusion

"Even in the silence, your love still speaks. One day, the heart that turned away may remember and find its way back. Until then, have faith, hold onto hope, stand in your truth, and never stop being the parent who loves unconditionally."

CHAPTER 17
A Message of Hope

Estrangement caused by a narcissistic son or daughter-in-law is one of the deepest emotional wounds a parent can experience. It's a grief that doesn't have a funeral, and an agony that lives in the background of everyday life. At times, you may have felt utterly powerless, rejected, and invisible - cut off from your child and possibly your grandchildren - left wondering how everything you poured into your family could disappear. I want you to know: this is not the end of your story.

Throughout this book, you've gained a better understanding of narcissistic manipulation, enmeshed relationship interactions, and the psychological dynamics that morph family love into estrangement. You've learned how to communicate more diligently, protect yourself emotionally and financially, and most importantly, how to rebuild your sense of identity outside of this pain. These are tools that will serve you for life - tools that hundreds of parents before you have used to regain their footing, rebuild positivity in the days ahead to come, and, yes, even reunite with their children and grandchildren.

I want you to hold on to something stronger than hope: I want you to hold on to faith. Hope says, "I wish my child would come back." But faith? Faith says, "I believe that even if I can't see it now, one day my child will find their way back to me." Faith is deeper. It's not just a feeling, it's a quiet strength, a steady current beneath the surface. It's what carries you through the silence when answers don't come, through the doubt that creeps in when nothing makes sense, and through the aching absence of certainty. Faith doesn't demand evidence; it holds you when there's nothing left to hold onto. It's the whisper that says "keep going" when everything in you wants to give up.

When rooted in faith, we open our hearts to something greater than ourselves: the grace of renewal, the unseen power of love, the timing of the universe, and yes, even the hand of God. You don't have to know the how or the when. You just have to believe that this story isn't over. It's your journey so embrace it.

Remember, this is also part of your child's journey. As painful as it is, sometimes it takes walking the wrong path to finally see the truth. People do leave narcissists, thousands of them have - if they didn't, I wouldn't be a divorce coach. Whether through awakening, by choice, or because the narcissist eventually discards them for a new supply, many do break free. ...and when they do, they often look back and realize exactly what—and who—they were dealing with, and who they had entrusted their life to. Be ready and stay rooted in faith.

I've coached parents all over the world through situations just like yours. I've seen reconciliations after months... and after years. I've witnessed grandchildren who were born into isolation later find their way back to their loving grandparents. These families didn't get there through begging, fixing, or pleasing. They got there by healing, setting healthy boundaries, changing the way they communicated with their child, and holding space for their child to grow and come back when they were ready. With patience and strategy, these reunions can and do happen.

Even if that day hasn't come for you yet, or never does, you have still reclaimed something invaluable: yourself. You've shown immense strength just by reading these pages, by doing the hard work of reflection, self-regulation, and transformation.

Acceptance doesn't mean giving up. It means honoring what's true and making peace with what you can't control, allowing you to finally start breathing again. It means learning to live again - fully, courageously, and with an open heart, even with that empty chair at your table, an unspoken reminder of what once was.

If you're still struggling, let me make it clear that help is here for you. I offer private coaching for parents navigating estrangement and host *Estranged Parents Educational Strategy Groups*—safe, supportive spaces to learn, grow, and feel less alone. All the resources you need are at your fingertips on my website: NarcissistAbuseSupport.com. You don't have to face this alone, and I would be honored to walk this journey with you.

As you close this book, take one last deep breath and remember: you are not broken. You are not alone. You are not done. This estrangement is just one season in the story of your life—a difficult and tearful one, but it is not the entire narrative. There is still time for healing, growth, and new beginnings, and this chapter, as challenging as it may be, will eventually be a part of your past, not your future. The next one is yours to write, with resilience, humility, and fortitude. Your love matters. Your story matters. And your life can still be full of meaning, even as you nurture the belief that, one day, your child may come home.

Time, on its own, does not mend a broken heart. It doesn't erase the sorrow or undo the loss. What time does is, gently teach us how to carry that ache, how to weave it into the fabric of our lives, and how to keep moving forward—not because we've forgotten, but because we've learned to live with the love that remains, even in their distance.

Grief never truly disappears. It may quiet down for a while, softening into the background of your days, letting you catch your breath. But then, without warning, it can rise up again—sharp, sudden, and overwhelmingly triggered by a memory, a moment, or even just the stillness of an ordinary day. It comes and goes in waves, reminding us of the depth of our love and the weight of our loss.

Grief ebbs and flows with the rhythms of life. Certain moments will stir it more deeply than others, an empty chair at a holiday gathering, a birthday or milestone celebration that feels incomplete, like something is missing, like someone is missing. These occasions can open a tender place in your heart, a space where longing lives. Expect these emotional waves. Anticipate the triggers. And when they come, meet them with compassion—for yourself, and for the love that still lives within you.

Learning the tools to navigate difficult moments—to shake off the heaviness of hard days and regain your balance more quickly—is truly invaluable. Over time, this inner strength begins to foster a healthy detachment, not from your emotions, but from the influence they once held over you. It's not about denying the heartache, but about no longer allowing it to shape your identity.

You've faced what no parent should ever have to, and yet here you are—still standing, still loving, still hoping. That is resilience, and it will carry you forward.

ABOUT THE AUTHOR

Tracy A. Malone is an international narcissistic abuse survival coach, author, and founder of NarcissistAbuseSupport.com, a global resource dedicated to empowering victims of emotional abuse. As a surTHRIVER of narcissistic abuse herself, Tracy brings personal insight, deep compassion, and years of experience to her work. For over eight years, she has specialized in coaching estranged parents, helping them navigate the heart-wrenching journey of disconnection—often due to narcissistic in-laws—and find strategies for healing, boundaries, and, when possible, reconnection.

Tracy leads a weekly educational support group for estranged parents, offering a safe, structured environment to explore solutions, process emotions, and build resilience. Her work has helped thousands of parents around the world find clarity and strength in the midst of family turmoil.

She is the author of best-selling book Divorcing Your Narcissist: You Can't Make This Shit Up! and multiple eBooks focused on narcissistic relationships—from divorcing a narcissist to surviving narcissistic family members, co-parenting challenges, and toxic friendships and workplaces. She has also authored 32 targeted healing journals to help survivors heal.

A frequent guest on podcasts and summits, Tracy has built a robust YouTube channel featuring more than 800 educational videos with over 36,000 subscribers and 4 million views. Her Narcissistic Abuse Support website reaches survivors in over 145 countries. She also manages a thriving Facebook community with over 17,000 members.

Tracy is available for parent/family coaching, groups, interviews, and speaking engagements globally.

To explore more of my work, visit NarcissistAbuseSupport.com. You can sign up for my mailing list to stay updated on new resources, blogs, videos, and upcoming free events like webinars and Q&A nights for parents. I'm always adding tools to help you heal, learn, and feel less alone.

BIBLIOGRAPHY

Bill Eddy - https://highconflictinstitute.com/

Psychology Today - https://www.psychologytoday.com/

Karl Pillemer - https://www.karlpillemer.com/